THE BURNING BUSH AND A FEW ACRES OF SNOW

The Presbyterian Contribution to Canadian Life and Culture

Edited by WILLIAM KLEMPA

The Carleton Library Series

A series of original works, new collections and reprints of source material relating to Canada, issued under the supervision of the Editorial Board, Carleton Library Series, Carleton University Press Inc., Ottawa, Canada.

THE BURNING BUSH AND A FEW ACRES OF SNOW

*The Presbyterian Contribution
to Canadian Life and Culture*

Edited by WILLIAM KLEMPA

CARLETON LIBRARY SERIES #180

CARLETON UNIVERSITY PRESS
OTTAWA, CANADA
1994

Printed and bound in Canada.

Canadian Cataloguing in Publication Data

Main entry under title:

The Burning Bush and a Few Acres of Snow :
The Presbyterian Contribution to Canadian Life and Culture

(The Carleton library ; no. 180)
Includes bibliographical references and index.
ISBN 0-88629-236-0 (bound) -
ISBN 0-88629-239-5 (pbk.)

1.   Presbyterian Church—Canada—Influence.
2.   Presbyterian Church—Canada—History.
3.   Canada—Intellectual life   I. Klempa,
William J.   II. Series

BX9001.B85 1994   285'.271   C94-900169-4

Carleton University Press   Distributed in Canada by:
160 Paterson Hall   Oxford University Press Canada
1125 Colonel By Drive   70 Wynford Drive, Don Mills
Ottawa K1S 5B6 Canada   ON M3C 1J9
(613) 788-3740   (416) 441-2941

Cover Design: Chris Jackson, Ottawa
Interior: EpiSet Corporation, Ottawa

Acknowledgements

Carleton University Press gratefully acknowledges the support extended to its
publishing programme by the Canada Council and the Ontario Arts Council.

The Press would also like to thank the Department of Communications, Government of Canada, and the Government of Ontario through the Ministry of Culture,
Tourism and Recreation, for their assistance.

To the Memory of

Three Remarkable Presbyterian Mentors

and Colleagues in Ministry

*

Donald J. M. Corbett

W. Gordon Maclean

James D. Smart

Contents

There's More to a Presbyterian than Meets the Eye

Presbyterians have played a conspicuous role in many aspects of Canadian life and culture. The close connection of the two is expressed in the title of the volume: the burning bush, with the Latin inscription *nec tamen consumebatur* ("nevertheless not consumed"), is the official emblem of the Presbyterian or Reformed faith and the "few acres of snow" ("quelques arpents de neige") is Voltaire's dismissive description of Canada in his novel *Candide* (1759). This collection of essays attempts to explore and assess the not inconsiderable part Presbyterians have played in the development of Canadian life and culture.

Over a century ago, Canadian literary figure and enthusiastic Scotophile W. J. Rattray concluded his four-volume study *The Scot in British North America* with the following assessment:

> The history of the Scot in British North America has virtually been the history of the country since its occupancy by the British ... By all the qualities of statesmanship, of leadership, of diplomacy, men of Scottish origin have proved their claim to the foremost place among those who have laid the foundations of Canadian nationality ... The strong religious instincts, the keen moral perceptions, the resolute will, tireless energy, and acute logical faculty of the Scot, tempered and modified by the qualities of the peoples who share our national heritage, will enter very largely into the fibre of the coming race.[1]

If this Scottish author's "gude conceit" of his own race (Margaret Laurence once said, "the Scots knew how to be almightier than anyone but God") has at least a measure of truth, then it is also the case that the history of Canada owes much to Presbyterianism, the characteristic faith of most of the Scottish Protestant settlers. To be sure, not all Scottish immigrants were Presbyterians. Many were Roman Catholics, and their contribution to Canadian life and culture was immense as is evidenced in R. MacLean's essay "The Highland Catholic Tradition in Canada."[2]

There were also Scottish Protestants who were Anglicans, Baptists, Congregationalists and Methodists, as well as those of no religious or denominational loyalties. Here one has in mind Anglicans of Scottish descent such as Bishop Charles Inglis, who became the first Anglican bishop of the diocese of British North America; Bishop John Strachan, founder of Trinity College, University of Toronto; Professor Daniel Wilson of the University of Toronto, who helped found Wycliffe College, Toronto; the Rev. R. A. Fyfe, a Baptist, who founded McMaster University; and historian Donald Creighton's father, W. B. Creighton, a Methodist, who edited the *Christian Guardian*, as well as political figures such as William Lyon Mackenzie, leader of the rebellion in Upper Canada, of no particular denominational affiliation, and Sir John A. Macdonald, nominally Church of Scotland, who described himself as a pillar of the Church, although an outside pillar.

Yet we must not assume that religious faith in those Scots, who called themselves Presbyterians, was always the most important dimension of their lives. For many it was central and dominating, and through them it exercised its influence in both the private and public spheres. In others, it was more peripheral. Yet even where this was the case, the ethical and moral principles which had become part of the Scottish character continued to operate with strength and vitality. Professor W. Stanford Reid has argued rightly that "the Scottish Calvinistic-Presbyterian outlook on life has formed one of the basic drives in the Scottish character."[3] This outlook instilled such virtues as industriousness, integrity, and thriftiness, expressed in the copybook maxims: "Waste not, want not," "A penny saved is a penny earned," "Time is money," "Early to bed, early to rise," and so on.

In support of this view, Pierre Berton has noted the profound impact of the Protestant work ethic on the Aberdeen-born Scot, Sir George Stephen, President of the Bank of Montreal and later of the CPR, and commented:

> It was this hard ethic ... that explains the dominance of the Scot in pioneer Canada ... For the Scots it was work, save and study; study, save and work. The Irish outnumbered them as they did the English, but the Scots ran the country. Though they formed

only one-fifteenth of the population they controlled the fur trade,
the great banking and financial houses, the major educational
institutions and, to a considerable degree, the government.4

These qualities of "work, save, and study; study, save, and work"
made the Scot the ideal colonist and Canada is much the richer for
that contribution.

Still, not only Scots but also French, Swiss, Dutch, German,
Irish, Welsh, English, Hungarians, and other nationalities have professed the Presbyterian or Reformed faith. Similar characteristics of
hard work, thriftiness, and a sense of divine calling may be found
in them also, and can be traced to their Calvinistic faith. The purpose of this volume is also to focus on their role and contribution to
Canadian life and culture.

Above all, it must be borne in mind that the Presbyterian
tradition is only one among many of the diverse traditions which
have gone into the making of the rich Canadian mosaic. We
must guard against a presumption about Presbyterianism
comparable to Mr. Thwackum's presumption about Anglicanism
in Henry Fielding's *Tom Jones*: "When I mention religion, I mean
the Christian religion, and not only the Christian religion, but the
Protestant religion, and not only the Protestant religion, but the
Church of England."5 Anglicans, Baptists, Congregationalists,
Lutherans, Mennonites, Methodists, Orthodox, Pentecostalists,
Roman Catholics, United Church and many others have made
their invaluable contributions to the Canadian nation.

If the writers of the following essays at times speak with
particular pride of the Presbyterian contribution, it is not in any
way to belittle those of others. Many diverse traditions, including
those of French Canadians, English, Irish, Welsh, Dutch, Germans,
Ukrainians, Chinese, Japanese, Scandinavians, and more recently
Koreans, Jamaicans, and Salvadoreans, have entered into the warp
and woof of the entity we call and celebrate as Canada. Surely, if
we are to understand Canada aright, we must know more than
just its geography and scenery. It is necessary to know and to
appreciate something of the diverse traditions which have gone
into the making of the Canadian nation, among which the
Presbyterian tradition has an important place.

To be sure, we must not exaggerate the importance and influence of the Presbyterian tradition which is the theme of this volume. Perhaps nothing is so distasteful as triumphalistic denominational flagwaving. Presbyterianism at its best, when it has taken seriously its *soli Deo gloria* principle, has not been self-aggrandizing. At the same time, it would be a mistake to underestimate the profound impact of Presbyterian ways of thinking, in both their positive and negative aspects, on the social, political, economic, intellectual, and cultural aspects of the Canadian nation.

It is not wrong, therefore, to take some pride in these achievements. A proper pride in and loyalty to one's own tradition are not the opposite of but rather the necessary complement to a wider ecumenical and national loyalty. Denominational loyalty can be a barrier and thus a problem when it is narrow and one sided. Yet it can be a rich resource when it is broad and balanced. Moreover, the important role of denominational traditions has generally had in view the great benefit of all Canadians. These traditions have become an integral part of the cultural riches we now enjoy as a Canadian nation.

At the same time, we must confess that the Scottish Presbyterian heritage is a burden and a shame as well as a glory to be celebrated. Canadian Presbyterians have had more than their fair share of internal conflict, ecclesiastical battles, and church divisions. Religious rigidity, petty theological squabbling, moral censoriousness, and an obsession with work have all too often been marks of the Presbyterian character. Writers such as Hugh MacLennan, Margaret Laurence, and Robertson Davies, all children of this heritage, have rebelled, each in his or her own way, against these unattractive features of Presbyterianism. The Presbyterian presence in Canada, in the words of Jesus' parable, is a mixture of wheat and tares.[6]

It may surprise some to learn that Presbyterians have had almost as long a connection with Canada as French Roman Catholics. Yet this is so. The first persons of Reformed or Presbyterian persuasion—French-speaking Huguenots—came to Canada with Samuel de Champlain in the early part of the seventeenth century. Yet the Presbyterian presence did not become strong and

significant until the eighteenth century after the cession of
New France in 1763.

Scottish settlements began in Pictou County, Nova Scotia, with
the Highland settlers who came on the ship, *Hector* in 1773,[7] and
with colonists who went to Prince Edward Island in 1777. This
stream of Scottish emigration deepened and widened in succeeding years.[8] Scottish settlers spread to other parts of the province and
to New Brunswick, and later to Lower and Upper Canada. Most of
these early settlers were Presbyterians but they were joined later by
Highland Catholic immigrants, many of whom found their way to
Cape Breton Island. These settlers often lived alongside French-
speaking Roman Catholic settlers. Historians have pointed to the
considerable evidence of a special understanding between the French
and the Scots as well as between the Presbyterian and Catholic
Scots, an understanding which did not develop between the French
and others who came to Canada. André Siegfried has observed that
the Scots "manifested a real goodwill towards the French and these
latter were the first to recognize it."[9]

Other Scots living in the American colonies were attracted to
British North America in the aftermath of the American Revolu-
tion. Among the attractions were the grants of land which were
given to soldiers of disbanded Scottish regiments who had fought
in the Revolutionary War and who wished to remain loyal to the
British Crown. For example, the "father of Presbyterianism in Up-
per Canada," the Reverend John Bethune, Chaplain to the Royal
Militia Regiment in North Carolina and later to the Royal Highland
Emigrants Regiment in Halifax, received a 3000-acre grant near
Williamstown in Glengarry where he built the first Presbyterian
Church in Upper Canada.[10] These and other settlements served as
nuclei for immigrants, attracting them to Quebec, Montreal and the
Ottawa Valley.

Churches and schools were erected and ministers were called
from the American colonies or from Scotland. Among the first
Presbyterian ministers were the Reverend James Lyon, a graduate
of Princeton Seminary, and the Reverend James Murdoch, an Irish-
man who trained in Scotland and was sent out by the Irish Associate Synod. Lyon arrived in 1764 and returned to the United States

in 1782. Murdoch came in 1766 and ministered for over thirty years. Those who came from Scotland were, to begin with, ministers of the Secession churches which had divided from the Church of Scotland in 1733 and in 1761 over whether a patron could intrude a minister into a parish against the desires of the people. Yet since many of the Scots were members of the Auld Kirk (Church of Scotland), its ministers also came to serve the settlers. Presbyterianism in its Auld Kirk, Secessionist and later Free Church forms, gradually gained a stronghold in British North America.

The first presbytery in what is now Canada was formed in Nova Scotia in 1770 when the two Presbyterian ministers, James Lyon and James Murdoch, joined with two Congregational ministers to form an ad hoc presbytery to ordain Bruin Romkes Comingo, a fisherman who had no formal theological education, but who had the required gifts for ministry. This unusual action displayed a commendable ecumenical spirit so that the German settlers in Lunenburg might have an ordained pastor. The first permanent presbytery was formed at Truro in 1786 by the Associate Synod to be followed in 1795 by the formation of the Associate Presbytery of Pictou.

Two names stand out prominently in early Nova Scotia Presbyterianism: Reverend James MacGregor and Reverend Thomas McCulloch. MacGregor arrived in Pictou in 1786 and ministered sacrificially until his death in 1830. It has been noted that his forty-four year ministry and the lives of his descendants typify the Presbyterian contribution to the new land. Among his direct descendants were four members of Parliament, one lieutenant-governor, one judge, four professors and eleven teachers, four ministers, eight lawyers, two doctors, seven engineers, one artist, fifteen merchants, eight nurses, and five authors. If one multiplies this achievement many times one can have some idea of the part played by Presbyterians in the building of the Canadian nation.

The other prominent minister, Thomas McCulloch, arrived with his wife and three children at Pictou in 1803. A man of singularly versatile learning,[11] he devoted himself, despite opposition from both the Church of England and the Church of Scotland in Canada, to the establishment of an academy and a theological seminary.

McCulloch is best known as the author of *The Mephibosheth Stepsure Letters*, published originally in *The Acadian Recorder* and collected in a volume after his death.[12] Literary critic Northrop Frye has described him as the "founder of genuine Canadian humour."[13] McCulloch became the first principal of Dalhousie College in 1838. His achievement in the establishment of Pictou Academy is chronicled by Professor B. Anne Wood in the first essay in this volume, "Schooling for Presbyterian Leaders: The College Years of Pictou Academy, 1816-1838," and his contribution to theological thought in Canada is considered in William Klempa's essay, "History of Presbyterian Theology in Canada to 1875."

Scots continued to migrate to the Atlantic Provinces and to the Canadas, settling in the Eastern townships of Lower Canada, in the Glengarry district of eastern Ontario, west and northwest of York (Toronto), and in the newly opened areas such as the Huron Tract. Thereafter, settlers moved to the west of the Great Lakes. In 1812 the Earl of Selkirk set up the first colony of Scottish settlers on the Red River in Manitoba. A Presbyterian congregation was established at Kildonan in 1851 by the Reverend John Black from among the Presbyterian Red River settlers who had previously been ministered to by an Anglican priest. From this church many settlers travelled to points further west. Missionaries under the direction of Dr. James Robertson, the first Superintendent of Mission in the North West, took the Presbyterian faith to Scottish and other settlements, in what are today the provinces of Manitoba, Saskatchewan, and Alberta.

Presbyterians of Scottish descent took a prominent role in government, commerce, and education. Their leadership in Canadian business in the early part of the nineteenth century is most evident in Montreal, which became the economic centre of the Province of Canada toward the end of the eighteenth century. Merchants such as James McGill and Simon McTavish, who were both Scottish born, and Canadian born Peter Redpath, dominated the scene. "A typical early millionaire living in what came to be known as the 'Square Mile,'" Donald MacKay has written recently, "was a Scottish Presbyterian who had left school at the legal age of fourteen, apprenticed himself to a business house, risen to the top largely through Calvinistic determination, invested in new railways and shipping, and served on the Bank of Montreal, which became something of a finishing school for commercial talent."[14] These Presbyterians of Scottish descent were the leading philanthropists of the city and were responsible for the founding of such institutions as McGill University, the Royal Victoria and Montreal General Hospitals, the building of churches, and the establishment of commercial organizations such as the Board of Trade and even the Mercantile Library Association. They served in the great fur companies and were involved in the founding of banks, the building of railways, and other commercial enterprises. It is a matter of regret that there are no essays chronicling the role of Presbyterians in government and commerce. This story needs to be told.

Individual Presbyterians or Presbyterian church bodies established schools and universities, including Pictou Academy in Nova Scotia, Queen's University, Kingston, Morrin College, Quebec, and Manitoba College, Winnipeg. Presbyterians provided the leadership of many academic institutions: Dalhousie College's first principal was the Reverend Thomas McCulloch; Sir William Dawson, a graduate of Pictou Academy and a staunch Presbyterian brought McGill University to life; Queen's was headed by ministers during its early years; Morrin College was founded and led by Dr. John Cook, and from 1907 to 1932 Sir Robert Falconer, former principal of Presbyterian College, Halifax, presided over the University of Toronto. Institutions of theological education were also founded: Presbyterian College, Halifax, Queen's Theological College, Kingston, Knox College, Toronto, and Presbyterian College, Montreal.

When the four branches of Presbyterianism representing Church of Scotland, Free Church, and Secessionist bodies united in 1875 to form The Presbyterian Church in Canada, the new church became the largest Protestant denomination in Canada, containing over 1,000 congregations, 88,000 communicants (600,000 Canadians identified themselves in the census as Presbyterians), and 634 ministers. During the next fifty years the newly formed church experienced remarkable growth. The 1921 Canadian census shows that there were 1,409,407 Presbyterians or 16 percent of the total Canadian population of 8,788,483. In 1925, the year of church union when two thirds of Presbyterians entered the new United Church of Canada, there were 380,000 communicant members and 1,708 ministers.

Presbyterians thus represent an important historical presence within Canadian society. Both in the colonial period and in the age of Confederation, Presbyterians were a vital, energetic, and influential force. They were quintessentially "mainstream" and they exerted their influence by virtue of the social, economic, political, educational, and cultural advantages they enjoyed. In 1925 the Presbyterian river divided into two weaker streams: the larger stream went into the United Church of Canada, while the smaller one has continued as The Presbyterian Church in Canada. The question facing both streams today is whether the Presbyterian presence in Canadian life and culture has declined so markedly that Margaret Atwood's central symbol for Canada—"survival"— is now the sole raison d'être of these two churches. Does the Reformed tradition still have a sense of mission to inform and transform Canadian society? That, of course, could be the theme of another volume.

In this volume we are concerned with what the Presbyterian presence was and its significance in the development of Canadian life and culture. One of Robertson Davies's characters in his novel, *The Manticore*, makes a revealing remark: "Mackenzie King rules Canada because he himself is the embodiment of Canada—cold and cautious on the outside ... but inside a mass of intuition and dark intimations."[15] Apart from his occasional dabbling in spiritualism, Mackenzie King, it must be remembered, was a staunch Presbyterian and a faithful member of St. Andrew's Presbyterian Church, Ottawa. When the United Church Act bill was debated in the House of Commons in 1924 he favoured the more cautious approach of referring the whole matter to the Supreme Court of Canada for a judgment. The Honourable Arthur Meighen, leader of the opposition, succeeded in persuading the House to pass the bill without reservation.[16] In many ways, Prime Minister William Lyon Mackenzie King was the quintessential Presbyterian—cold and cautious on the outside but on the inside full of dark intimations. Yes, there *is* more to a Presbyterian than meets the eye!

*   *   *

This collection of essays is a modest attempt to record the Presbyterian contribution to Canadian life and culture. Much still remains to be learned, and it is hoped that this collection will stimulate further research not only with respect to the role of Presbyterians, but also of persons of other faiths, in the development of the Canadian nation.

The twelve essays in this volume were selected from a total of twenty-five papers which were originally delivered at two symposia, one at Presbyterian College, Montreal, in October 1988, and the other at Knox College, Toronto, in May 1989. To all who participated, and especially to those who gave papers and chaired the sessions, we express heartfelt thanks. We are especially grateful to the Social Sciences and Humanities Research Council of Canada for its generous grant and to the Senates of Knox College, Toronto, and Presbyterian College, Montreal, for their financial support of the two symposia and of the publication of this volume. Dr. George Harper was responsible for much of the organization of these symposia, correspondence with the speakers, and the preparation of the manuscript, and to him I express sincere gratitude for his invaluable work. I would like to thank my secretary, Mrs. Cathy Unger McInnis for her assistance, Professor J. C. McLelland who collaborated in the selection of the essays, Professor Ramsay Cook for his valuable advice, and Professor Margaret Ogilvie of Carleton University for all her help in facilitating the publication of these essays. Two anonymous readers for Carleton University Press have made constructive and helpful suggestions. Frances Rooney copy-edited the manuscript and Jennie Strickland guided it through Carleton University Press. I hope the final text embodies most of their corrections and enough of their valuable suggestions for strengthening the edited volume.

Presbyterian College, Montreal
April 1, 1994

NOTES

1. W. J. Rattray, *The Scot in British North America* (Toronto: Maclear and Company, 1880), vol. 4, 1191-92. Cf. also to the similar judgment by W. Stanford Reid, "the history of Canada is to a certain extent the history of the Scots in Canada," in *The Scottish Tradition in Canada*, ed. W. Stanford Reid (Toronto: McClelland & Stewart, 1976), ix.

2. R. MacLean, "The Highland Catholic Tradition in Canada," in *The Scottish Tradition in Canada*, ed. W. Stanford Reid, 93-117.

3. W. Stanford Reid, "The Scottish Protestant Tradition," in *The Scottish Tradition in Canada*, ed. W. Stanford Reid, 120. Professor Reid refers to Robert Louis Stevenson and W. Notestein, *The Scot in History* (New Haven: Yale University Press, 1946), who have made this judgment.

4. Pierre Berton, *The National Dream* (Toronto: McClelland & Stewart, 1971), 319ff.

5. Henry Fielding, *The History of Tom Jones, A Foundling* (New York: Modern Library, n.d.), Book 3, Chapter 3, 82.

6. Matthew 13:24-30.

7. The story of the Highland Scots who sailed to Pictou is related by Donald MacKay in *Scotland Farewell: The People of the Hector* (Toronto: McGraw-Hill Ryerson, 1980). See also D. Campbell and R. A. MacLean, *Beyond the Atlantic Roar: The Nova Scotia Scot* (Toronto: McClelland & Stewart, 1974).

8. Cf. George Patterson, *A History of the County of Pictou Nova Scotia*. Canadiana Reprint Series No. 31 (Belleville, ON: Mika Studio, 1972), 82. "We venture to say," says Patterson, "that there is no one element in the population of these Lower Provinces, upon which their social, moral and religious condition has depended more than upon its Scottish immigrants, and of these that band in the hector were the pioneers and vanguard."

9. André Siegfried, *Le Canada, les deux races*. Paris: 1906, 73, quoted by Henry B. M. Best, "'The Auld Alliance' in New France," in *The Scottish Tradition in Canada*, ed. W. Stanford Reid, 15. It is worth noting that the Scottish Presbyterians in Montreal worshipped in the Recollet Church from 1791 until 1792 when the edifice of St. Gabriel Street Presbyterian Church was built. Robert Campbell in *A History of the Scotch Presbyterian Church, St. Gabriel Street, Montreal*, refers to this fact and the role of the Roman Catholic Bishop Alexander Macdonnell in settling a dispute between the Reverend John Bethune and his Glengarry congregation as something that "was general at that time throughout the country" (Montreal: W. Drysdale, 1887), 31. No rent was paid but the St. Gabriel Street congregation rewarded the Recollets with a barrel of wine and some candles.

10. Cf. Donald N. MacMillan, *The Kirk in Glengarry* (Montreal: n.d.), chapter 2.

11. McCulloch's student, George Patterson has said the following in tribute to his teacher: "He had a multifarious learning, so that he might be regarded as a whole *senatus academicus*. He could have taken any branch included in the faculties of Arts and Theology, and taught it in a respectable and efficient manner." *History of the Pictou County* (Belleville, ON: Mika Studio, 1972), 331.

12. A new edition of the *Letters* has been edited by Gwendolyn Davies: *The Mephibosheth Stepsure Letters* (Ottawa: Carleton University Press, 1990).

13. H. Northrop Frye in "An Introduction" to Thomas McCulloch, *The Stepsure Letters*, General editor, Malcom Ross. New Canadian Library No. 16 (Toronto: McClelland & Stewart, 1960), ix.

14. Cf. Donald MacKay, *The Square Mile: Merchant Princes of Montreal* (Toronto: Douglas & McIntyre, 1987), 7.

15. Robertson Davies, *The Manticore* (Toronto: Macmillan, 1972), 99.

16. N. Keith Clifford, *The Resistance to Church Union in Canada, 1904-1939* (Vancouver: University of British Columbia Press, 1985), 158-160.

I

PRESBYTERIANS AND CANADIAN EDUCATION

Presbyterians have always attached great importance to education. In 1560, in the *First Book of Discipline*, reformer John Knox introduced the ideal of a church and school in every community as one important aspect of the reformation of the Scottish Church and society. Knox's dream of a nationwide parish school system was not carried out until a century and a half later and even then imperfectly. Still, as G. M. Trevelyan has noted, at the union of Scotland and England in 1707, the Scots were among the best-educated people in Europe.[1] Their system of popular education made them, at home and abroad, a cultured, resourceful, and industrious people.

Scots strongly emphasized post-secondary education. Even though Scotland was small and relatively poor, it boasted four excellent universities: St. Andrew's, Aberdeen, Glasgow, and Edinburgh. These centres of learning began to flourish in the eighteenth century, during the period known as the Scottish Enlightenment. Major thinkers such as David Hume, Frances Hutcheson, William Robertson, and Adam Smith addressed a whole range of issues concerning individual and social obligations, politics, economics, and religion. Scottish Common Sense philosophy or Scottish realism, represented by such major thinkers as Thomas Reid, Dugald Stewart, and Sir William Hamilton, and which focused on questions of knowledge, the moral sense, and conscience, came to be a prevailing philosophical influence in nineteenth century Scottish, United States, and British North American universities and seminaries.

The Scottish universities proved to be far more open than their English counterparts, Oxford and Cambridge, to the new and growing interest in the sciences and technology. Chemistry and physics advanced under such scientists and teachers as Joseph Black (1728-99) of Edinburgh University, who laid the foundations of chemistry as an exact science in his investigations on magnesium carbonate, during which he discovered carbon dioxide. Technology also expanded as a result of the work of James Watt (1736-1819), a Scottish

inventor at Glasgow University. Some of these Scottish developments provided the foundations for education in nineteenth century British North America.

In the opening essay in this section, "Schooling for Presbyterian
Leaders," B. Anne Wood describes and analyzes the first Presbyterian venture into higher education in Atlantic Canada. It was made
by the Reverend Thomas McCulloch, the notable Nova Scotian
divine of *Stepsure Letters* fame. Since King's College, Windsor, effectively barred non-Anglicans from its faculty and student body,
McCulloch, a Presbyterian minister of the Antiburgher, Secessionist
Church, sought to make higher education available to the largely
non-conformist population of Nova Scotia by establishing Pictou
Academy in 1816. His efforts to obtain provincial grants and degree-granting status for the Academy were strenuously resisted.
Initial opposition to the new Academy came from the Anglican
Tory establishment, which wanted to keep education in the hands
of the Anglican church. Later, however, Church of Scotland
ministers, annoyed by McCulloch's anti-patronage views, joined
the Anglicans in opposing his plans. The divisions which plagued
Presbyterianism in Scotland were carried over to the new Scotland,
Nova Scotia. McCulloch's strong and severe personality probably
exacerbated the situation. Nevertheless, Thomas McCulloch initiated a movement in higher education among Presbyterians and
other non-conformists which continued in the establishment of
Dalhousie College and other institutions of higher learning.

Professor Wood analyzes the contrasting ideologies of the
Presbyterian groups, their underlying motives, and the nature
of the schooling each group established in Pictou Academy.
Unlike King's College, Windsor, which was modelled on
Oxford, the Academy sought to imitate the Scottish universities.
Science, mathematics, logic, and moral philosophy were given
equal weight to the classics. McCulloch was convinced that
the Scottish model offered a system of university education
which was better adapted to the needs of the province and
the active purposes of life. Above all, McCulloch, unlike his
Church of Scotland counterparts, was motivated by the need to
train an indigenous ministry, convinced as he was that

Nova Scotia could no longer depend on Scotland for its supply of ministers.

Thomas McCulloch, Professor Wood concludes, left three important legacies from this Presbyterian venture into higher education. First, partly as a result of his advocacy of the rights of nonconformists, Nova Scotia entered an era of reform in government, providing the first model of responsible government in British North America. Pictou Academy graduates became leaders in the Reform party and a few participated in the Confederation debates of the 1860s. Second, McCulloch was one of the earliest pioneers of higher as well as theological education in British North America. He set a high standard of academic excellence. His students played important roles in the establishment of common schooling in Nova Scotia, and as Professor Wood notes William Dawson, later Principal of McGill, held his first teachers' institute at the Academy. Third, as the Pictou area entered its golden era of shipbuilding and industrialization during the 1840s many Pictou graduates became successful entrepenuers.

McCulloch's major intellectual legacy to his students and to Canadian Presbyterianism, Professor Wood believes, is epitomized in the controversy over Darwinian evolution. Opposition to Darwin's theory was led by Sir William Dawson, a graduate of the Academy who held that Darwinian evolution posed a real threat to morality and religious authority. Unlike the theological progressives in the church who emphasized social action rather than doctrine, both McCulloch and Dawson recognized the dangers to traditional Protestant teachings. They "warned in vain," Professor Wood says, "the path they [the progressives] now blazed led not to the kingdom of God on earth but to the secular city." Many historians would disagree or would want to qualify this judgment in a number of ways. In the first place, McCulloch and Dawson addressed rather different historical contexts, the former in the first half and the latter in the second half of the nineteenth century. Second, neither McCulloch nor Dawson felt that he had to choose between doctrine and the social application of the gospel, though naturally Dawson saw the dangers for morality of social Darwinism. Professor Wood is correct, however, in pointing out that McCulloch was of a rather conservative bent, and his conservative approach persists to this day in Pictou County.

Reference has already been made in the introductory essay to the contribution of Presbyterianism to Canadian higher education. D. C. Masters has noted that there were two kinds of colleges headed or taught by Presbyterians.[2] The first sort were schools founded and led by Presbyterians of Scottish descent such as Pictou Academy in Nova Scotia, Queen's in Kingston, Manitoba College in Winnipeg, and Morrin College in Quebec City. Dalhousie was in reality a Presbyterian college for much of the nineteenth century, even though it was non-sectarian in name. Theological colleges such as Knox in Toronto, Presbyterian College in Montreal, West River Seminary in Pictou, and Presbyterian College, Halifax, were of course distinctively Presbyterian. The second sort were schools where Scots and Presbyterians had an important influence, such as McGill, King's College, Fredericton (later to be the University of New Brunswick), King's College, Toronto, and the University of Toronto. Among administrators there were such distinguished Presbyterian educators as Thomas McCulloch at Pictou Academy and the later Dalhousie, Sir William Dawson at McGill, George Munro Grant at Queen's, Donald H. MacVicar at Presbyterian College, Montreal, Sir Robert Falconer at Presbyterian College, Halifax, and later the University of Toronto. Among notable Presbyterian teachers were John Watson at Queen's, Clark Murray at McGill, William Lyall at Dalhousie, and George Paxton Young at Knox College and later the University of Toronto.

In the second essay in this section, Michael Gauvreau considers the relationship of Presbyterianism, liberal education, and the research ideal by focusing on the career of Sir Robert Falconer, President of the University of Toronto from 1907 to 1932. Through a close analysis of Falconer's theological and educational writings, Professor Gauvreau seeks to place his religious and educational concerns within the context of late Victorian attempts to accomodate evangelical theology and the naturalistic explanations of human behaviour. He argues that this was not a rearguard action but that it arose from a confidence in the power of the gospel to Christianize both individuals and society. Falconer had learned in the Scottish universities to subordinate all forms of intellectual endeavor to the explicit criterion of Biblical doctrine.

According to Gauvreau, Falconer's leadership of the University of Toronto was marked by his allegiance to the evangelical creed, with its suspicion of the evolutionary explanations of mind and society. Falconer relied on the humanistic canons of the older liberal education. His Presbyterian theology and also his ambivalence to the "research ideal" made him resist the specialization and fragmentation of knowledge and the growing gulf between the sciences and the humanities. All this leads Professor Gauvreau to question the prevailing view that between 1910 and 1940 there was a rapid secularization of the English Canadian university.

NOTES

1   G. M. Trevelyan, *English Social History* (London: Longmans, Green, 1942), 426-28.

2   D. C. Masters, "The Scottish Tradition in Higher Education," in *The Scottish Tradition in Canada*, ed. W. Stanford Reid (Toronto: McClelland & Stewart, 1976), 250-51. See also D. C. Masters, *Protestant Church Colleges in Canada: A History* (Toronto: University of Toronto Press, 1966), and Robin S. Harris, *A History of Higher Education in Canada, 1663-1960* (Toronto: University of Toronto Press, 1976).

Schooling for Presbyterian Leaders: The College Years of Pictou Academy, 1816 – 1832

B. Anne Wood

Scholars have long acknowledged that education and religion were closely related in nineteenth-century Atlantic Canada. Although a number of good religious histories in recent years have dealt with this relationship, as Terrence Murphy recently stated, there are only three major new histories of one of the largest denominational groups—the Presbyterians—and only one of these works, Laurie Stanley's *The Well-Watered Garden: The Presbyterian Church in Cape Breton, 1798-1860*, deals with schooling in any depth.[1] Murphy also notes that there is little recent work on Presbyterianism in mainland Nova Scotia. This is particularly surprising when the birthplace of its native ministry and Presbyterianism's first British North American college was at Pictou in northeastern Nova Scotia.

Founded in 1816, Pictou Academy epitomized "the fusion of education and religion which characterized [the] Scottish social philosophy of [the] age," in the words of Susan Buggey and Gwendolyn Davies. As Buggey and Davies note, by 1825 the Academy "was widely recognized for the quality of its instruction, the commitment of its principal, and its acceptance among dissenters in meeting their needs for higher education."[2] Unable to gain degree-granting status from the Halifax Tory establishment which controlled the Council, the trustees sent the Academy's first three graduates to the University of Glasgow where they passed the qualifying examinations, were awarded their masters degrees, and were praised for their scholarship. McCulloch was appointed the first professor of divinity by the Presbyterian Church of Nova Scotia in 1820 and taught the theological courses for the rest of his life. By 1825 the Secessionist[3] sect of the Presbyterian Church had such strength over its rival, the established Church of Scotland, that it looked upon Nova Scotia, particularly its northeastern portion, as its domain. McCulloch was the undisputed leader of the Presbyterian Church of Nova Scotia.

In an important study of Presbyterian higher education in the United States between 1707 and 1837, Howard Miller points out the strengths and weaknesses of Presbyterianism.[4] Its hierarchical structure of government was designed to promote social unity, thus giving the religion its strength. On the other hand, its divisive theology, vacillating between evangelical and rational strains, weakened the effectiveness of Presbyterianism as a religion and led to numerous schisms as each theological camp attempted to gain control of the governmental structure. Under external attack, Miller claims, these internal tensions were exacerbated, and when a sole figure represented one camp, he was exposed to undue vituperation in order to defeat his side. By the late 1820s McCulloch and Pictou Academy became the centre of a bitter political dispute between the Secessionists of Nova Scotia and the evangelical part of the Church of Scotland. The Kirk ministers in the province used their missionary activities and attacks on the elitism of Pictou Academy in order to win supporters for the policies of the Glasgow Colonial Society [GCS] and its Scottish promoters who were to lead the evangelical wing to disruption for the Church of Scotland in 1843. They were aided in this strategy by the large number of Highland immigrants to the province at this time (most of whom were evangelical Church of Scotland adherents) and by the transition of the economy from a resource to an industrial base (the 1829 opening activities of the General Mining Association at New Glasgow launched this initiative).

From its early days as a major port the town of Pictou had spread its liberal, modernizing influence over the more remote hinterland not only through its religious and commercial activities but now through its school policies. The differences between the two Presbyterian groups were highlighted by their opposing policies regarding the training of future leaders of their community. Their "petty feuds" affected all aspects of Presbyterian society in the region for the next forty years and strongly influenced the rise and fall of Pictou Academy. This paper will analyze the contrasting ideologies of the rival Presbyterian groups, their underlying motives, and the nature of schooling which each group established in the Academy, and it will conclude with a brief analysis of the legacy McCulloch bequeathed to his students.

By 1803 when Thomas McCulloch arrived in Pictou, the area had passed through forty years of pioneer life and was entering a more settled mode of existence. There were approximately 1,300 people in the Pictou district, most of them emigrants from Scotland. Harbour Village (later Pictou Town) consisted of about a dozen houses, but it was already developing as a major commercial centre. There were several taverns, a store, blacksmith's and carpenter's shops, and a jail. Two trades were to dominate the economy for the next twenty years, the fishery with the West Indies and the white pine timber trade. They were not unrelated. Rum was imported in the empty hulls returning from the West Indies. This was used by local merchants in lieu of cash. Edward Mortimer, Pictou's leading timber merchant, claimed that it took 300 to 400 puncheons of rum consumed per season by workmen, approximately one third of the cost of the timber, to move it from the woods to the ships. At the height of the timber trade during the Napoleonic Wars, Mortimer was estimated in one year to have furnished cargoes of timber for seventy vessels sailing out of Pictou Harbour. An average of 120 vessels yearly took away 40,000 tons of timber for which Harbour merchants received about £2 per ton.[5]

There were three Antiburgher Secessionist Presbyterian ministers in Pictou at McCulloch's arrival, two of whom would become strong Academy supporters, the Reverend James MacGregor and the Reverend Duncan Ross. They were concerned about the effect of the timber trade on the social habits and moral condition of the community. In their letters home to Scotland they described the extravagant and intemperate habits of the farmer-woodsmen, who in spring found themselves in debt to the merchants, their farms mortgaged, and with no hope of relief except to go back to the woods in the fall. Sailors from the many ships in the port frequently made the streets of Pictou scenes of drunkenness and riot. Clear-cut logging without stump removal rendered the clearings unfit for ploughing and, to Lowland agricultural improvers such as MacGregor, Ross, and McCulloch, a ruinous Highland system of farming impoverished the land already under cultivation. The many Presbyterians in the region were alarmed at the severe losses in their ranks to revivalist preachers who swept through the area as part of the late eighteenth-century Second Great Awakening.

The Secessionist ministers and town leaders felt that the solution to these dangerous trends was to train a native ministry and to educate professionals who would lead the way toward modernization, much as in Lowland Scotland, but would protect the community from the severe social and economic dislocations of the Industrial Revolution. MacGregor began a branch of the British and Foreign Bible Society and got the British office to send 500 Gaelic Bibles to Pictou in 1808. McCulloch began a school in his house. By 1817 he was renowned as a grammar school teacher; fifty-three boys from all parts of the province were attending his school. He and his friends launched a subscription drive in 1815 for an institution of higher learning which would carry no religious distinctions and would exclude no Christians. The group particularly resented the exclusive nature and privileged degree-granting status of King's College in Windsor, which was given a royal charter in 1802 and was liberally financed by the imperial and colonial governments. The Pictou Academy Bill passed unanimously in the House of Assembly in 1816. When it reached the Council, however, it was strongly opposed by extreme Tory members. To gain passage it was amended by the insertion of a clause requiring all trustees and masters to swear that they were members of the Church of England or professed the Presbyterian religion. The Council refused requests for a permanent grant and for degree-granting status. What had been planned as a nondenominational college was turned into a Presbyterian academy. McCulloch's Presbyterian enemies would use this weakness to their advantage in the near future.

During this time hundreds of Highlanders were moving into the Pictou district, many from Skye, Sutherland, and Ross-shire. They were leaving their homeland because, in the words of J. M. Bumsted, they wished "to preserve the old ways—economic, social and cultural—which were being threatened in Scotland. This essentially conservative purpose led most prospective emigrants to prefer to join their compatriots already established rather than striking out in new directions."[6] Bumsted notes important characteristics of Highland settlements in British North America. They were all located in isolated places off the mainstream of transatlantic commerce, and they were insulated by location and heavily wooded terrain from alien cultural influences. The Pictou district was on the north side of the province, well removed from Halifax and the bulk of the population centres of the province. Many of the Highlanders withdrew to intervales or upland regions where they continued their traditional subsistence farming and cattle-grazing practices. As Marianne McLean points out in a study of Glengarry County immigrants, by maintaining these traditional agricultural patterns of life, the Highland settlers could achieve a balance between the physical environment and their farming techniques on one hand and social considerations on the other.[7] The Highlanders who settled in the Pictou district were largely Gaelic-speaking and were mainly supporters of the established Church of Scotland. Through their isolation and strong clan, religious, and linguistic ties, then, homogeneous communities were formed based on traditional Highland values. Both Bumsted and McLean note that the eighteenth-century Highland immigrants left by choice and had sufficient capital from their tenant farms to bring all the members of their immediate family to the New World. They were a protest group reacting to the radical transformation of the Highlands under the impact of commercial land development. At first they accepted the infrequent visits of the three Secessionist Presbyterian ministers to their communities. Only MacGregor, however, spoke fluent Gaelic. McCulloch's scathing denunciation of the patronage practices of the established Church of Scotland alienated many of these Highlanders; they were unfamiliar with the tenets of the Antiburgher sect, which in Scotland was confined largely to towns and cities in the Lowlands. They began to regard McCulloch's efforts to supply a native ministry as calculated to destroy the established Church of Scotland, and they quickly became hostile to Pictou Academy.

Meanwhile, in Scotland the evangelicals within the established church were becoming actively involved in pleading for the rights of the poor, especially in the industrial cities of the Lowlands. Robert Burns, a Church of Scotland minister in Paisley, had heard from his brother, the Reverend George Burns in Saint John, New Brunswick, that there was a great need for settlers in the region. Burns became president of a number of immigration societies which sought to help impoverished families by facilitating their passage to British North American, New Zealand, and Australia. He began to write for the *Christian Instructor*; the major arm of the evangelical party within the Church of Scotland, it waged war on the incumbent moderates in every issue. Burns soon used Pictou's Highland discontent to aid his cause.

In 1817 the Reverend Donald A. Fraser, another Church of Scotland minister, arrived in the colony. At first he was friendly to the Academy supporters but he soon retired to McLellan's Mountain where he ministered to forty scattered, Gaelic-speaking Highland families for eleven years. His charismatic personality and commanding appearance quickly won over the hearts of his congregation, who regarded him with "the reverence and awe with which Highlanders approached the chief of their clan. He enjoyed this," claims the Reverend Alexander Maclean, "in a larger measure than perhaps any other Presbyterian minister in Nova Scotia."[8] In 1824 Fraser and the Reverend John MacLennan travelled to Cape Breton and gathered the hundreds of High-landers there to renewed allegiance to the Church of Scotland. Burns was to publicize this mission in the *Seventeenth Report of the Edinburgh Bible Society* (1826), and the evangelicals quickly decided in 1825 to use this missionary success to launch a new humanitarian organization, The Society (in connection with the Established Church of Scotland) for promoting the religious interests of Scottish settlers in British North America, or the Glasgow Colonial Society. Its patron was George Ramsay, ninth Earl of Dalhousie, who had been Nova Scotia's lieutenant governor (1816-20) and was now Governor General of the Canadas. Many of its twenty-four directors were key ministers and community leaders in Scotland.

The by-laws restricted all directors and helpers to members of the established Church of Scotland.

These Scottish missionary endeavours were imitated in Nova Scotia. An effort was first made to revive the moribund church in the colony. While in Halifax, Dalhousie laid the foundation for another non-denominational college, which was to be modelled on Edinburgh University. He used customs revenue seized during the War of 1812 with the United States to begin the erection of a new building on the Grand Parade in Halifax. The 1821 Dalhousie College bill contained a chair in theology, which would duplicate McCulloch's divinity classes in Pictou. Two years later a Scotch presbytery was organized in Halifax. One of the first resolutions of its four Kirk ministers was to undertake missionary work to deprived settlements. There was no compunction about either encroaching on Secessionist territory or maligning the efforts of McCulloch to train a native ministry. As a result of Fraser's successful proselytizing, the Church of Scotland became the dominant body in Cape Breton. He and MacLennan possessed two qualities not held by their Secessionist rivals. They spoke fluent Gaelic and they were backed by the evangelical zeal and highly successful missionary efforts of the GCS. Fraser considered that McCulloch and his followers had strayed far from their evangelical roots: "The amalgamated Burghers and Antiburghers of these colonies are no more like the Erskines and the Fishers of former days, than the generality of modern occupiers of Scotch pulpits are to such as Knox and Cargill."[9]

Resentment of McCulloch grew within the town of Pictou by the early 1820s. For several years a number of Presbyterians had been denied admission to Harbour Church, where McCulloch was the minister. They tried unsuccessfully to introduce the Church of England into the town. In 1823 another Kirk minister, the Reverend Kenneth John MacKenzie, arrived and stayed in Pictou. In order to make up a congregation MacKenzie, who was also fluent in Gaelic, persuaded a number of Highlanders from remote settlements to join the Pictou malcontents. By 1824 this group had gathered enough support against the Secessionists that McCulloch was forced to resign his pastoral duties at Harbour Church. He explained that he had done this in part "to avoid the ill-will of those whom he was occasionally obliged to offend in the discharge of his ministerial duties and who counted the Academy with him in expressions of their dissatisfaction."[10] McCulloch even contemplated joining forces with the evangelical wing of the Church of Scotland to form one Presbyterian body in Nova Scotia. But he was determined to retain his major policies in connection with the Academy which, he wrote, should have a curriculum suited to "the sons of the middle classes ["poor men" crossed out] who are enabled to procure for themselves an education but who cannot afterwards obtain such stations as in a pecuniary respect they justly deserve."[11] McCulloch's principal goal for his students was to give them such a rigorous liberal education that their merit would enable them to break the control on patronage held by the Halifax oligarchy, thereby allowing Dissenters in the province to attain positions of leadership.

But the meritocratic admission standards of the Academy, its philosophical and scientific curriculum, and above all the scarlet gowns (like those worn by students at Glasgow University), which Pictou Academy students wore as they paraded around the College Green, offended the Kirk group.[12] A long-standing court case over ownership of the Green, which at times was used as a garbage dump by Academy opponents, continued to exacerbate relations between the two sides. In a letter written to Council by Hugh Denoon, the Academy was described as "unpopular in this place, and ... attended only by 'clowns.' "[13] Burns, it would appear, was directing MacKenzie to exploit this discontent in order to gain adherents for the Kirk. In a letter of 1825 MacKenzie reassured Burns that despite his poor stipend (£120 per annum) and McCulloch's increasing attacks on him, "in the name of your Triumvirate [Fraser, MacKenzie, and the Reverend John Martin of Halifax] ... all within our power shall be done to meet your wishes and expectations."[14] Writing to Burns from Halifax in 1827, Martin described the "wanton and unprovoked attacks of Dr. McCulloch in the newspapers of this province during the past six to seven weeks," but it was "in endeavouring to assist you that we have drawn down upon ourselves the indignation of one of the most abusive writers that ever lived."[15] The Reverend Dugald McKichan, a Kirk minister sent out in 1829 by the GCS as a missionary to Barney's River and Merigomish in eastern Pictou, also alluded in a letter to Burns to "an idea which dropped from you when I had the honour [of] being entertained at your table" about bringing the Pictou Academy under the wing of the Church of Scotland. He was instructed to gather humorous documents, newspaper reports, and statistics about the Academy, "its character and conduct," and forward these to the secretary of the GCS. He even reported rumours about McCulloch's avarice and his wife's extravagance and suggested that these would be the greatest barriers to union between the Secessionists and the Church of Scotland.[16]

One of the reasons for the attack on Pictou Academy was its success. By 1825 it had gained widespread support among Dissenters of the province as a high quality institution. McCulloch was renowned as an excellent teacher. One of his 1820 students, George Young, described McCulloch's incisive intellect and clear exposition as follows:

> The lectures which I have heard Dr. McCulloch deliver this week in Natural and Moral Philosophy class have tended to produce in my mind a very high opinion of his abilities. Notwithstanding all his peculiarities of character he is really a man of profound and accurate knowledge. His lectures are to me a treat. They are delivered in plain almost homely language but at the same time display an intimate acquaintance with his subject. He takes a clear view of everything—sees the very bottom of his question & illustrates it so fully that if a due attention be paid it is impossible that you can leave the room without understanding clearly his elucidation. His examples are all taken from nature—they are strong but I must confess to me they sometimes appear coarse. He either despises the imagination or... If he has one it is a jaded old plough horse—not a fiery & foaming steed.[17]

In contrast to King's College, modelled on Oxford University and whose curriculum emphasized the classics, the program of the Academy was modelled on that of Scottish universities. Science (or natural philosophy), mathematics, logic (which included general grammar and rhetoric), and moral philosophy were given equal weight as the classics (Latin and Greek). As early as 1794 in Ayr, Scotland, a new type of scientific education was emerging in re-organized post-secondary institutions called academies. Scottish universities soon viewed their curriculum as a direct attack on their own programs of study, which were painted by academy promot-ers as cultivating speculative and indolent habits in their students as well as preparing them only for the learned professions. Similar to the earlier science curriculum of Perth Academy (established 1759-60), these later eighteenth-century academies were aimed at sons of tenant farmers and growing numbers of middle-class mer-chants who were thriving from Scotland's rapid commercial and economic growth. Besides the advantages of this more practical curriculum, the Scottish promoters argued that academies offered cheaper education, better supervision of students, and teachers who were less conscious of rank and behaved more as schoolmasters.

There were two major differences, however, between the ear-lier Perth Academy and these later institutions. Like Pictou Acad-emy, Perth had a separate local college for higher education, and it was equivalent to the universities in its level of instruction. Pictou Academy's program imitated the Bachelor of Arts degree require-ments for Glasgow University.[18] McCulloch's class, wrote Young, tended "to preserve the dignity of the Professor. He sits on an elevated seat above the class & wears now a black gown similar to those in which our attorneys appear at the bar. It has really a very imposing & respectable appearance."[19] Not only did this dignified stance and McCulloch's demand of rational, logical arguments evoke fear among his students, it also weeded out the inept. McCulloch's surviving lecture notes on moral philosophy and epistemology are highly scholastic. He drew clear distinctions, for instance, between sensation and perception; definitions were given for logic, con-sciousness, generalization, judgment, and modes of reasoning. Terms, logical definitions or propositions were thoroughly explained, the eleven classical types of argument outlined. Reference was made to Francis Bacon's four types of illogical judgments. For a gifted student destined for the legal profession, such as nineteen-year-old George Young, these analytical distinctions would have been meaningful. But even though McCulloch included numerous examples to illustrate the implication of these abstract concepts, the lectures remain highly abstract and must have daunted all but the brightest of his students.[20]

Ironically, McCulloch's goal, like that of his Scottish Common Sense mentors, was very practical. He shared with other Protestant Dissidents in Nova Scotia a hatred of the irrational, authoritarian culture epitomized both by the Roman Catholic Church, which they believed had led inevitably to the French Revolution, and by the Anglican oligarchy in Halifax, which was trying to impose a uniformity of religious instruction on the population. Denying charges that their type of liberal education would lead to sentiments of disloyalty, these Dissidents argued that instead the population would be educated toward positive doctrines based on principles of common sense and merit. Further, McCulloch suggested, a higher seminary which gave a liberal education would prepare lawyers, for instance, with methods of classification and with habits of abstraction and generalization which would lead to a more enlightened profession. Ministers would gain an improved intelligence with respect to their daily experience, especially as "religion and political influence of the clergy, go hand in hand."[21] In contrast to the Oxford model, McCulloch argued in his 1818 newspaper debate against the Reverend Dr. William Cochran of King's College, the Scottish universities offered a system of university education adapted to the present needs of the province and "the active purposes of life." These included knowledge about the duties of their students in the community, the operations of their own minds, the modes of communicating their ideas and sentiments and, finally, "those just views of the various social relations ... and that knowledge of mathematical and physical science, which would be every day useful to the community and honorable to themselves."[22] Not only the program, but even the style of life of the professors, McCulloch stressed, should convey the learning and respectability which their Scottish colleagues epitomized. In contrast to the "monkish" boarding school practices of King's, which McCulloch judged to be harmful for the character of its students, the professors at Pictou Academy and their students lived in the community. Since the Academy was open to all members of the community regardless of their religion, the institution could concentrate on competition and instill in its students an incentive to improve themselves and the community around them which would benefit both these future leaders of society and the province.

Neither these laudable educational ideals nor McCulloch's increasingly aggressive defence of his Academy convinced his enemies that they should support the current structure of the Academy or the hegemony of the Secessionist Presbyterians over all affairs in the region. MacKenzie seized on the original charter of the Academy and used the later Scottish academy model to argue for a composite school unit, which would place the Pictou grammar school in the building. The curriculum he and his Kirk allies promoted in numerous petitions to the legislature would be more practical, at a level between the grammar school and the college. In an 1826 petition organized by Fraser and MacKenzie, for instance, they claimed that McCulloch's curriculum was not useful to the majority of the people in the district who were debarred from admission to the Academy because of its high standards. In "a Commercial community like Pictou," subjects such as arithmetic, navigation, book-keeping, geography, geometry and French— useful subjects like those taught in the Scottish academies— were seriously needed, they said. The petitioners further argued that not only was the Academy inefficiently managed but its entire direction had fallen into the hands of persons not connected with the established church, contrary to its charter, thus giving the institution an "exclusive and sectarian appearance ... a sect of the Seceders is at variance with the object of its foundation and has besides a tendency to create ... clerical division and disunion in the Community."[23] They asked that the House of Assembly prohibit everything that gave the Academy a sectarian appearance, including the divinity class, that it offer a program of studies similar to those of the Scottish academies, and that the Academy be made available to all classes in society.

Between 1828 and 1831 the Council rejected the trustees' requests for a permanent grant and even for the annual grant. Under attack, McCulloch and MacGregor attempted to organize Dissident support for the Academy, but their political aggressiveness alienated both the Baptists, who founded their own Horton Academy at that time, and moderate supporters of the Academy in the Council. The unfortunate politicization of Presbyterianism and the Pictou Academy question came to a tragic climax in 1830 in Pictou over the riot associated with the Brandy Election.[24] Joseph Howe watched incredulously as a party of armed sailors and Highlanders, led by MacKenzie and carrying banners inscribed with the names of the Council's candidates, paraded before the Academy and the homes of Jotham Blanchard, the Assembly candidate, and George Smith, the sitting member. MacKenzie then led his forces to the polls armed with sticks and afterwards to the tavern where he harangued them in Gaelic. His blandishments proved successful. The Council candidate, Lawrence Hartshorne, outpolled Blanchard in the district of Pictou by 142 votes. In the province at large, however, all Assembly supporters, including Blanchard, were voted in. Howe was aghast at the conduct of the Kirk ministers. He saw at last that they were the chief villains in the politico-religious disputes of the district.

MacKenzie and his allies achieved their goals also as far as the Academy was concerned. In 1832 a new "Act to Regulate and Support the Pictou Academy"[25] was passed. It expanded the trust to twelve members, seven trustees including McCulloch from the old board, and five new trustees, including the Roman Catholic bishop, the Right Reverend William Fraser, to be appointed by the lieutenant governor. The previous religious declarations required of trustees were repealed and theology classes were barred on the premises. A permanent annuity of £400 yearly was to be granted, out of which McCulloch was to receive £250 per year as principal. The Academy now was to offer a grammar school level of instruction as well as the higher branches of learning, and a master was to be appointed to teach the lower branches at a salary of £100 a year. This structure would prove unworkable; the warring parties were forced to sit together on the Academy board but they were given little financial leeway to pay off the mounting debt. Its future direction as a Union Academy, however, was now established. All the Kirk demands for a more practical curriculum were implemented, and the hegemony of the Secessionists was to be seriously undermined.

Over the next six years the previous high reputation of the Academy was destroyed. Although the committee of management, consisting of two Kirk members including MacKenzie, made it clear that the £974 debt was to be paid off, they could not get their community to pay their share of the burden, and the Secessionists gradually drew back their promised support. They did manage to have a former Pictou Academy graduate appointed as master of the lower branches, but George Blanchard soon discovered that he could not control his thirty-nine students, who were "running over the benches, playing ball, or cutting wood in the room."[26] The noise was so bad that McCulloch and his son Michael could not properly teach their eighteen students. Michael appealed in vain to the trustees and within a year threatened to resign. Blanchard's 1834 class only had eighteen students (McCulloch's had eleven that year), and his limited fees of £14.2.6 and salary of £100 left him so short that he tendered his resignation. McCulloch found the attacks by the Kirk board members intolerable and stayed away from all further meetings. In 1833 the Legislature appointed Judge W. Q. Sawyers as a one-man commissioner to examine the affairs of the Academy. MacKenzie's scurrilous attacks on McCulloch at the hearings were so venomous that the judge rebuked him as a member of the cloth for speaking in this manner. McCulloch remarked in a letter to his brother William, now master at Yarmouth Academy, that these attacks by Fraser and MacKenzie were made because they knew their congregations would not contribute to the Academy and wanted the province to pay off its debts. Judge Sawyers concluded:

> The Board as it now exists not only exhibits a striking example of the extent to which party spirit may be carried, but also must, by the contentions of its Members ... frustrate the design of their Incorporation ... Its prosperity can be insured only by relieving it from present embarrassments [debt], placing it under direction

which will insure the harmony and co-operation of the Board of Trustees, and granting it such other patronage as similar institutions in other countries obtain.27

Howe and his fellow educational commissioners supported these recommendations when they examined the Academy in early 1838. By this time McCulloch had been offered the post as president of the newly opened Dalhousie College in Halifax. Enrolment in the Academy had fallen to nine students in the higher branches and only seventeen in the lower. Voluntary contributions had dwindled to only £11.2.6 in 1837, resulting in the resignation of the second teacher appointed as master to replace Blanchard. Kenneth John MacKenzie died in November 1838 and Fraser moved away from the district. Petitions continued to flood the Legislature praying that a generous grant of money be given to pay off the debt of the Academy. A new union committee had organized these renewed efforts to keep the Academy open. Its recommendations for financial support from the two Presbyterian groups, for a higher grammar school curriculum and for guaranteed legislative grants of £230 annually, would establish the framework for a Union Academy in 1845. Within three years the debt was largely paid off. Further fights were to ensue between extreme factions of the two Presbyterian groups over the next fifteen years, but the union moderates now were supported by a much strengthened provincial educational system which led eventually to the establishment of a normal school in 1855 and to the Free School Acts and compulsory assessment legislation in 1864-66. By this time Pictou Academy had been re-established as a high quality institution, but it was more a superior grammar school than a college.

McCulloch left three important legacies to British North America from this Presbyterian college experiment. Partly as a result of his early political battle for the rights of Dissenters, the province entered an era of reform in government which culminated in the first model of responsible government in British North America in 1848. Many Pictou Academy graduates became important leaders in the Reform Party, and a number also took an active role in the Confederation debates of the 1860s. McCulloch was one of the earliest pioneers of Presbyterian theological education in British North America. With the departure of all but two of the Kirk ministers from Nova Scotia after the 1843 Disruption in the Church of Scotland, most of his divinity school graduates were called to fill the many vacant ministries throughout the Maritimes, and they played a crucial role in establishing the Presbyterian Church in Nova Scotia. McCulloch set a high standard for his many students who were to become teachers in northeastern Nova Scotia. The Academy and its graduates played important roles in the establishment of common schooling in Nova Scotia; the first superintendent of the province, William Dawson, held his first teachers' institute at the Academy and for several years it was proposed as the major contender for the provincial normal school. As the Pictou area entered its golden era of ship-building and industrialization during the 1840s, many Pictou Academy graduates became successful entrepreneurs and important businessmen. Unfortunately, a few of the graduates used McCulloch's ideal of liberalism to continue their political battle with the more traditional Kirk group; this became translated into a long-lasting political polarization of the region into two parties, the Liberals and the Conservatives. A number of McCulloch's students countered this parochialism with a scientific ideal which they advanced to justify their promotion of a national economy.[28]

McCulloch's major intellectual legacy to his students and to Canadian Presbyterianism can best be epitomized in the scientific battle of Dawson with Charles Darwin in the later nineteenth century. Dawson recognized that Darwinian evolution had the potential to break apart the moral authority of our civilization which was founded on religion. In this he was the true disciple of McCulloch and in his world-famous championing of anti-Darwinism Dawson became as implacable against his foes as McCulloch had been against his political and religious enemies. Both men recognized the dangers to traditional Protestant teachings of the intellectual and social transformation taking place in British North America. As the evangelicals and later the social gospellers gained power and attempted to correct the injustices of the emerging industrial capitalist order, they reformulated Christian social thinking. Social action, rather than a rethinking of theological doctrine, became a priority for these theological progressives. But as McCulloch and Dawson warned in vain, the path they now blazed led not to the kingdom of God on earth but to the secular city.

NOTES

1. Terrence Murphy, "The Religious History of Atlantic Canada: The State of the Art," *Acadiensis* (Fredericton) 15 (Autumn 1985), 152-74. Murphy describes Laurie Stanley's book, *The Well-Watered Garden: The Presbyterian Church in Cape Breton, 1798-1860* (Sydney: University College of Cape Breton, 1983), as "among the most original contributions to the religious history of Atlantic Canada published in the last decade" (158).

2. Susan Buggey and Gwendolyn Davies, "Thomas McCulloch," in Francess G. Halpenny, ed., *Dictionary of Canadian Biography*, vol. 7, 1836-1850 (Toronto: University of Toronto Press, 1988), 534-41. The entry on McCulloch is the longest biography in this volume.

3. In 1732 the Secession Church was formed in Scotland by evangelicals who objected to the abolition by the Assembly of the Church of Scotland of popular election of ministers. In 1747 the Secession Synod in Scotland itself split into two branches. The Burghers regarded the oath required of burghers in Scottish corporate towns as merely an abjuration of Romanism, not as recognition of the Church of Scotland; the Antiburghers felt that the oath included approval of the Church of Scotland and all of its abuses. In 1795 the Presbytery of Pictou was organized by three Antiburgher ministers and McCulloch joined their presbytery when he was inducted as minister of Harbour Church, Pictou, in 1804. In 1817 the two Nova Scotia secessionist branches, the Burghers concentrated at Truro and the Antiburghers at Pictou, buried their differences and formed the Presbyterian Church of Nova Scotia.

4. Howard Miller, *The Revolutionary College, American Presbyterian Higher Education 1707-1837* (New York: New York University Press, 1976).

5. Frank H. Patterson, *John Patterson: The Founder of Pictou Town* (Truro: Truro Printing, 1955), 27-28. Mortimer's business extended to Prince Edward Island and Baie Verte, and included a thriving fishery trade. Sealing was another flourishing business carried on in James Patterson's Cove. Mortimer largely controlled all trade and did not hesitate to crush any intruders. He had almost every inhabitant of the district relying on his credit system. From 1799 to 1819 he represented the district of Pictou in the House of Assembly and successfully represented the "country party" against the entrenched merchantocracy of Halifax. As Patterson notes, it was not surprising that he was dubbed the King of Pictou.

6. J. M. Bumsted, *The People's Clearance: Highland Emigration to British North America 1770-1815* (Winnipeg: University of Manitoba Press, 1982), 65.

7. Marianne McLean, "Peopling Glengarry County, The Scottish Origins of a Canadian Community," Canadian Historical Association, *Historical Papers* 1982 (Ottawa: CHA, 1983), 160.
8. Rev. Alexander Maclean, *The Story of the Kirk in Nova Scotia* (Pictou: The Pictou Advocate, 1911), 58.
9. Donald Fraser to Dr. Scott, Saint John, June 29, 1826, 2, in Micro: Misc., Societies, GCS, Reel 1, Vol. 1, Item 56, Public Archives of Nova Scotia [PANS].
10. McCulloch quoted in Report of the annual meeting of the Trustees, Pictou Academy, January 25, 6, in Micro: Places, Pictou Academy, Reel 1, Item 32, PANS.
11. Ibid., 3.
12. James Munro to [Chipman] Commissioners appointed to look into the affairs of Pictou Academy, Pictou, July 20, 1827, 4 pp., MG1, Vol. 554, Item 52, PANS.
13. Excerpt in letter John MacKinlay to George Smith, Pictou, March 30, 1825, Micro: Places, Pictou Academy, Reel 1, Vol. 554, Item 52, PANS.
14. Kenneth John MacKenzie to Robert Burns, Pictou, November 8, 1825, 2, in Micro: Misc., Societies, GCS, Reel 1, Vol. 1, Item 27, PANS.
15. Rev. John Martin to Robert Burns, Halifax, April 24, 1827, 1, 2, Reel 1, Vol. 1, Item 88, PANS.
16. Dugald McKichan to Robert Burns, Merigomish, November 4, 1829, Reel 1, Vol. 2, Item 95, PANS.
17. George Young to Father, Pictou, December 2, 1821, MG2, Vol. 719, F1/10, George Young Papers, PANS.
18. The Bachelor of Arts degree program of Glasgow University in 1826 was very similar to that of Pictou Academy at the same time:

	Glasgow University	Pictou Academy
Year 1:	Latin and Greek	Latin I & Greek I
Year 2:	Logic (including General Grammar & Rhetoric), Latin, Greek	Latin II, Greek II, Math I
Year 3:	Moral Philosophy, Math (with practical applications), Algebra	Math II, Logic (including Rhetoric)
Year 4:	Natural Philosophy, Math, Algebra	Natural Philosophy, Moral Philosophy

19. Young to Father, December 2, 1821.
20. See for example, Thomas McCulloch, "A writing on the Epistemology of Mind," MG1, Vol. 555, Item 32, and,"A Lecture on Moral Philosophy," Item 33, PANS.
21. "Investigator," *Acadian Recorder*, Halifax, January 24, 1818.
22. *Acadian Recorder*, February 28, 1818. And see B. Anne Wood,"Thomas McCulloch's Use of Science in Promoting a Liberal Education," in *Acadiensis* 17 (Autumn 1987), 56-73.
23. Petition to the Legislature by Kenneth MacKenzie, et al. (142 names), [July 20, 1826], Micro: Places, Pictou Academy, Reel 1, Vol. 554, Item 52, PANS.

24. Gene Morrison clearly outlines the complex issues which since the 1826 election led to deteriorating relations between the Council and the Assembly. The dispute itself was over a question of whether a tax on foreign brandy was legal or not. It was allied to the old dispute between the Assembly and the Council over control of the purse. In his lead editorial of June 19, 1830 in Pictou's *Colonial Patriot* Blanchard also connected the dispute to the oppression of the Pictou Academy by the Council. When one of the Council-sponsored candidates declared against the Academy, Jotham Blanchard decided to run against him. Unfortunately, when the polls were moved to Pictou violence erupted and one man was killed. See Gene Morrison,"The Brandy Election of 1830," *Collections of the Nova Scotia Historical Society* 30 (1954), 151-83. See also J. Murray Beck, *Joseph Howe, Conservative Reformer, 1804-1848*, vol. I (Kingston and Montreal: McGill-Queen's University Press, 1982), 78.

25. William IV, c.5. It was passed March 26, 1832.

26. Michael McCulloch to Reverend Duncan Ross, Pictou, May 20, 1834, MG1, Vol. 554, Item 111, PANS.

27. "Report W. Q. Sawyers," Halifax, March 3, 1834, Appendix 74, *Journals of the Nova Scotia House of Assembly 1837*, 112.

28. Suzanne Zeller, *Inventing Canada: Early Victorian Science and the Idea of a Transcontinental Nation* (Toronto: University of Toronto Press, 1987).

Presbyterianism, Liberal Education and the Research Ideal: Sir Robert Falconer and the University of Toronto, 1907-1932

Michael Gauvreau

"I believe," proclaimed Robert Falconer at his inaugural as President of the University of Toronto in 1907, "that the highest type of citizenship cannot be permanently trained apart from a sense of obligation to and reverence for the moral order which is Divine. Religion is the crowning function of our manhood, for in religion we reach out to that which completes this fragment of the present."[1] That the new president should choose to affirm so forcefully the centrality of religion was not surprising. Falconer had been trained as a Presbyterian minister, and although he had never occupied the pulpit of the regular ministry, he had spent much of his career teaching in the theological colleges of the Presbyterian Church. Indeed he was particularly concerned to remind his audience of faculty, students, businessmen, and government officials that even within the precincts of a secular university, there was no antagonism between the free pursuit of learning and what he termed "essential Christianity."

Falconer's insistence on the centrality of Christian belief and the moral basis of education in a modern university was reinforced by his continued concern for the supremacy of the liberal arts in an age of science and specialization. Despite the proliferation of new faculties and professional schools, the new president maintained, the ideal of the university should remain "the attainment of that mental and moral efficiency which comes through intellectual discipline and culture." The arts course, Falconer, informed his audience, "will always retain the central position in a university, because in it mental discipline and intellectual culture are found in purer quality. A well-sustained Arts Faculty gives balance and proportion to the University, and we hope that it will become increasingly the preparation for professional study."[2]

Robert Falconer's forceful articulation of the cultural supremacy of Christian belief and liberal education in the context of a university environment ostensibly devoted to specialization and professionalization compels us to question the supposed dominance of the research ideal[3] over the older moral concerns of college education. His address also raises a number of important issues concerning the relationship of Protestant religion and English Canadian culture. President Falconer delivered his inaugural address at a critical juncture, at the very point where many Protestant clergymen and their congregations were attempting to define the relationship of their traditional creed to the social problems attendant upon rapid industrialization. At first sight, it might well be claimed that the new president was involved in a hopeless rearguard action. Surely, clergymen like Falconer were simply misguided in their belief that the traditions of their religious creed could be strengthened through contact with the new scientific spirit.

Any such accommodation, it might be argued, was based upon the intellectually flimsy conventions of "theological liberalism" which, historians have maintained, encouraged many Protestant clergymen to neglect the traditional theology of evangelicalism in favour of a vague, reformist social activism directed to achieving the Kingdom of God on earth.[4] Yet if we are to place Falconer among the "liberals," a number of perplexing questions need to be addressed. First, was his peroration concerning the supremacy of the religious spirit in university education characteristic of one who had unwittingly abandoned the vital doctrines of the faith and simply capitulated to naturalistic explanations of human behaviour? Second, did the fact that he so forcefully desired to impress his creed upon his audience indicate that his outlook was irrevocably destined to be marginalized in the cultural life of twentieth-century Canada?

My questioning of this perspective is not based upon a denial of the secularization of English Canadian society in the early twentieth century. Rather, my concern is with the historical teleology by which the religious thought of late nineteenth-century evangelicals like Robert Falconer can only be interpreted from our modern, secular vantage point. This, in my estimation, has contributed to a neglect of the sources, motives, and context which lay behind Falconer's reconciliation of Christian belief and the spirit of modern research, and between the moral and cultural goals of an arts education and the specialization of the twentieth-century university. Rather, through a close analysis of his theological and educational writings, this study seeks to place his religious and educational concerns within the context of late Victorian attempts to accommodate evangelical theology and the naturalistic explanations of human behaviour supplied by science and biblical criticism. Falconer's synthesis, this paper argues, cannot be seen as simply a rearguard action or one that was intellectually misguided. It was derived not from any perception of Protestantism's weakness in the face of the intractable social and industrial problems of the early twentieth century but from a confidence in the power of evangelism to Christianize both individuals and society. This outlook flowed from his sense of place within a specifically Presbyterian, evangelical cast of mind, and his contact with a powerful synthesis of theology and history developed in the universities of Victorian Scotland, one which directed him to subordinate all forms of human intellectual endeavour to the explicit criteria of biblical doctrine.

Robert Falconer was born at Charlottetown, Prince Edward Island, in 1867, the eldest son of a prominent Free Church Presbyterian minister. He remembered his father as "an unusually good preacher, well educated and thoughtful," but a clergyman who "rarely exhibited emotion, was reserved as to his inner life, and was suspicious of overwrought sentiment."[5] Faith was not merely a matter of emotion, but was securely anchored in intellectual comprehension and sound doctrine. Yet the young Falconer's theology did not consist in lifeless dogmas. His intellect was quickened and invigorated by the passion and zeal of the evangelical creed, which stressed the constant redeeming and transforming presence of a personal God in both the individual sinner and in human society.[6] The combination of intellect and reverence, instilled at an early age, was the foundation of his religious outlook. It was the expression of a Christian conviction well braced to withstand the encounter of the traditional creed with scientific thought and the higher criticism of the Bible.

In 1885 the young man's devotion to classical studies was rewarded with the prestigious Gilchrist Scholarship, which enabled him to continue family tradition by pursuing his studies at Edinburgh University. Although by his own account his formal studies did little to change his early religious or moral convictions, his contemptuous dismissal of the Edinburgh philosophy class is open to serious question. From the distance of nearly fifty years, he characterized the teaching of philosophy under the elderly A. Campbell Fraser and the unimaginative Henry Calderwood as "fossilized,"[7] but it is evident upon closer scrutiny that the synthesis of religion, science, and philosophy proposed by these scholars was central in forming Falconer's own reconciliation of evangelical conviction and modern thought.

Despite Falconer's assertion that the questions raised by evolutionary science were absent from the Edinburgh curriculum, it should be pointed out that neither Fraser nor Calderwood was ignorant of the impact of modern science on the traditional agenda of the Scottish philosophy. Indeed, Calderwood was the author of an influential study entitled *The Relations of Mind and Brain*, and he frequently devoted his moral philosophy lectures to discussing issues raised by the new physiological psychology.[8] Nor were these men hostile to the idea of evolution. Although they certainly rejected the Darwinian position that physical forces were sufficient to account for the development of the human mind, they were confident that "design is a conception in harmony with, and even involved in, natural evolution."[9] Providential purpose and divine law, according to these philosophers, continued to rule nature, the human mind, and society, a conviction which conveyed the assurance that evolution was, ultimately, a moral process ruled by spiritual forces. It was an acceptance of evolution which acknowledged the continued supremacy of the basic concerns of the evangelical creed.[10]

What the young student experienced in the philosophy classroom was the subtle, moderate balance which had been worked
out by the Edinburgh philosophers between 1850 and 1880. Unlike
Edward Caird (their Glasgow counterpart), Fraser, Calderwood,
and their successor, Andrew Seth Pringle-Pattison refused to accommodate religion and science by adopting an ironclad, Hegelian
metaphysic which imposed a naturalistic dynamic on revelation,
faith, and theology.[11] Against the inflexible rational process of Hegel
and Caird, which submerged the Christian doctrines of free will,
sin, immortality, and the independence of divine activity into an
all-encompassing universal mind, they were insistent, like their
Common Sense predecessors, upon the empirical reality of each
individual personality.[12] The Edinburgh school posited an intermediate philosophy, an eclectic form of "idealist-realism" which preserved the primacy of the evangelical outlook, and blunted the
neo-Hegelian attempt to resolve theology into philosophy.

Robert Falconer always termed himself an "idealist," yet this
description requires explanation and qualification in light of his
encounter with the moderate philosophers of Edinburgh. By idealism he meant not a formal philosophical system, but the belief that

> moral forces are finally dominant; that law is not a convention or
> pact that may be broken for the sake of interest; that it does not
> draw its sanction from any legislature, class in society, or auto-
> crat, but is the antecedent condition on which society domestic,
> national, or international must rest. By law we do not mean
> particular laws which change, but the permanent moral relation-
> ship which holds mankind together.[13]

For Falconer, unlike the adherents of the Hegelian tendency,
represented in Canada by John Watson of Queen's University, philosophical idealism did not emerge as a substitute for faith or as a
theory of religious knowledge, but was always subordinate to firm
religious conviction. He treated philosophy as a mere intellectual
exercise, and not as a quest for faith.[14] Indeed, he preserved a suspicion of philosophical speculation, and feared the tendency of
idealism to degenerate into pantheism and agnosticism, to deny
the central Christian doctrines such as the divinity of Christ and

"the problems of moral evil." Christian faith, he maintained, could not, as some philosophers claimed, simply be equated with the worship of nature or humanity.[15]

Falconer's presence at Edinburgh in the late nineteenth century coincided with the rising importance of the research ideal, which resulted in what one historian has termed the "knowledge revolution."[16] University education gradually began to emphasize the creative pursuit of new knowledge for its own sake, and the specialization of both the natural and human sciences forced a rethinking of the older liberal belief that by discerning underlying principles or laws, the unity of the sciences and the humanities might be preserved.[17] At first sight it might be assumed that the young scholar's decision to pursue the classics, this most traditional of the liberal humanistic disciplines, would simply encourage a reactionary, rearguard defence of the older moralistic canons of liberal education. Falconer was, however, fortunate in his apprenticeship to S. H. Butcher, Edinburgh's Professor of Greek, who was a central figure in the transformation of what the historian Frank Miller Turner has termed "the critical and moral tradition of humanism." For many educated Victorians, the study of classical culture implied conservatism and stability, as the ancient past was used as a normative guide to the human condition in the present.[18] By 1900 such views had been revised under the impact of evolutionary interpretations of human behaviour and society and researches in sociology and archaeology. There emerged among classicists like S. H. Butcher a "dynamic or evolutionary humanism," a determination to associate Greece with positive forces for change and human improvement as well as with the preservation of enduring moral and social values.[19]

This balance of progress and stability, the belief that Greek civilization rested upon a "ordered liberty" which harmonized the commitment to rational freedom with reverence for the past, was distilled into a volume of Butcher's lectures entitled *Some Aspects of the Greek Genius*, published in 1891, Falconer's last year at Edinburgh.[20] This essential lesson, argued the Edinburgh classicist, was one which must be learned and applied by modern industrial civilization. What was more significant for Falconer's latest concerns, however, was the fact that Butcher used the Greek notion of the unity of learning to synthesize the older liberal humanism with the research ideal. Although specialization was one of the most desirable features of modern culture, it was necessary, Butcher maintained, to broaden the basis of education "to emancipate the mind from what is narrow, local, partial," an injunction to avoid "the disintegrating tendencies" of extreme specialization.[21] It was important for the university to preserve the unity of knowledge by recognizing that although the methods of the natural and human sciences might differ, "the method of learning is one,"[22] a point of departure that enabled him to assert the fundamental unity of literature, art, and science, based upon a common search for the universal principles of order underlying all knowledge.

This reconciliation of the research ideal and the older concern for morality and culture can be dismissed as an impossible attempt to harmonize the old liberal education with the demand of the research ideal for the pursuit of knowledge unrestrained by moral or religious conviction. Yet committed young Presbyterians of Falconer's generation took Butcher's moderate position seriously because it argued that the research ideal, far from being detrimental to religious and moral concerns, was conducive to moral ends since it rested upon the attempt to elucidate "truth," or the fundamental principles underlying each branch of knowledge. Thus the arts faculty, what Butcher informed his audience was the successor to the Greek idea of philosophy, need not surrender its position to the social sciences or the professional schools, but would remain the vital centre of the university, the "connecting link" uniting academic learning with professional study.[23] The message of ancient Greece, appealingly presented as conducive to both intellectual progress and social stability, was one which substantially informed Falconer's own attempt to moralize the research ideal at the University of Toronto.

His theological study at New College, Edinburgh, however, provided the context in which Falconer articulated his later educational concerns. In the late 1880s, young Free Church Presbyterians were faced with the task of somehow reconciling the traditions of their theology with Biblical criticism, philosophical idealism, and a wave of revivalism unleashed by the efforts of the American evangelist Dwight Moody.[24] Of these developments, perhaps the most intractable issue was the problem of Biblical criticism, yet between 1850 and 1880, leading Scottish clergy-professors like Robert Candlish, A. B. Davidson, Robert Rainy, and Robert Flint worked out an intellectually sophisticated reconciliation of the older evangelical creed and the demands of the historical criticism of the Bible.[25] The central premise of the new relationship of revelation and reason was that theology itself must be made historical. Thus, while agreeing with the German higher critics that the Bible— like any ancient text—must be viewed historically and that revelation had its human side and "conforms rigidly to the usual laws of history and progress,"[26] these scholars also refused to banish God from the Bible and fought to retain the idea of Scripture as sacred history ruled by an active and independent divine providence.

The "historical theology" young preachers like Robert Falconer learned in the Free Church colleges provided an intellectually respectable alternative to the unrestrained naturalistic assumptions underlying both neo-Hegelian idealism and the more radical higher criticism emanating from Germany.[27] Specifically, clergymen influenced by historical theology denounced the tendency of both Hegelians and higher critics to discard the creeds and systems elaborated by earlier ages. They maintained that progress was, rather, "the continuous and consistent development which brings the new out of the old instead of parting with the old for the new."[28] They also preserved a basic loyalty to the Baconian premises of the Free Church theology and urged their students to remain close to the "facts," structure, and traditional meaning of the Biblical text.

As Falconer later recalled, his encounter with historical theology and the "reverent criticism" of A. B. Davidson dovetailed neatly with Henry Drummond's revivalist message. Drummond, who joined devotion to evolutionary science and the search for the natural laws underlying spiritual life with a lifelong association with Dwight Moody,[29] neatly epitomized the cautious and reverent yet open atmosphere of the Free Church colleges. The new Biblical and historical knowledge caused no crisis of faith or dissolving of his evangelical creed, but rather, according to Falconer, "helped me to remove loose deposits and to get further down to bedrock. The more intellectually secure I became the more consistent was my inner life."[30] Indeed, the historical criticism espoused by his mentors, A. B. Davidson in Old Testament literature and Marcus Dods in the New Testament, challenges the conventional categories of liberal, conservative, and modernist. Far from being a conscious adaptation of evangelical theology to modern culture or a simple capitulation to the naturalistic assumptions of higher criticism, historical theology was specifically directed to constraining the impact of these ideas on the evangelical creed. Its approach was not to exalt the critical method but to reinforce the living faith of the student, who after all was to be a preacher, not a cloistered scholar.[31] Respect for the community of the church and its theological traditions thus closely circumscribed critical method.

Nothing more aptly illustrated the continuities of the evangelical creed and historical theology than Robert Falconer's ambivalent reception of German theological ideas. A Scottish theological training allowed for a period of summer study on the continent, and in the early 1890s this meant a pilgrimage to Berlin to sit in the classroom of that most brilliant disciple of Albrecht Ritschl, Adolf von Harnack, the celebrated author of the massive *History of Dogma*.[32] In his 1893 inaugural address as Professor of New Testament Exegesis at Presbyterian College, Halifax, Falconer declared, *"Theology and religion have one ultimate source and standard. What is this? Everything revolves around the Person of Christ."*[33] By this statement Falconer appeared to have accepted the "liberal," humanized Jesus and the purely ethical gospel so attractively presented in the writings of the German Ritschlians. Indeed, in his emphasis upon ethics Harnack, in both his widely publicized *What is Christianity?* and his study of dogma, had removed the doctrinal element from the Gospels themselves, arguing that Jesus had not intended to found a religious community based on notions of his own divinity. Rather, the "essence" of his message was ethical and social, consisting of the preaching of the moral and spiritual Kingdom of God, the infinite value of the human soul, and the commandment of love. The German scholar actually denied the physical resurrection of Jesus, dismissing the miraculous and the mystical as an evasion of the moral kernel of the Gospel. The dogmas of the church he regarded as dessicated, petrified relics of the imposition of Greek metaphysics on a warm and vibrant Christian faith oriented to the primacy of the moral and the ethical.[34]

A surface glance at Falconer's teaching at Presbyterian College in the 1890s might lead the modern observer to identify him as a leading Canadian disciple of the Ritschlian tendency.[35] Indeed, he always praised Harnack's emphasis on the believer's personal experience of Jesus as the historical essence or core of the Christian faith.[36] For a young man who had grown to maturity in the Darwinian age where "science" and "religion" sometimes appeared diametrically opposed, the writings of Ritschl and Harnack offered an exciting prospect. They gave the sanction of historical study to an irreducible "minimum" of belief, a reality that lay in human feeling and experience, beyond the corrosive speculations of philosophy and the criticisms of evolutionary science.

On several crucial points, however, Falconer parted company with his Ritschlian mentors. The first was the issue of doctrine itself, which Harnack clearly regarded as merely incidental to personal feeling and experience in faith. Despite his great admiration for Harnack's genius, Falconer took his stand within the precincts of the Scottish historical theology when he declared:

> The second main result of Christianity having a personal centre is that *doctrines are an essential part of it*. This is denied by some, and they have raised a great hue and cry to rid religion and theology of metaphysics ... But doctrines cannot be removed from our religion, for the very reason that it is based on a living Christ. If religion were a mere sentiment, nothing but a feeling of dependence, or even if it were a code of morals, there might be some plausibility in attempting to remove what is regarded as an encumbrance. But since the Christian religion is a union of the whole person, mind, heart, and spirit, and intellect, will and affections with the entire consecration of every faculty to the Christ of God, we can never have a doctrineless religion.[37]

Falconer's use of the term "Christ," rather than "Jesus," also implied a critical divergence from Ritschlian tenets. Philosophers like
Harnack believed that historical study would strip away the Christ
of the creeds and restore the essential Jesus to late nineteenth-
century Protestants. Presbyterians like Falconer, however, could
not accept this division, for it denied the divine origin of the church
and, more important, threatened to undermine the central evangelical doctrine of the divinity of Christ.

Indeed Falconer's theology probably owed more to the Scottish
"Back to Christ" movement represented by Alexander Balmain Bruce
of Glasgow and Andrew Martin Fairbairn of Mansfield College,
Oxford, than to Harnack.[38] Falconer strove to preserve the identity
between the "Jesus of History" and the "Christ of the Church" and,
in a broader sense, the connection between doctrine and historical
fact. In his estimation, the doctrinal element was not simply a late
addition that must be stripped away but was itself essential to a
sound and reverent evangelical faith. The implications of this view
for Falconer's own religious outlook were evident in his writings at
Presbyterian College between 1893 and 1907, first as Professor of
New Testament and after 1904 as principal. Although it is possible
to see this period as one when the Protestant churches watered
down a number of key evangelical doctrines under the impact of
philosophical idealism, liberal humanism, and higher criticism,[39]
this is not apparent in Falconer's own theology.

Viewing the Bible and theology through a Scottish evangelical
perspective rather than from the standpoint of a German critic, he
coldly rejected the idea that doctrine should simply be altered to
bring Christian faith up to date with modern scientific or philosophical assumptions. Ministers of the gospel should not identify
with every whim and fancy of the times, but must remain "true to
the legitimate old, resisting changes that are not progress." Falconer deplored the tendency toward what he termed "undue liberalism" in doctrinal matters, for he feared that without a definite
faith there could be little spiritual growth. Though insistent on the
practical application of Christian principles to life, social reform
was not a substitute for evangelical religion. The Kingdom of God

could only be realized in the world through acceptance of vital truths of religion.[40] On the two key articles of the evangelical creed, the authority of the Bible and the issue of sin, his views placed him firmly within the evangelical camp. His Biblical studies, while praising the historical method of criticism, stressed the basic reliability of the New Testament text as a source of both doctrine and history.[41] At the same time, he refused to countenance the naturalistic or social explanations of human sin popularized by idealist philosophers and social thinkers. He forcefully maintained a strong sense of individual sin, which he defined in traditional terms as "an act of antagonism to a personal God,"[42] requiring a personal saviour.

The persistence of the evangelical creed in this Presbyterian minister-professor raises serious questions concerning the customary categories liberal and conservative. Falconer's religious outlook, like that of many other Presbyterian and Methodist clergy in the early twentieth century,[43] cannot be simply categorized as a watered-down ethical Christianity or creed of practical good works which he constructed in response to evolution, materialism, and secularism. Indeed, historical theology provided the evangelical creed with an intellectually respectable method of containing and limiting the naturalistic assumptions of higher criticism. More important, his attempt to strike a balance between individual regeneration and social action rested less upon philosophical idealism than on the fulcrum of the evangelical creed[44]—a high view of the factual accuracy and authority of the Bible in which the central doctrines of a personal sense of sin and the need for individual regeneration must motivate true Christian social action. The continued loyalty to the evangelical creed demonstrated by Falconer and most of his colleagues defeats any attempt to place them within the American spectrum of conservative, progressive, and radical wings of the social gospel imported by Richard Allen, a difficulty which points towards the urgent need to revise the concept of the "social gospel" in Canada.

Viewed from another perspective, Falconer's historical theology, formulated amid the changes confronting Scottish evangelicalism in the 1880s, itself applied the most powerful brake to the pursuit of the research ideal in the university. With its emphasis upon the primacy of faith in the interpretation of the Bible, it acted as a firm barrier to evolutionary naturalism and, further, proclaimed the subordination of Biblical criticism to the task of preaching and the spiritual life of the congregation. It remains to be asked to what extent these beliefs influenced the wider academic culture of early twentieth-century Canada, a question rendered more significant by the fact that in 1907 Robert Falconer resigned the principalship of Presbyterian College, Halifax, to assume the presidency of the University of Toronto, a post which he occupied until his retirement in 1932.

On the surface, it might be assumed that there could be simply no continuity between the leadership of a small theological college and the management of a large, secular university. Indeed, between 1900 and 1932 the University of Toronto expanded from about 1,500 students to over 8,000,[45] a revolution of numbers accompanied by even more dramatic changes. The establishment of new professional faculties and the expansion of the graduate school altered the orientation from the classics and humanities and the liberal notion of the cultured person to one in which the scientific ethos and the spirit of research prevailed. The achievement of equality in numbers of students by the professional faculties after 1920 imparted a utilitarian note and marked what many historians have believed was the final transformation of the old college dominated by the classics to the modern university.[46]

For one of Falconer's temper, these changes raised a number of serious questions. Between 1890 and 1930 the old liberal notions of the professor as moral tutor and the university as a place for the development of character were challenged by the scientific temper with its emphasis on research and professionalism.[47] Could the traditional ideal of a liberal education, the training of cultured character, be grafted onto the modern specialized professions? Was it possible to find a harmony between the new human sciences of sociology, political economy, and psychology and the older humanities philosophy, history, and classical study? More important, the emergence of specialized and professionalized academic disciplines after 1900[48] seemed to threaten the belief in the unity of knowledge—the cornerstone of the Victorian ideal of liberal education—and called into question the primacy of morality and culture both in the university and in the wider society.

From the moment of his arrival in Toronto, Falconer realized that the forces shaping the modern world were irreversible; the era was one of "industrial development, of scientific discovery, of new social conceptions. It is an age of world-wide commerce and of restless movement." The university, he declared, "must produce an efficiency for quite a new environment." Efficiency, in Falconer's vocabulary, did not simply mean the wider application of the research ideal, the quest for scientific objectivity. Rather it implied the combination of the spiritual and the practical, uniting the moral values of service to the community with the highest technical efficiency. The university was not merely the focus of knowledge and intellect, but a school for the acquisition of character and standards. This vision rested, in the final analysis, on the firm subordination of the research ideal to liberal education, a hierarchy founded on Falconer's consistent belief in the power of moral imperatives to rule the physical and material world.[49]

Speaking in 1922, Falconer defined the university as "one of the stable institutions of society and is both conservative and progressive."[50] Both the language and the underlying assumptions of this careful attempt to strike a stable balance might be read as the effort of a beleaguered university president to harmonize the competing demands of various departments and to satisfy the government and business sponsors of the university. But Falconer's statement drew specifically for its intellectual sustenance upon the canons of historical theology elaborated at the University of Edinburgh in the 1880s. His Scottish training had armed him with a profound suspicion of evolutionary naturalism, the theoretical structure underpinning many of the new developments in the natural and the human sciences. His addresses, warning students and faculty against the application of biological hypotheses to questions of individual and social morality,[51] continued to reflect the opposition of the evangelical creed to the extension of evolutionary interpretations into the realms of human behaviour and social organization.[52] Like his Presbyterian mentors, he maintained that scientific law and moral law occupied distinct spheres, a separation which enabled him to emphasize

> the fact that evolution and progress are not the same. The latter concerns the intrinsic value of the life we possess. Progress is not to be narrowly defined in terms of material well-being, or of the growth of scientific knowledge and its applications to the external equipment of the human race. It is determined by the essential quality and worth of the ideals that man sets before himself, by the measure in which he realizes them and by the harmony that this accomplishment induces both in himself, and in the society of which he is a member.[53]

Indeed, "progress" was equated, not with the new spirit of objective, scientific research, which sought to extend natural law into the realms of human psychology, religion, and social organization, but with the older moral values taught by the liberal humanities.

The evangelical creed restrained the research ideal in another important respect. In Falconer's estimation, the university was founded like the rest of society upon reverence for an inviolable "moral order which is Divine."[54] Free enquiry comprised only one aspect of his educational vision, and it was constantly bounded by tradition, the pursuit of the beautiful, and the faith and practice involved in religion.[55] The research ideal was hedged about in this quadrilateral with the same informal restrictions as was Biblical criticism in the Free Church of the 1880s; that is, its practice was widely praised so long as it did not offend against or alter to any significant degree the faith and practice of the community. In a similar vein, Falconer inveighed against irresponsible inquiry, for tradition must not be "bundled out bag and baggage by emotional youth acting on mass impulses."[56] What was most praiseworthy in Falconer's view was not dazzling theorizing or speculative forays into the human mind and social customs, but the slow and patient labour with "facts," the "exact and orderly method," which he was certain would ultimately testify to the "reign of law" and the existence of an orderly, beneficent universe.[57]

The separation of the natural and moral spheres enjoined by the evangelical creed, however, was potentially troublesome for one like Falconer, whose view of university education was premised upon the unity of knowledge, the essential harmony of science and the humanities. His resolution of this difficulty involved a fine balance, for his Presbyterianism forbade a simple conflation of the two approaches, which would imply the extension of inflexible scientific metaphysics into areas supposedly governed by free will and responsible moral choice. The answer lay in another aspect of his early education, in the image of Greece he had gained in the classroom of S. H. Butcher. Following the lead of his classics mentor, he often reminded the students that there was a proper division of labour between the sciences and the humanities. Yet while these disciplines followed different methods, specialization did not mean the fragmentation of knowledge. The diverse subjects and professional schools within the university were partners, not only in the quest for knowledge for its own sake, but in a shared idealism founded upon a search for standards and principles. Writing in 1925, he defined humanism as "an earnest contact with reality," the concern for truth, beauty, and goodness.[58] Even in the utilitarian environment of the professional schools, this idealism was possible, for the student could both attain "a wide and liberal knowledge of the subject," and acquire the sense of a "vocation for service."[59]

The humanities, sciences, and professional studies, in Falconer's definition of the university, all had a part in discovering the natural and moral laws of the universe, and each in its own way was conducive to order. For this leading Presbyterian, the scientific temper clarified man's understanding of the divine purpose in the natural world, it was compatible with the moral concerns of the humanistic disciplines. It was, however, not simply a question of broadening the idea of liberal education to include the sciences and the new professions. Falconer's views afforded an additional safeguard for the fragile unity of knowledge. Adopting almost verbatim Butcher's concept of the arts faculty as the "connecting link" within the university, Falconer consciously articulated the supremacy of the humanities. In the arts faculty, he confidently declared, "mental discipline and intellectual culture are found in purer quality."[60] Only through literature, philosophy, and history, he claimed, could the student arrive at an appreciation of the good. Without contact with these humane subjects, science was exposed to the lure of materialism and wealth.[61] Thus these subjects would necessarily remain at the core of the curriculum, not so much because of the new knowledge they produced, but because of their role as moral arbiters; the research ideal could be tempered and constrained through the very structure of the university itself.

Robert Falconer's leadership of the University of Toronto was marked by his allegiance to the evangelical creed, with its suspicion of evolutionary explanations of mind and society, and a reliance upon the humanistic canons of the older liberal education. This alliance, forged in the Scottish intellectual transformation of the 1870s, redefined the research ideal in such a way as to resist the specialization and fragmentation of knowledge and the growing gulf between the sciences and the humanities. It is not enough, however, merely to note the persistence of a powerful spirit of moral concern within the University of Toronto.[62] To understand Falconer's cast of mind, it may be argued, is to afford insight into both the organization of knowledge and the research agenda of a number of key disciplines within the university after 1910, especially when it is borne in mind that as president, Falconer had final responsibility for the hiring of both senior and junior staff.

Why, for example, until the 1960s were the social sciences at the University of Toronto organized in such a way as to preserve the unity of politics, economics, and sociology, rather than following the pattern of separate departmental structure characteristic of American universities? More important, why did social science, rather than adopting a rigid model of objectivity derived from the natural sciences, affirm its links with the humanistic disciplines, history and philosophy?[63] And why, it might be asked, did Falconer deliberately recruit men like Robert MacIver, Edward Urwick, and Harold Innis, all of whom rejected the possibility of an objective, value-free science of society? Answers to these questions must be tentative, but Falconer's Presbyterian theology and his ambivalence toward the "research ideal" at least encourage us to question prevailing views which assume, all too easily, that the period between 1910 and 1940 witnessed a rapid secularization of the English Canadian university.

NOTES

1. "Inaugural Address of President Falconer," *University of Toronto Monthly* [UTM] 8 (1907-08), 12.

2. "Inaugural Address of President Falconer," 7.

3. See A. B. McKillop, "The Research Ideal and the University of Toronto," in A. B. McKillop, ed., *Contours of Canadian Thought* (Toronto: University of Toronto Press, 1987), who argues that the research ideal was well established at the university by the time of Falconer's appointment in 1907.

4. The link between theological liberalism and social activism, usually termed by historians the "social gospel," has been explored from a variety of perspectives by a number of Canadian cultural historians. An optimistic view of the transformation of the older evangelicalism into twentieth-century movements of social reform is taken by Richard Allen in his classic study, *The Social Passion* (Toronto: University of Toronto Press, 1973). Allen's view was reinforced, although from a slightly different perspective, by A. B. McKillop in *A Disciplined Intelligence* (Montreal: McGill-Queen's University Press, 1979). The more pessimistic view, that Protestant clergymen, by accommodating their theology to the evolutionary insights of evolutionary biology and the social sciences, surrendered the vital foundations of belief, has been most recently and most eloquently stated by Ramsay Cook in *The Regenerators: Social Criticism in Late Victorian English Canada* (Toronto: University of Toronto Press, 1985).

5. Robert Falconer, *Religion on My Life's Road*. The Rockwell Lectures delivered at the Rice Institute, April 1938, 45-46; Robert Falconer, "From College to University," *University of Toronto Quarterly* [UTQ] 5 (October 1935): 2. Additional biographical details may be found in the fine study by James G. Greenlee, *Sir Robert Falconer: A Biography* (Toronto: University of Toronto Press, 1988), which is particularly strong on Falconer's role as a university administrator.

6. University of Toronto Library, George M. Wrong Papers, Robert Falconer to G. M. Wrong, January 25, 1942; "From College to University," 3.

7. Impressions of his Scottish education are given in Robert Falconer, "In Edinburgh Fifty Years Ago," *Queen's Quarterly* 44 (Winter, 1937): 441-54. It is interesting to note that Falconer's biographer, Greenlee, uncritically accepts Falconer's estimate of his teachers. It should be noted that Falconer wrote this assessment in 1938, at a time when he himself sensed that the convictions of his youth were under assault from the forces of secularism and materialism. His rejection of their philosophy was not characteristic of the earlier phases of his career. See Greenlee, *Sir Robert Falconer: A Biography*, 24.

8. See Henry Calderwood, *The Relations of Mind and Brain* (London: Macmillan, 1892; first published 1879); W. Calderwood and D. Woodside, *The Life of Henry Calderwood, L.L.D., F.R.S.E.* (London: Macmillan, 1900), 176-77, 193.

9. A. Campbell Fraser, *Philosophy of Theism, being the Gifford Lectures delivered before the University of Edinburgh in 1895-96* (Edinburgh: Blackwood, 1896), 92; Calderwood and Woodside, *Life of Henry Calderwood*, 191.

10. In recent years, historians in Britain and the United States have moved beyond the traditional model of conflict between religion and science. Specifically, they argue, one must distinguish between "Darwinism" and other, competing forms of evolutionary thought which continued to insist upon the teleological nature of the evolutionary process and which were available to late Victorian clergymen and scientists. See, for example, James R. Moore, *The Post-Darwinian Forgotten Defenders: The Encounter Between Evangelical Theology and Evolutionary Thought* (Grand Rapids, MI: Eerdmans, 1987).

11. For an analysis of Caird's neo-Hegelian perspective, see John Passmore, *A Hundred Years of Philosophy* (Harmondsworth: Penguin, 1966), 55; Sir Henry Jones and John Henry Muirhead, *The Life and Philosophy of Edward Caird* (Glasgow, 1921), 74, 333-34, 347-48.

12. It is significant that even the latest representative of this school, Andrew Seth Pringle-Pattison, wrote in 1887 a forceful critique of neo-Hegelianism entitled *Hegelianism and Personality*. Originally delivered as the Balfour Lectures at the University of Edinburgh, the themes explored would have certainly been familiar to Robert Falconer, who would have been an undergraduate at the time.

13. Robert Falconer, *Idealism in National Character* (Toronto: University of Toronto Press, 1920), 23.

14. W. R. Taylor, "Religion and Scholarship," in H. J. Cody, Malcolm Wallace, and W. R. Taylor, "In Memoriam Sir Robert Alexander Falconer, K.C.M.G.," *UTQ* 13 (January 1944): 159.

15. Robert Falconer, "A Study in Emerson," *The Theologue* 2 (April 1891): 5-7; "Ideals of Religion: Review Article,": *UTQ* 10 (January 1941), 231.

16. See Sheldon Rothblatt, *Tradition and Change in English Liberal Education: An Essay in History and Culture* (London: Faber & Faber, 1976), 165. For other aspects of this important cultural transition, see T. W. Heyck, *The Transformation of Intellectual Life in Victorian Britain* (London: Croom Helm, 1983).

17. For the characteristics of the early Victorian ideal of liberal education, see Rothblatt, *Tradition and Change*, 148-50. This little-known work actually contains a superb discussion of the changing meaning of this ideal in relation to its cultural and social context.

18. Frank M. Turner, *The Greek Heritage in Victorian Britain* (New Haven: Yale University Press, 1981), 15-16.

19. Richard Jenkyns, *The Victorians and Ancient Greece* (Cambridge, MA: Harvard University Press, 1980), 17, 74-76.

20. S. H. Butcher, *Some Aspects of the Greek Genius* (London: Macmillan, 1904; first published, 1891), 28-29.

21. Butcher, *Some Aspects*, 213, 220-21.

22. Butcher, *Some Aspects*, 223.

23. Butcher, *Some Aspects*, 214-16.

24. For a recent account of these developments, see A. C. Cheyne, *The Transforming of the Kirk: Victorian Scotland's Religious Revolution* (Edinburgh: St. Andrew Press, 1983).

25. See Cheyne, *Transforming of the Kirk,* and for the experience of Canadian Presbyterians who attended the Scottish universities in this period, see Michael Gauvreau, *The Evangelical Century: College and Creed in English Canada from the Great Revival to the Great Depression* (Montreal: McGill-Queen's University Press, 1991).

26. Quoted in James Strahan, *Andrew Bruce Davidson* (London: Hodder and Stoughton, 1917), 197. See also Cheyne, *The Transforming of the Kirk,* 37-38.

27. Here I dissent from the position advanced by Brian Fraser in his recent work *The Social Uplifters* (Waterloo: Wilfred Laurier University Press, 1988). Fraser argues that neo-Hegelian idealism formed the intellectual underpinning of the social activism of the prominent Presbyterian clergymen Robert Falconer, T. B. Kilpatrick, J. A. Macdonald, and C. W. Gordon, George Pidgeon, and J. G. Shearer. All these men attended the Free Church Presbyterian colleges between 1870 and 1890, and would have encountered a rival system of theology which had been consciously constructed in order to refute the evolutionary views of Edward Caird and his followers. For a further elaboration of this point, see Michael Gauvreau, *The Evangelical Century,* chapter 4.

28. See Donald Macmillan, *The Life of Robert Flint* (London, 1914), 262-64; Robert Rainy, D.D., *Delivery and Development of Christian Doctrine* (Edinburgh: T. & T. Clark, 1874), 35-36, 40.

29. For the influence of Drummond, an associate of the evangelist Dwight Moody and author of *Natural Law in the Spiritual World,* see James R. Moore, "Evangelicals and Evolution: Henry Drummond, Herbert Spencer, and the Naturalisation of the Spiritual World," *Scottish Journal of Theology* 38 (September 1985), 383-417.

30. Falconer, *Religion on My Life's Road,* 52.

31. Falconer's impressions of Davidson and Dods are provided in two articles written later in his career: "Reminiscences of Professor A. B. Davidson," *Constructive Quarterly,* 6 (June 1918): 385-400; "New Testament Scholarship in My Time," *UTQ* 14 (January 1945): 135-49.

32. Falconer's reminiscences of this episode can be found in "My Memory of Harnack," *Canadian Journal of Religious Thought* 7 (1930): 380.

33. "Christ the Personal Source of Religion and Theology," *The Theologue* 5 (December 1893): 4.

34. Adolf von Harnack, *History of Dogma,* vol. I (London: Williams and Norgate, 1887), 16; Harnack, *What is Christianity?* (London: Williams and Norgate, 1901), 51, 199-214. For a modern study of Harnack, see G. Wayne Glick, *The Reality of Christianity: A Study of Adolf von Harnack as Historian and Theologian* (New York: Harper & Row, 1967).

35. This is the position advocated by Falconer's biographer, James Greenlee. My reservations will be apparent from the body of the text. See Greenlee, *Sir Robert Falconer: A Biography,* 44-45.

36. Prof. R. A. Falconer, "Christian Theology Spiritually Discerned," *Presbyterian College Journal,* 15 (January 1896): 176-77.

37. Falconer, "Christ the Personal Source of Religion and Theology," 8. This view was supported by the chief intellectual leaders of Canadian Presbyterianism. See, for example, Principal MacVicar, "Dogma and Current Thought," *Knox College Monthly* 17 (May 1893): 691; United Church Archives, John Mark King Papers, Reel 1, "Inaugural Lecture," *The Manitoba College Journal* (1893): 127-34.

38. For A. B. Bruce's views, see J. E. McFayden, "Alexander Balmain Bruce: An Appreciation," *The Westminster*, April 7, 1900, 394; Andrew Martin Fairbairn, *The Place of Christ in Modern Theology* (London: Hodder and Stoughton, 1893), viii, 3, 47-49, 187-88. The copy consulted in the John P. Robarts Research Library was Robert Falconer's personal copy.

39. This view has been most compellingly articulated by A. B. McKillop, *A Disciplined Intelligence*, chapter 7.

40. Robert Falconer, "Preaching to the Times," *The Theologue* 14 (November 1902): 460-66; *The Ideal of Immortality in Western Civilization*. The Ingersoll Lecture, 1930 (Cambridge, MA: Harvard University Press, 1930), 33.

41. Robert Falconer, *The Truth of the Apostolic Gospel* (New York, 1904); "The Gospel According to Peter," *The Theologue* 4 (April 1893): 119-27; "The Burning Question of New Testament Criticism," *The Westminster*, ns, 2 (January 1903); "The Church and Unity According to the New Testament," *The Presbyterian Witness*, June 3, 1905.

42. Robert Falconer, "Sin As a Religious Concept," *The Theologue* 18 (February 1907): 65.

43. On the larger context, see my *The Evangelical Century*, chapter 5. A similar perspective on the "social gospel" among Canadian Presbyterians has been advanced by Brian Fraser in *The Social Uplifters*.

44. James Greenlee's biography advances the argument that Falconer was uncompromisingly hostile to the "social gospel." This is not quite accurate. Writing in 1930, in a passage not noted by his biographer, Falconer criticized the old evangelical insistence on the securing of individual salvation as too narrow in its neglect of widespread moral aspirations for a better social order. He praised, rather, the more modern evangelical balance of individualism and social action provided by the historical interpretation of the Gospels and "the conception of the Kingdom of God as a Realm in which the Divine Will is to be realised by the redemption of men as a society of the sons of God." See Falconer, *The Ideal of Immortality and Western Civilization*, 33.

45. H. J. Cody, et al., "In Memoriam Sir Robert Alexander Falconer," 139-43.

46. Robin S. Harris, *A History of Higher Education in Canada, 1663-1960* (Toronto: University of Toronto Press, 1976), 352, gives enrolment statistics, illustrating the trend was the fact that by the late 1920s the classics course, once the major humanistic study, had been reduced to a minor department struggling for survival. On this point, see Alan Bowker, "Truly Useful Men: Maurice Hutton, George Wrong, James Mavor and the University of Toronto, 1880-1927," Ph.D. thesis, University of Toronto, 1975, 283-88.

47. S. E. D. Shortt, *The Search for an Ideal: Six Canadian Intellectuals and their Convictions in an Age of Transition* (Toronto: University of Toronto Press, 1976), 6-7.

48. Recent American studies of this transformation of the organization of knowledge include: Thomas L. Haskell, *The Emergence of Professional Social Science: The American Social Science Association and the Nineteenth Century Crisis of Authority* (Urbana, IL: University of Illinois Press, 1977); Laurence Veysey, "The Plural Organized World of the Humanities," in Alexandra Oleson and John Voss, eds., *The Organization of Knowledge in Modern America, 1860-1920* (Baltimore: Johns Hopkins University Press, 1979), 51-106; Dorothy Ross, "The Development of the Social Sciences," in Oleson and Voss, 107-38. For an overview, see John Higham, "The Matrix of Specialization," in Oleson and Voss, 3-18. For the study of the emergence of sociology in the Canadian university, see Marlene Shore, *The Science of Social Redemption* (Toronto: University of Toronto Press, 1987).

49. "Inaugural Address of President Falconer," 7.

50. Robert Falconer, *The Progressiveness of the Modern University*. The President's Address at the Opening of the Session, 1922-23, 1.

51. Falconer, *Idealism in National Character*, 121-22.

52. My interpretation of the opposition of the perspective of the evangelical creed and that of the late Victorian social sciences was suggested by a reading of a forthcoming study by Nancy J. Christie, *The Cosmology of New Societies: Evolutionary Thought and the Writing of History in Canada and Australia, 1880-1920*. Christie argues that late nineteenth-century colonial historians and social thinkers drew upon a wide range of evolutionary assumptions promoted by British and American biologists, philosophers, and social scientists, all of which emphasized the identity of the moral and the material. For the view offered by evangelical clergymen, which stressed the separation of the moral and the material, see Gauvreau, *The Evangelical Century*, chapter 5.

53. Gauvreau, *Evangelical Century*, 108-9.

54. "Inaugural Address of President Falconer," 12-13.

55. Robert Falconer, *Some Factors in the Making of the Complete Citizen*. The Rice Institute Pamphlet 21 (January 1934), no. 1, 5.

56. Falconer, *Some Factors*, 23-24.

57. Falconer, "The Place of Authority in the University Spirit," *UTM* 9 (November 1908): 16.

58. Falconer, "Humanism," *The Hibbert Journal* 24 (October 1925): 123.

59. University of Toronto Archives, Robert Falconer Papers, Box 71, "What Should the Dental Student be Taught so that he may Have a Correct Appreciation of his Relation to Affairs of Life? Ethical, Political, Economical, Financial? (1921), 4-5, 12-14.

60. "Inaugural Address of President Falconer," 7.

61. Falconer, "Humanism," 128-32.

62. See A. B. McKillop, *A Disciplined Intelligence*, Epilogue, for the argument that the "moral imperative" continued to shape English Canadian thought and culture during the inter-war years.

63. A. B. McKillop, in "The Research Ideal and the University of Toronto," suggests that this peculiar organization was largely in place by the time Falconer took office in 1907. Yet the great expansion of the university and the multiplication of departments and schools took place during Falconer's presidency.

II

Canadian Presbyterians and the State

Few issues have been as contentious as the relation of church and state. The history of the Christian Church is, in part, a record of how Christians have sought to understand aright and to apply wisely Jesus's dictum, "Render to Caesar the things which are Caesar's and to God the things which are God's" (Matthew 22:21) as well as the Apostle Paul's injunction, "Let every person be subject to the governing authorities; for there is no authority except from God and those authorities that exist have been instituted by God" (Romans 13:1).

In the sixteenth century, Martin Luther, John Calvin, and the other reformers were forced to rethink the relation of secular and spiritual authority. The two jurisdictions had become hopelessly confused. On the one hand spiritual rulers claimed both spiritual and secular authority, and on the other hand civil rulers also insisted on having a twofold jurisdiction. The Middle Ages had witnessed a long and intense struggle between the two authorities regarding their respective rights and particularly which jurisdiction was superior. In contrast to these views and in the interests of safeguarding true religion, Luther drew an important distinction between the proper jurisdictions of secular and spiritual governments. He allowed the secular authority power over "a merely external" righteousness and accorded to the church charge over true piety and religion.[1]

John Calvin followed Luther's example. For him there was one absolute sovereignty, God's. All rightful authority in church and state is derived directly or indirectly from God. In a struggle with the Geneva Council, Calvin sought to carve out an independent sphere for the church to exercise authority in the spiritual realm, particularly in matters of doctrine and discipline. Yet because of the obstinancy of individuals, he was not averse to obtaining the backup of the power of the sword wielded by the civil authorities, as the execution of the heretic, Servetus, tragically shows.[2]

Two things should be noted about Calvin's view of civil government, as each bears on the essays in this section. The first concerns Calvin's insistence on the necessity and importance of civil order. Calvin held that there is a dual government to which humanity is subject. In addition to the spiritual government which rules over the soul or the inner person and has to do with eternal life, there is a second order of government whose province is the establishment of civil and external justice.[3] The two governments differ in character and must not be confused. Calvin sought to find a middle way between the spiritualists and "fantasts" of his day and those whom he called "the flatterers of princes." The former wished to overturn the civil order, while the latter championed the power of princes without acknowledging any bounds to it and even opposed it to the sovereignty of God. Anyone who knows how to distinguish between body and soul, between this present transitory life and the eternal life of the world to come, Calvin said, will not find it difficult to understand that the spiritual government of Christ and civil government are things far removed from each other. Still, while the two governments are distinct they are in no way incompatible with each other. Christ's spiritual rule, while we are on earth, prepares us for the coming kingdom. The aim of secular government, while we remain on earth is "to foster and protect the external worship of God, defend pure doctrine and the good condition of the Church, accommodate the way we live, mould our conduct to civil justice, reconcile us one to another, and uphold and defend the common peace and tranquillity."[4]

The second matter concerns Calvin's view that "popular magistrates" may collectively resist "tyrants." On the analogy of the Spartan ephors and the Roman tribunes of the people, Calvin put forward the view that modern estates general or parliaments may resist tyrannical rulers and even wage war against them. Calvin made a distinction between private and public persons. Private persons have a duty to obey and suffer. Yet public persons or "popular magistrates" may legitimately oppose and even have the duty to resist "the licentiousness and frenzy of kings." Indeed Calvin goes on to say: "On the contrary; if they connive at their unbridled violence and insults against the poor common people, I say that such negligence is a nefarious betrayal of their oath; they are betraying the people and defrauding them of that liberty which they know they were ordained by God to defend."[5] Later, Calvin's followers extended the right of resistance to private persons. This was the case with Théodore de Bèze, Calvin's successor in Geneva, and John Knox in Scotland. Further developments occurred in France and Holland where a full-scale doctrine of resistance was worked out by Reformed thinkers such as Althusius, Grotius, and others.[6]

John Moir in his essay explores the way in which Canadian Presbyterians have related to the state. According to him, the problematic relationship of church and state has been at the heart of every division and every reunion in the history of Presbyterianism in both Scotland and Canada. He believes that the arguments used in Canada owed more to John Knox than to John Calvin. This may be the case, and yet there was little difference between Knox and Calvin on the question of the spiritual independence of the church for which they both contended. This Knoxian tradition of resistance lingered on in Scotland and in those lands overseas where Scots settled. The 1707 union of England and Scotland protected the rights of the Church of Scotland and established equality with the Church of England in their respective kingdoms. Yet it did not define their status outside of Britain and this had its consequences in British North America. Two developments in Scotland had far-reaching effects. The first was the re-establishment of the power of patrons to appoint parish ministers, thus negating the congregation's right to call and compromising the spiritual independence of the church. The second was the gradual polarization of the Church of Scotland into two competing parties: the Moderates and the Evangelicals. These last two developments played a part in the 1733 and 1761 secessions from the Church of Scotland.

Three positions on the relation of church and state emerged from these controversies: (1) the idea of endowed church establishment in which the patron pays the piper and calls the tune; (2) the notion of the separation of church and state represented by the Secession churches in which the congregation pays the piper and calls the tune and; (3) the mediating view of the independence of the church yet its acceptance of support from the state represented by the Free Church (separated from the Church of Scotland in 1843) position, in which the state may pay the piper but cannot call the tune.

Professor Moir shows how these views affected the Canadian situation, first, in the controversy over the Clergy Reserves, second, in the 1875 union of the Presbyterian bodies in Canada; third, in the social gospel movement; fourth, in the 1925 Church Union; fifth, in the Declaration Concerning Church and Nation of 1955; and finally, in the 1989 Memorandum of Agreement between the University of Toronto and the Toronto School of Theology. The mediating Free Church position of the independence of the church from state interference and the presumption that the state is obligated to support "true religion" even materially with public funds, Professor Moir contends, has won out: "Despite all the pressures and precedents of North American voluntarism and of secularism in the twentieth century, one Scottish tradition will be honored by Canadian Presbyterians. The piper should still be paid but he who pays the piper is not yet permitted to call the tune. *Nec tamen consumebatur.*" Small wonder! It is the best of both worlds.

In the other essay in this section, "Canada's Sunday," Paul Laverdure shows how church-state struggles were focused in the issue of Sabbath observance. He believes that what could or could not be done on the Canadian Sunday was largely shaped by the Presbyterian Church. This is evident in the leadership of the Lord's Day Alliance founded in 1888 in Ottawa. Principal William Caven of Knox College headed the Ontario Lord's Day Alliance while the Reverend W. D. Armstrong, another Presbyterian, presided over the national organization. Half the executive were Presbyterians. In 1899 the Reverend John G. Shearer, a Presbyterian, was appointed the first full-time paid field secretary. While the Methodists made prohibition their main concern, Presbyterians concentrated on the observance of the Lord's Day.

Dr. Laverdure proceeds to tell the story of the successful opposition between 1875 and 1900 to Sunday business and the railways, and from 1900 to 1925 the successful struggle with

Quebec, business, and the state. After 1925 the Presbyterian river split into two weaker streams. War, depression, and again war took the initiative out of Presbyterian hands. The Lord's Day Act remained in effect until 1985 when the Charter of Rights made all religious legislation unconstitutional. The state finally resolved the issue by deciding that it would not impose "Presbyterian Sunday morality" on Quebec or any province or any business. It was up to individuals to follow the fourth commandment in their own way.

To many people today, the question of how Sunday is to be observed may appear trivial. Compared to such pressing contemporary issues as abortion, human sexuality, civil rights, and especially oppression in Latin America or South Africa, the question of how one spends Sunday may seem rather archaic and insignificant. Even if it were desirable, there is no possibility of going back to the way Presbyterians observed Sunday in 1892. But that does not make it an unimportant matter. While we must deplore the extremes to which the supporters of Sunday observance went, yet it was a right impulse that motivated them. Spiritual practice, of which Sunday worship and the proper use of the Lord's Day are for Christians an integral part, is no trivial matter. As recent events in Ontario and Quebec and other provinces show, it is for this reason, at least in part, that the issue of how Sunday is to be observed will not simply die or go away.

NOTES

1. For what follows see particularly, *Luther and Calvin on Secular Authority*, ed. and trans. Harro Höpfl. Cambridge Texts in the History of Political Thought (Cambridge: Cambridge University Press, 1991), xviiiff.

2. This event more than any other has coloured Calvin's posthumous reputation. Many critics of Calvin have sought to discredit his whole theological enterprise on account of the Servetus affair. This is manifestly unfair. Three brief points should be noted. First, executions for heresy were exceedingly common in the sixteenth century, and in this respect Calvin was a child of his age rather than some kind of horrible initiator of this practice. Second, the trial, condemnation, and execution of Servetus, including the particular mode of execution, were the work of a tribunal of which Calvin was not a member but only an expert theological witness. Third, Calvin appealed to the Council against unnecessary cruelty in employing burning alive as the form of punishment rather than beheading, but his appeal was rejected. To

make these points is not to excuse Calvin of his involvement. He was not averse to employing the aid of the civil magistrate in support of the authority of the church. Moreover, there were contemporary theologians—Sebastian Castellio, for one—who argued for toleration in matters of religion. Calvin failed to come to this insight. For a helpful recent discussion see Alister McGrath, *A Life of John Calvin* (Oxford: Basil Blackwell, 1990), 114-20. See also Roland H. Bainton, *Hunted Heretic*, and J. T. McNeill, *The History and Character of Calvinism* (New York: Oxford University Press, 1962), 173-77.

3.   John Calvin, *Institutes of the Christian Religion*, 4.20.4.

4.   Calvin, *Institutes of the Christian Religion*, 4.20.2.

5.   Calvin, *Institutes of the Christian Religion*, 4.20.31. The translation is Harro Höpfl's in *Luther and Calvin on Secular Authority*, 83.

6.   Cf. Quentin Skinner, *The Foundations of Modern Political Thought*, vol. 2 (Cambridge: Cambridge University Press, 1978), 230ff.

'Who Pays The Piper...':
Canadian Presbyterianism and
Church-State Relations

John S. Moir

The problematic relationship of church and state has been at the heart of every secession and every reunion in the history of Scottish Presbyterianism, and in Canada that same issue, like so many other features of Presbyterian identity, has been shaped primarily by those Scottish precedents and traditions. Most of the arguments used in Canada and in Scotland owe more to John Knox than to John Calvin, but the ultimate appeal to authority leads back to the Bible. Scripture contributes several often-cited proof texts, but these are both inconclusive and even conflicting. The exhortation "Render unto Caesar" (Matthew 22:21) provides no assistance in determining what belongs to Caesar and what to God. Probably more influential in shaping Presbyterian attitudes have been Jesus's statement to Pilate, "You have no power over me unless it had been given you from above" (John 18:11) and the interjection by the disciples at the Last Supper, "Look, Lord, here are two swords" (Luke 22:38), a gratuitous comment freely misinterpreted and misused in every century since.

The latter two texts have been regularly taken to mean that sacred and secular authority are both of divine origin and are parallel but distinct and unequal spheres. In his classic study, *The Holy Roman Empire,* James Bryce notes that the Holy Roman Church and the Holy Roman Empire were like two sides of a single coin, "the co-operation of both being needed in all that concerns the welfare of Christendom at large."[1] This accord between papal and imperial powers, between the sacred and secular swords, rested on a theory ("as sublime as it is impracticable") that required a co-operation "attained only at a few points in their history."[2] The symbolism of the two swords was embodied in the coronation ritual of post-Carolingian emperors, but already by the middle of the ninth century Pope Nicolas I was trying to tilt the balance of power in favour of the church. Quoting St. Paul that the secular ruler is God's servant for the general good—"If you do wrong, be afraid, for he does not bear the sword in vain" (Romans 13:4)—Nicolas claimed that the emperor's right to rule came from the pope because the power to use the secular sword was intended "for the exaltation of his mother, this holy apostolic church."[3]

This concept of the two spheres of jurisdiction passed into Calvin's theology. Calvin stressed the king's responsibility as God's anointed, but he also allowed for the removal of a bad king by the lesser magistrates. John Knox agreed that civil government was divinely instituted and that the authority of rulers was limited by divine law, but he also recognized that the feudal kingdom of Scotland was not the republican city-state of Geneva. He asserted that ordinary citizens shared the power and duty to remove and execute a tyrant—"the sword is in their own hand"—and so both people and king shared the sword committed to them by God.[4] The operating base for this popular resistance grew from Knox's concept of covenanting, and for this his model was the Scottish custom of bonding.

The development of the Church of Scotland as a national, endowed, and protected institution reduced any reality of popularly based power, yet the Knoxian tradition of resistance lingered on in Scotland and in those lands overseas where Scots settled. The union of 1707 promised to protect the church's rights in Scotland and establish its equality with the Church of England in their respective kingdoms, but it failed to define their status outside Britain, an oversight fraught with future difficulties for British North America. Within Scotland itself, two other developments also influenced the religious development of the country and of the colonies. Just five years after the union the United Parliament re-established the power of lay patrons, whether individual landowners or the state itself, to appoint parish ministers, thus negating the congregation's right to call. The second development was the gradual polarization of the Church of Scotland into two competing parties, the strict Calvinist "Evangelicals" and the deistic and latitudinarian "Moderates."

These last two developments played a part in the secession of 1733 when Ebenezer Erskine and his followers separated from the established church over the patronage issue. For the Church of Scotland, particularly the Moderates, it was acceptable that the patrons who paid the piper should call the tune by appointing their chosen candidates to pulpits. The next secession, in 1761, saw three Church of Scotland ministers carry opposition to state interference with the church to its logical conclusion by demanding complete separation of church and state and the adoption of voluntarism. Under the voluntary system the piper would receive only the free-will offerings of the audience—a practice which might leave the party without any music!

The third tradition of church-state relations came immediately from the Disruption of 1843. Once again the seceders—this time more than 400 members of the General Assembly—left the established and endowed church because of the state's support for the patronage system. The new Free Church did not, however, believe in voluntarism. Reiterating chapter 23 of the Westminster Confession, the new church proclaimed that the state must not interfere in the church's separate and sacred sphere of authority. Nevertheless, the church still insisted that the state is under divine obligation to support it materially. Now the piper must still be paid, but whoever pays the piper will not be allowed to call the tune. For the Free Church the two swords still existed, but whereas state intrusion into the church's jurisdiction was anathema, the church could claim to be not only the conscience of the state but by logical extension the final arbiter in all matters involving church-state relations.

The similarity of this anti-Erastian position to the contemporary political arguments of the Oxford Movement and Roman Catholic ultramontanism is striking and results from the events and philosophy of the French Revolution.[5] Reacting to the emergence of modernism and secularism, and specifically to Napoleon's treatment of the papacy, ultramontanes asserted that because the Church is divine, infallible, and soul-saving where the state is human, fallible, and materialistic, the Church is superior to the state and is the

God-appointed conscience of the state. Anti-Erastianism was the bedrock of the Romantics' opposition to statism, whether voiced in Edinburgh, Oxford, Rome, or Paris, yet anti-Erastianism per se is not necessarily voluntaristic.

The three traditions—endowed church establishment, separation of church and state, and finally the church independent of but superior to the state—were carried from Scotland to British North America, but here circumstances and personalities created interesting mutations. The ideal of a national establishment, based on the Reformation principle of *cuius regio, eius religio* (the ruler's religion becomes the nation's religion) assumes the existence of religious uniformity—an assumption not applicable here because of de facto religious pluralism. Although the Church of England was legally established in the Maritimes, there was little cause for jealousy or cupidity among other denominations because no endowment was provided. Similarly, when the Church of Scotland did claim social and religious superiority over the Secessionists in the 1820s, no demand for co-establishment with the Church of England was ever put forward.

In Upper and Lower Canada, however, the relations of church and state became a Presbyterian *cause célèbre*, complicated by conditions and traditions inherited by the government from the French regime. The Quebec Act of 1774 was designed to integrate a French-speaking and Roman Catholic population into an anglophone and Protestant empire, in part by giving legal recognition to the religion of the "new subjects." The so-called Constitutional Act of 1791 recognized the right of Loyalists to representative government and English law, but it also established the Protestant religion and endowed the clergy with lands equal to one-seventh of Crown land grants. "Protestant Clergy" was not defined, but subsequent clauses referring to rectories and rectors "of the Church of England" are accepted by historians as sufficient evidence that the Church of England was now established in the two Canadas, as in the Maritime colonies. The difference in the two regions, however, was the creation of the Clergy Reserves—3,750 square miles of prime agricultural land—

a delayed fuse for church-state relations in the St. Lawrence-Great Lakes basin.

Among Presbyterians in the two Canadas the church-state issue arose soon after the arrival of the Loyalists. The controversy, however, did not begin with the Clergy Reserves. In 1786, when Presbyterians petitioned against the Church of England's monopoly on marriages, their claim for equal treatment of the Church of Scotland was based on the loyalty of Scots. No group in Britain deserved more appreciation from the House of Hanover for their steady support of the Protestant succession during the Glorious Revolution that had prevented "tyranny by High Churchmen."[6] Lieutenant-Governor Simcoe blamed John Bethune, the Presbyterian Loyalist chaplain, for this petition which he denounced as "the product of a wicked Head and a most disloyal Heart." Nevertheless, the petition produced a revised marriage act that added clergy of "the church of Scotland, or Lutherans, or Calvinists" to those licensed to solemnize matrimony.[7]

Two generations passed before church-state relations again attracted Presbyterian attention. This time the issue was government aid to St. Andrew's at Niagara-on-the-Lake after its church was burned by the Americans in the War of 1812. The petition of the Niagara congregation made no claim to co-establishment—it merely suggested that the Clergy Reserves might supply the £100 the Presbyterians wanted.[8] No money was forthcoming, but four years later resolutions of the legislatures of both Canadas called for co-establishment of the Church of Scotland as a legal right, with endowment from the Clergy Reserves or some other public source.

Despite the creation, at government prompting, of a Canadian synod of the Church of Scotland in 1831, John Strachan's successful defence of the Church of England's control over the Clergy Reserves and the campaign by Methodists and other voluntarists to end denominational privileges and religious favouritism in the Canadas by the separation of church and state prevented the achievement of co-establishment.[9] The closest the Church of Scotland ever came to establishment and endowment in the Canadas was its inclusion as an inferior partner in the 1841 compromise division of the Clergy Reserves funds—a division that also made the Church of Rome a beneficiary of the support promised a half-century early to the "Protestant Clergy"! That 1841 solution to the issue of state endowment for religion lasted only fifteen years before the Clergy Reserves were secularized by an act that proclaimed its purpose to be the removal of "all semblance of connexion between Church and State,"[10] the only such reference in the legislative history of Canada.

Before this victory of voluntarism was achieved, however, Canadian Presbyterianism had already faced its own moment of truth regarding church-state relations. In the wake of the Napoleonic wars a flood of Scottish immigrants fled depressed conditions at home to settle in the colonies, and particularly in the area north of Lake Erie which received an estimated 10,000 persons per year.[11] As important as their numbers was the religious persuasion of these immigrants—most supported the Evangelical party in the Church of Scotland. The issues of "patronage" and "intrusion" did not exist in British North America, yet the Disruption in Scotland called for a sympathetic response, particularly among these more recent immigrants. If Disruption was good enough for Scotland, it should be good enough for the colonies. To an Evangelical, continued connection with the Church of Scotland constituted guilt by association.

Orchestrated by that peripatetic advocate of the Free Church cause, the Reverend Robert Burns, the Disruption spread to British North America in 1844, bringing with it that third version of the church-state relationship—pay the piper but do not call the tune. Burns had fought valiantly and written voluminously against voluntarism in Scotland in the late 1820s,[12] and not surprisingly he found clerical allies in the Canadas among those ministers who had so recently begun to receive supplementary stipends from the Clergy Reserves funds. Unfortunately for the Free Church ministers, the government ruled that those leaving the church in Canada would lose their claim to the monies. The upshot was that the new colonial Free Church became unwillingly voluntarist, but eventually even those clergy who remained in the Church of Scotland also lost their stipends thanks to financial mismanagement by church authorities.[13]

In the short run the Free Church interpretation of church-state relations seemed fated to disappear in the North American climate of voluntarism. Immediately after the local Disruption the voluntarist Secession synod approached the new Free Church with a view to union. Despite the fact that the Free Church clergy had lost their government stipends, ministers such as Burns and Michael Willis, the principal of Knox College, were able to delay the union by insisting that Secessionists acknowledge that the civil magistrate is obligated to support "true religion" because Christ is head over the nations. Their rearguard action denying the de facto existence of voluntarism in British North America is the more surprising in light of the victory by the growing forces of voluntarism within the Free Church itself in 1848.

That year the government invited denominations to apply for surplus money in the Clergy Reserves Fund. The reaction in the Free Church was like Atalanta's when confronted with the golden apples. Some clergy applied for a share of the money because "endowment of the Church by the civil magistrate is lawful," but voluntarists countered with the argument that offering and accepting public funds for denominational use ought to be determined "on the grounds of Christian expediency."[14] Because synod decided to forbid applications by either ministers or congregations, the voluntarist version of church-state relations triumphed, and union with the Secessionists was possible.

The Basis of Union that created the Canada Presbyterian Church in 1861 required seven years of protracted discussion about the headship of Christ, but in the end it provided a compromise that became the official Canadian Presbyterian position on church and state for the next eighty years. The Secessionists agreed that Christ is king, but denied that he delegates power to "earthly Kings." Burns broke this log-jam with a resolution asserting that the Basis already embodied "the grand principle of national responsibility to Christ," and it should not be clogged with "an enumeration of the varied practical applications of that principle."[15] In its final form the fourth article of the Basis states that Christ is "King of the Nations" and therefore, like all people, "the Civil Magistrate ... is bound to regulate his official procedure ... by the revealed will of Christ."[16]

In the negotiations that led to the union in 1875 of all Canadian Presbyterians, the doctrine of Christ's headship posed no serious obstacle. The doctrine was, however, further broadened by invoking the practice of "forbearance." Article 2 concluded that nothing in the Westminster Confession or either catechism regarding the power and duty of the civil magistrate "shall be held to sanction any principles or view inconsistent with full liberty of conscience in matters of religion."[17] This produced a very Canadian formula— the headship of Christ simply means whatever you want it to mean!—a formula that satisfied all but a very few and became an enduring tradition until World War II.

In the late 1880s Canadian Presbyterians did become vocal and involved in the equal rights movement when they and other Protestants accused the Jesuits of having divided loyalties that prevented them from being good Canadians. This issue certainly involved church-state relations in terms of denominational equality—expressed in the slogan "A Free Church in a Free State" that accompanied a series of resolutions on the separation of church and state by the General Assembly of 1890. At least in those days before multiculturalism and religious pluralism the solution seemed simple—keep the long arm of the Vatican out of Canada, and let the Jesuits be more like Presbyterians![18]

Although the bases of union in 1861 and 1875 had denied the right of civil government to intrude in the church's affairs, Presbyterians saw no reason the church should not use the power of the state to achieve its own aims through legislation. Promoters of the various programs that historians lump together under the umbrella-term "social gospel" believed that morality could be legislated into existence or that at the very least immorality could be legislated out of existence. Professor Robert Law of Knox College declared that the church is "the conscience of the community."[19] In terms of moral reform, said George Pidgeon, the welfare of the nation must override personal rights.[20] Prohibition and sabbath observance are the two most obvious examples of campaigns to usher in the here-and-now kingdom by employing the power of the civil sword. As Brian Fraser has pointed out, social gospellers fostered a naive belief that social evils could be eliminated and instant millennium reached thanks to the simple panacea of more laws.[21]

No discussion of Canadian Presbyterianism and church-state relations (indeed no discussion of Canadian Presbyterianism) would be complete without some reference to the church union of 1925. For Presbyterians the major consideration was the continuance and integrity of their church. Despite the willingness of some Presbyterians to use the civil sword for religious ends, the independence of the ecclesiastical sword had been jealously guarded in the past. The Presbyterian Church in Canada, although recognized as a legal entity by many statutes, had never been incorporated,[22] and any hint of state intrusion was as feared in Canada in 1925 as it had been in Scotland in 1843. Yet the new church was to be created not by water and the word but by legislative action of the civil state. A contemporary parody of the union process, entitled "In Lege Unitas," derided the work of Gershom W. Mason, the legal *éminence grise* of the unionist forces. Sung to Samuel Wesley's tune, "Aurelia," the parody began:

> Our Church's one foundation
> Is Mason's Union Bill,
> She is his new creation
> By legal craft and skill;
> From Parliament he sought her,
> To force into his fold
> And for law-fees to slaughter
> The Scottish kirk of old.

Four more verses in the same vein attacked the Erastianism of the union. E. Lloyd Morrow, the early archivist of nonconcurrency, summarized this perceived danger of state control in one Actonian dictum, "*An incorporated church will tend to autocracy.*"[23] Ephraim Scott, probably the most vocal opponent of union, made the same point even more strongly in a small pamphlet postscript to his book

Church Union in Canada. "In Canada, in 1925, over three years ago, as in Scotland, in the days of the Covenanters, nearing three centuries ago, came the climax and failure of a long attempt to blot out, by civil power, Presbyterian democracy, with its liberties and rights of the people, and replace it by unpresbyterian autocracy where the rights of the people are no more."[24]

The question of defining Christ's headship over the nations might have slumbered longer among Canadian Presbyterians but for the rise of Nazism. In 1942 the issue was placed before the General Assembly by a deliverance of the Presbytery of Paris, pointing out the contradiction between the 1875 "forbearance" statement and the Westminster Confession. By that statement the church had so effectively stopped its own mouth that it could neither authoritatively condemn Nazism nor affirm Christ's headship over Canada! An overture from the Synod of Hamilton and London to the same General Assembly declared that the church had thus been left without guidance as to "how to affirm their loyalty to the State; and the State ... without assured knowledge of its powers and duties, under the Lord Jesus Christ, towards the Church."[25] The result of this episode was the appointment in 1943 of a Committee on Articles of Faith to consider the problem as it concerned church-state relations. That committee laboured long to produce the Declaration of Faith concerning Church and Nation adopted by the Assembly of 1955.

As the most recent official statement of the Presbyterian Church in Canada on the question of church-state relations, the declaration draws heavily from history but not always with harmonizing results. Reminiscent of the Free Church position, Article 1 recites that Christ is "both Head of the Church and Head of the Civil State." Article 2 recalls the doctrine of the two swords by stating that Christ has given power to both the Church and the Civil State, "entrusting to each its own distinctive function." The next three articles repeat the traditional statements that civil authority is commissioned by Christ and as a stewardship under Him civil authorities must be obedient to His revealed word. Article 6 directs the church to denounce and resist all forms of tyranny, although a citizen's right of resistance is not so clearly stated as it was by John Knox.

Article 7, "The Relation of Church and State," in part restates the earlier reference about the distinct functions of church and state but comes even closer to the concept of the two swords. Both church and state are subordinate to Christ—they must be mutually supportive but neither has a right to "domination over the other." The church therefore cannot be the religious agent of the state nor is the state the political agent of the church. The church must also not mix the Gospel with nonreligious creeds, but at the same time it is obliged to "confront the Nation with Christ's judgment and grace." This might be interpreted as acting as the conscience of the state, an implication that becomes clearer in the section on the duty of the civil government towards the church. There the state is advised that it must "pay serious attention whenever its office-bearers are addressed by the Church ... concerning the kingdom of God and His righteousness."

Taken as a whole the Articles of Faith concerning Church and Nation certainly do not approach the Church of Scotland's traditional position of advocating establishment and endowment, whereby whoever pays the piper has the right to call the tune. On the other hand the Secessionist insistence that the piper must not be paid with public funds is also implicitly rejected. In fact, Article 7 explicitly denies the separation of church and state—"We reject all doctrines which assume ... that the Church's life should be or can be completely dissociated from the life of the Civil State." Of the three versions or interpretations of the church-state relation that can be found historically in Canadian Presbyterianism, the Articles come closest to the Free Church's position: the state must pay attention and perhaps money to the ecclesiastical piper, but it is forbidden to call the tune.[26]

A recent and very real question of the application of this doctrine of church-state relations arose in 1987 when the memorandum of agreement between the University of Toronto and the Toronto School of Theology was to be renewed. The changes demanded by the university threatened the independence of the church, and nonconcurrence by the churches would bring an end to government grants for the theological colleges. The university was pressing the issue of academic freedom by insisting that its rules governing hiring, discipline, and firing of faculty members must be enforced in the constituent colleges of the Toronto School of Theology. Given the Canadian Presbyterian tradition of the independence of the church from state interference, this episode posed a potentially serious threat to Knox College.

The University of Toronto is state financed and therefore ultimately state controlled, but Knox College is the creature of the General Assembly of the Presbyterian Church in Canada. Like its sister theological colleges, Knox College's purpose, structure, requirements, and rules are different from those of a secular university. Despite the limited government aid the church receives for theological education, it cannot, by principle or tradition, admit any right of the civil power to control faculty or teaching in its college. Here was an apparent impasse in church-state relations. If the university insisted that the college submit unreservedly to the university's rules, Knox College would have to be withdrawn from any connection with the university in order to preserve the independence of the church. Such a move might also entail withdrawal from the Toronto School of Theology if other member colleges and their churches did accept this state-imposed limitation on their independence.

Long and difficult negotiations have seemingly defused this crisis. The university has apparently acknowledged the different and distinct nature and requirements of theological education, while Knox College has moved to create a church-controlled review procedure for such cases involving its faculty. This supposedly meets the concerns of the university regarding academic freedom without impairing the independence of the church. Knox College's Bylaw 17 required the de facto, immediate, and automatic firing of any professor removed or deposed by his or her presbytery. The compromise accepted by the General Assembly of 1989 permits, on appeal, the creation of a peer-group review committee to consider the faculty member's "competence to continue to fulfill the professorial office notwithstanding such resignation or deposition."[27] The committee reports to the college senate which will recommend to the next General Assembly that the appointment be continued or terminated. This formula supposedly satisfies the university's insistence on a review procedure, while meeting Presbyterian insistence on the historical independence of the church from state interference. The test of this pudding will obviously be in the eating if a conflict of interpretation ever arises between the state-controlled university and the Presbyterian Church in Canada.

This latest development of Canadian Presbyterian concern over the relation of church and state exemplifies once again the basic issue of the independence of the church from state interference and the presumption that the civil magistrate is obligated to support "true religion," even materially with public funds. The parallel with the Free Church position after the Disruption is self-evident in the attempt of the Presbyterian Church in Canada to reconcile secular academic freedom with ecclesiastical sovereignty while continuing to receive public funds for denominational purposes. Despite all the pressures and precedents of North American voluntarism and of secularism in the twentieth century, Canadian Presbyterianism will honour one Scottish tradition. The piper should still be paid, but the one who pays the piper is not yet permitted to call the tune. *Nec tamen consumebatur.*

NOTES

1. James Bryce, *The Holy Roman Empire*, 2nd. rev. ed. (New York: A. L. Burt, 1887), 103.

2. Bryce, *Holy Roman Empire*, 105.

3. Walter Ullmann, *A History of Political Thought: The Middle Ages* (Harmondsworth: Penguin, 1965), 75.

4. David Laing, ed., *The Works of John Knox*, 6 vols. (Edinburgh: Wodrow Society, 1846-64) 4: 506; W. C. Dickinson, ed., *Knox's History of the Reformation in Scotland*, 2 vols. (London: Nelson, 1949) 1: 136-37.

5. In two of a series of lectures delivered during World War I, Harold Laski first drew the parallel between the anti-Erastianism of the Free Church and Oxford movements. Historians have generally not followed up this line of analysis as applied to religious history of the first half of the nineteenth century. See Harold Laski, *Essays in the Problem of Sovereignty* (New Haven: Yale University Press, 1917).

6. John S. Moir, ed., *Church and State in Canada 1627-1867*, The Carleton Library No. 33 (Toronto: McClelland & Stewart, 1967), 144.

7. Moir, *Church and State*, 146.

8. Moir, *Church and State*, 161.

9. John S. Moir, "'Loyalty and Respectability': The Campaign for Co-Establishment of the Church of Scotland in Canada," *Scottish Tradition* 9/10 (1979-80): 64-82.

10. John S. Moir, *Church and State in Canada West* (Toronto: University of Toronto Press, 1959), 38.

11. John S. Moir, "'The Quay of Greenock'—Jurisdiction and Nationality in the Canadian Disruption of 1844," *Scottish Tradition* 5 (1975): 38-53.

12. R. F. Burns, *Life and Times of the Rev. R. Burns, D.D., Toronto* (Toronto: James Campbell, 1871), 133-35.

13. *Historical Report of the Administration of the Temporalities' Fund of the Presbyterian Church in Canada ... 1856-1900* (Montreal, 1900).

14. Moir, *Church and State in Canada 1627-1867*, 213.

15. A. F. Kemp, ed., *Digest of the Minutes of the Synod of the Presbyterian Church of Canada, with a Historical Introduction and an Appendix of Forms and Procedures* (Montreal: John Lovell, 1861), 309.

16. Kemp, *Minutes of the Synod*, 307.

17. *Acts and Proceedings of the General Assembly of the Presbyterian Church in Canada 1875*, 5.

18 J. F. MacCurdy, ed., *Life and Work of D. J. Macdonnell, Minister of St. Andrew's Church, Toronto, with a Selection of Sermons and Prayers* (Toronto: William Briggs, 1897), 259-74; J. R. Miller, *Equal Rights: The Jesuits' Estates Act Controversy* (Montreal: McGill-Queen's University Press, 1979), 63, 106. By the terms of the Quebec Act, Roman Catholic canon law forms part of the *code civile* of the Province of Quebec, a fact that excited Protestant concern in the early decades of this century over the implementation of the *Ne Temere* decree. See John Moir, "Canadian Protestant Reaction to the *Ne Temere* Decree," *Study Sessions*, Canadian Catholic Historical Association 48 (1981): 78-91.

19. *Pre-Assembly Congress of the Presbyterian Church in Canada, 1913* (Toronto: Board of Foreign Missions, 1913?), 44-45.

20. George Pidgeon, "Problems of Moral Reform," in W. R. McIntosh, ed., *Canadian Problems* (Toronto: Committee on Young People's Societies, Presbyterian Church in Canada, 1910), 66.

21. Brian J. Fraser, *The Social Uplifters: Presbyterian Progressives and the Social Gospel in Canada, 1875-1915* (Waterloo: Wilfrid Laurier University Press, 1988), 173-78.

22. G. W. Mason, *The Legislative Struggle for Church union* (Toronto: Ryerson, 1956), 7; because relevant statutory and other legal references were so scattered as to be virtually inaccessible. Thomas Wardlaw Taylor had collected and published all these materials soon after the union of 1875. See T. W. Taylor, *The Public Statutes relating to the Presbyterian Church in Canada: with Acts and Resolutions of the General Assembly, and By-Laws for the Government of the Colleges and Schemes of the Church* (Toronto: Willing & Williamson, 1879).

23. Presbyterian Church Archives, Daniel Strachan Papers, file 2.

24. E. L. Morrow, *Church Union in Canada: its History, Motives, Doctrine, and Government* (Toronto: Thomas Allen, 1923), 205.

25. Ephraim Scott, *Postscript to "Church Union and the Presbyterian Church in Canada"* (Montreal: John Lovell & Son, 1928), 1. The appeal to the Covenanter tradition has little historical basis in the Canadian experience but it is such a recurrent theme in both religious and secular life that it deserves closer examination.

26. *Acts and Proceedings* 1942, 112-13; 1943, 130-31. G. A. Peddie, *"The King of Kings": The Basis of Union of the Presbyterian Church in Canada and its relationship to the present need of the Church for a Confession of Faith in Jesus Christ as Lord of Church and State, together with The Petition of a Memorial of the Presbytery of Paris to the General Assembly, 1941* (Toronto: Age Publications, 1942?), unpaged.

27. *An Historical Digest of the Work in Articles of Faith 1942-1967* (Don Mills, Ont: Presbyterian Church in Canada, 1967?), 97.

28. *Acts and Proceedings* 1989.

Canada's Sunday:
The Presbyterian Contribution,
1875-1950

Paul Laverdure

Remember the sabbath-day, to keep it holy. Six days shalt thou labour and do all thy work: But the seventh day is the sabbath of the Lord thy God: in it thou shalt not do any work, thou, nor thy cattle, nor the stranger that is within thy gates. Exodus 20:1-8

What can or cannot be done on the Canadian Sunday has been largely shaped by Presbyterian church-state struggles during the early twentieth century. Why politicians have debated Sunday laws can only be answered by studying the Presbyterians—William Caven, John Charlton, John G. Shearer, and William Rochester—who were involved in shaping a national Canadian Sunday. Canada's Sunday, however, also tells the story of declining Presbyterian influence and of a Presbyterian retreat to southwestern Ontario. Finally, Presbyterians have shown that they do not believe in freedom of conscience where Sunday is concerned.

With the Westminster Standards of 1646-48, Presbyterians strictly identified the Sabbath of the fourth commandment with Sunday. The Westminster Confession and both the Shorter and Larger Catechisms declared that every seventh day for Christians was Sunday and that all were to rest from all employment and recreation in order to worship God. Only works of necessity and mercy were allowed.

In 1875 these confessions became the subordinate standards of the Presbyterian Church in Canada. The young church formed the first Committee on Sabbath Observance. Synods sent petitions to the federal Parliament to restrain railway business. Open government post offices, Sunday funerals in Ontario, and the holiday atmosphere in Quebec were denounced. Presbyterian elder and member of Parliament, John Charlton, clamoured for a federal

Sunday law. John A. Macdonald claimed that Sunday legislation was a provincial matter, since only provinces could make laws dealing with customs. Three groups—the state, the province of Quebec, and business—opposed Presbyterian righteousness.[1]

In 1888 a bold step in creating a Canada-wide and Christian Sunday was taken. Following a call from the 1886 Hamilton conference to save "the precious heritage of the Sabbath," the church was asked to "rouse public interest on an issue so momentous, secure legislation ... and provide funds for the purpose of having the law enforced." Presbyterians planned to turn the moral law into a government law so that the State would enforce it. Letters went out to the Christian denominations, and in 1888 at Ottawa's city hall, under the Reverend W. D. Armstrong, convener of the Presbyterian Church's Sabbath Observance Committee, the Lord's Day Alliance of Canada was founded.

The important Presbyterian Sabbath Observance Committee disbanded in favour of the Lord's Day Alliance. Officially, temperance appeared to be the cause nearest to Presbyterian hearts, because it received the greatest amount of space in the minutes of Assembly. This was only apparent. Principal Caven of Knox College headed the Ontario Lord's Day Alliance, while the Reverend W. D. Armstrong presided over the Dominion Alliance. Half the executives of the non-denominational Lord's Day Alliance were Presbyterians.[2] Year after year, the General Assembly of the Presbyterian Church sent resolutions to Sir John A. Macdonald and money to the Lord's Day Alliance.

The Alliance took over the battle against Sunday streetcars, pleasure driving, reading secular literature, sleeping, games, fishing, skating, Salvation Army parades, mining, farming, railway activities, and secret Sunday tippling.[3] As far as Presbyterians were concerned, however, the Alliance was not working fast enough. So in 1899, again in Hamilton, a new Committee on Sabbath Observance was launched with the Reverend John G. Shearer in charge. Shortly afterward, at the Christian Endeavour Conference in Montreal, Shearer gave an impressive speech on how legislation could be passed and how the Lord's Day Alliance could improve its organization to stop the railways on Sundays.[4] The Alliance took Shearer up on his offer and appointed him their first full-time paid field secretary.

John Shearer was born in southwestern Ontario. He studied what would now be called political science at the University of Toronto, and theology at Knox College under Dr. William Caven. Like Caven, Charlton, and social reformers elsewhere, Shearer believed that legislative reform of society would restrain individuals from breaking God's commandments.[5] When Shearer left the security of his Hamilton pastorate, he was at the cutting edge of Canadian social and political reform.

After a whirlwind tour of the Maritimes, Shearer called the first convention of the Lord's Day Alliance in the summer of 1901. There, old John Charlton thundered, "Christ's teaching depends upon the church and the church upon the Sabbath."[6] There could be no simpler summary of sabbatarian concerns. The older Presbyterians trusted Shearer's leadership; the convention ratified all of Shearer's decisions. The appointment of Methodist minister T. Albert Moore as an associate secretary was to have major consequences for the future of Protestant ecumenism in Canada. Moore would look back, after a career as General Secretary and Moderator of the United Church of Canada, to remember Shearer as his inspiration when Moore had been a Methodist pastor in Hamilton. Together, Shearer and Moore filled the young dominion with Lord's Day Alliance branches, of which there were 512 by the end of 1902. Ominously, Quebec had ten. Only Prince Edward Island had fewer.[7]

The Alliance convention of 1901 shifted its administration from Ottawa to southwestern Ontario. Although Hamilton was the heart of the Canadian Sabbath controversy and home to the Presbyterian Free Church tradition seeking control of the state, Toronto had more money and more Presbyterians. As in so many other Canadian movements, notably the temperance and women's movements of the twentieth century, Toronto became the new centre of power. Hamilton watched it closely.

In 1903 the case of the *Hamilton Street Railway v. the Attorney-General of Ontario* went to the Privy Council in England, which decided that the power to enact Sunday laws, like all religious laws, belonged to the federal Parliament. The judges reasoned that since Sunday laws were based on the fourth commandment, and as the commandments against perjury, murder, and theft had become part of the criminal legislation of the Christian world, all religious legislation was part of criminal law. Under the British North America Act, criminal legislation was a federal responsibility.[8] Thus all provincial Sunday laws passed after Confederation in 1867 were void. The Hamilton Railway could run on Sundays. Only the laws from Charles I and II forbidding sports, individual travelling, bull- and bear-baiting, seemed to be still in force.[9] Sunday quiet melted away; workers were forced to their jobs; labour and the churches were in an uproar. The drive for one law for all Canada began.

The Alliance tried to be nondenominational; in reality, Shearer made contacts "either with an existing Sabbath observance association or with a Presbyterian minister whom he knew from General Assembly meetings."[10] He expected little from any except Presbyterians, Methodists or Congregationalists, the three churches which formed the United Church of Canada.[11] When Shearer reached out to Anglicans for a western secretary, he was unsuccessful; in the early twentieth century, most Anglicans were not interested in social reform.[12] Instead, the Lord's Day Alliance hired the Reverend William Marshall Rochester. Born in southwestern Ontario, he had been in sabbatarian circles since 1893, and moreover had actually served in some western pastorates.[13] He was, of course, a Presbyterian. Shearer made few attempts to contact Baptists. Roman Catholics were practically ignored, so sure were Protestants that Roman Catholics would not be interested.[14] The just-established newspaper, *The Lord's Day Advocate*, which quickly reached a circulation of 40,000, was consciously modelled on the size and format of *The Presbyterian Record*. The *Advocate* gave prominent space to prominent Presbyterians. The Reverend C. W. Gordon, or Ralph Connor to his many literary fans, reported on "The Necessity of the Sabbath to the West."[15] The resolutions of the Presbyterian Church were always faithfully reproduced. When the Reverend W. D. Armstrong, the former Ottawa-based Alliance

Secretary, became Moderator of the General Assembly for 1905-06, Presbyterian support for the Sabbath could not be more complete. Clearly, the Lord's Day Alliance, under Shearer, was a Presbyterian organization with Methodist help.

The Alliance moved on Ottawa in the guise of an interdenominational and labour-supported mass movement. Seventh-day Adventists and Jews were dismissed as insignificant foreign minorities, American heretics, vicious Europeans, and "strangers within our gates" who had to conform to the Christian majority's wishes.[16] In 1906, the Laurier government announced an "Act respecting the Lord's Day," which prohibited "sales, the prosecution of ordinary work or business, excursions, games for prizes, [and] the opening of places of public amusement for which an admission fee is charged."[17] The catechisms' teachings could hardly be better translated into legal terms.

In Parliament, however, the debate cut across party lines. Presbyterians and Methodists fought ferociously for every item. Roman Catholics, most Anglicans, and some Baptists opposed the law. Henri Bourassa denounced the bill as absurd and objected to making "people virtuous by law." David Henderson, a Presbyterian, saw any amendments to the law as a sacrilegious attempt to amend the fourth commandment. Laurier admitted that the choice of Sunday created a religious law, but workers needed protection for the natural law of rest. In spite of Laurier's conciliation, the debate escalated into a confrontation between French-Catholic and English-Protestant Canada.[18] In the Senate, one Presbyterian challenged French Catholics to measure themselves by the standard God set up and Queen Victoria had once exemplified. An Irish Catholic senator replied that Catholics were in peril for their souls when they missed Sunday mass; this Protestant law fined people only one dollar for failing to observe the Sabbath. Was this any indication of how much the fourth commandment was worth to Protestants?[19]

Hard bargaining went on. Quebec insisted on the sale of articles at the church for charitable purposes and the notarizing of deeds for people, usually farmers, who often could not take a weekday off to go into town to buy or sell land. Ontario got continuous manufacturing processes and through trains to transport perishable goods or livestock. Both sides denounced the Jews until Henri Bourassa realized that French-Canadian interests had more in common with religious minorities than with the English-Protestant homogenization of Canada. Nonetheless, an exemption clause for the Jews or others who conscientiously observed another day as the Sabbath was thrown out. No liberty of conscience was allowed.

The law was passed. Shearer rejoiced that corporations as well as individuals could be fined. The state, Catholic Quebec, and business, the three foes of the 1875 Sabbath committee, had been beaten. The "railway men are about the maddest crowd you could find in this Dominion," Shearer wrote, "It is something new for them to be beaten and to be beaten by preachers and their like is too humiliating altogether."[20] Canadian Presbyterians rejoiced with Shearer, and Knox College gave him a Doctorate of Divinity. He was promoted out of the Alliance to head the new Presbyterian Department of Moral and Social Reform.[21]

One day before the federal law came into force, Quebec rammed through a provincial Lord's Day Bill to take precedence over the federal law. It incorporated the Jewish exemption clause and also allowed everyone to "be and remain entitled to do on Sunday any act not forbidden by the" laws of Quebec.[22] The Sunday forces expanded to go after Quebec. This meant hiring more Presbyterians. Although Shearer had left, the Reverend W. G. Hanna, another southwestern Ontario Presbyterian minister, was hired for eastern Canada. In 1909 a special Quebec secretary was brought on staff. The Reverend George W. Mingie had been an academic whirlwind at McGill University and at Presbyterian College. His bilingualism and legal studies made him an obvious choice for Quebec.

Although older faces were fading away—John Charlton died in 1910—more Presbyterians took their places. When T. A. Moore left in 1910 to become secretary of the Methodist Board of Temperance and Moral Reform, Rochester replaced him as general secretary and began a fifteen-year reign. Only Alberta and B. C. enjoyed the services of a Methodist organizer.[23] The Alliance Presbyterians fought against the laws forcing Toronto municipal workers to work at toboggan slides on Sunday, the sale of ice cream in Hamilton and of American Sunday newspapers in Windsor, band concerts in Regina, and Prime Minister Borden's habit of Sunday golf in Nova Scotia.[24]

But despite sometimes stooping to spy on men buying American papers off a Napanee train, the Lord's Day Alliance lawyers won important court battles. Judge William Middleton, a Presbyterian, ruled in 1911 that for the sale of food to be an act of necessity or mercy, the purchaser had to eat the food on the spot, in order to demonstrate need.[25] No one could carry any food out of a store on Sunday. More important, however, in 1912 the Supreme Court declared the Quebec Lord's Day Act unconstitutional, thus forcing the Quebec government to observe the stricter federal Lord's Day Act and to prosecute the Jews. Rochester was rewarded with a Doctorate of Divinity.

After 1914, nothing seemed to go right. The forces for moral reform watched with horror as the war ripped away the illusions of peace and progress the long Victorian era had fostered. In a joint war effort, business and the state ignored the Sunday laws. Within months, military necessity justified parades, theatres for the weary soldiers, Sunday newspaper war extras, full-blast seven-day manufacturing, and patriotic entertainments to raise money and recruits. War justified it all, and the Methodists and the Anglicans who turned toward England both blessed the Canadian war effort[26] and stopped supporting the Lord's Day Alliance. Even some Presbyterians thought that the Alliance "might possibly lose caste with the public if we insisted too strongly on the letter of the law."[27] Quebec openly ignored the federal law and reimposed its own more lenient and unconstitutional legislation.

All of Canada's resources were thrown into the Great War. Unless ammunition was manufactured on Sunday, Canadians would die defenseless. The war needed clothing, shoes, and Sunday work on farms for food. Above all, the war and the Red Cross demanded Sunday shows, vaudeville, cigarettes, military band instruments and alcohol.[28] Stopping the "thin edge of the wedge" in the Maritimes, where the soldiers were stationed before going overseas, was impossible.[29] When Rochester questioned the means Canadians were using to win the war, the Winnipeg *Free Press* manager pointedly suggested that useless clergymen might find some work with patriotic fund-raising events.[30] Rochester, however, had already campaigned for these causes. Two of his four sons were already in the field, and by the end of the war, two would be dead and one would be home with wounds. The abuse from the war boosters still piled up on Rochester's desk.[31]

There were few consolations. One Lord's Day Alliance employee wrote to Ontario's attorney general that Sunday newspapers were:

> Sixty-nine pages of rubbish,
> Twenty-two pages of rot,
> Forty-six pages of scandal vile
> Served to us piping hot.
>
> Thirty-four comic pages
> Printed in reds, greens and blues:
> Thousands of items we don't care to read
> But only two columns of news.

Governments stopped Sunday newspapers because they upset people with inaccuracies in their casualty lists, and had no right to inform families of casualties before the official telegram arrived.[32] During the 1918 Spanish influenza, the newspapers retaliated by suggesting that churches should remain closed on Sundays in order to prevent the spread of disease.[33] Some churches obediently closed. Sunday problems in Canada were blamed on American branch plants, and anti-Americanism seemed to help the Sunday forces, but when the United States entered the war, complaints about the allied Americans became rare. When recruiting dropped off, so did Sunday recruiting shows.[34] It was clear, however, that the war, not morality, controlled everything.

As the war dragged on, people listened to the Presbyterian ministers, E. Leslie Pidgeon and Dr. Rochester, about the need of the men for rest after the war. They claimed that "one of the most apparent reasons for the Divine chastisement of the nations is that Europe had, to a shocking degree flung away the Christian Sabbath."[35] Sabbath desecration, not a murdered Austrian arch-duke, seemed a more appropriate reason for such a terrible war.

Whatever the cause of the war, a new world order rose from the ashes. From 1919 to 1925 a new attempt at world peace and progress was made. The Paris Peace Conference declaration for "a weekly rest of at least twenty-four hours, which should include Sunday wherever practicable" was incorporated into the League of Nations 1921 labour recommendations. The Government of Canada in 1925 followed suit in declaring one day's rest in seven.[36] Rochester was elected chair of the World Commission on the Christian Sab-bath at the World's Christian Citizenship Conference. He thanked God for the survival of the Canadian Sunday as a day free from newspapers, theatres, and paid sports. The Presbyterian General Assembly thanked Rochester for the reputation Canada's Sunday had around the world.[37] In 1924 Canadian Presbyterians celebrated the Olympic victory of the Scots Presbyterian, Eric Liddell, in the 400 metre race after he refused to run the 100 metre trial held on a Sunday.[38] It seemed a golden age; it was a fragile dream.

Criticisms came from all parts of the country. The Calgary *Albertan* ran a letter begging for the Sunday opening of libraries. Was their closing, "like the bagpipe, an unwelcome and noisome legacy from bonnie Scotland?" There were altogether too many Scots and, probably, Presbyterians in Calgary for this letter writer.[39] Complaints of seven-day workweeks reached J. S. Woodsworth in Parliament, who commented that the Alliance should bother the employers more and the ice-cream salespeople less.[40] Montreal's *La Presse* said the Alliance held a minority opinion and could be ignored. *Le Canard* said they could not be ignored; they should be kicked out of town.[41] When the past moderator of the Presbyterian Church, C. W. Gordon, sold the film rights to his novels in 1922, he had to suffer seeing them turned into films shown on Sundays in the U.S. Toronto newspapers attacked him mercilessly.[42] Alberta declared gasoline a necessity and allowed its sale on Sunday. Concerts and dancing spread across the Prairies. Finally, in 1923, the Manitoba government allowed excursion trains to run in Manitoba.[43] Governments, Quebec, and businesses successfully ignored the 1906 law.

The idea of a righteous Canada propelled some Presbyterians to form a powerful church to influence Canadian life. As the *Montreal Star* humorously reported, "Church Union Will Never Be Successful Until the *Fordites*, and—The Sabbath *Recreationists*, and—The Seventh Day *Golfites* and Similar Denominations Come Into the Union."[44] Names prominent in Presbyterian social reform movements and the Lord's Day Alliance disappeared from the General Assembly lists and reappeared in the United Church minutes. C. W. Gordon, the Pidgeon brothers, and the Alliance's own solicitor went the United way. Shearer would have joined the United Church to promote God's Kingdom in Canada, but he had died just a few months prior to union.[45]

When Rochester remained with the continuing Presbyterian Church, the news went across the country. The Reverend George Mingie wrote bluntly to Rochester, "I think your stand may help in Ontario where the large number of Presbyterian Churches are," but not with donations elsewhere.[46] With religious loyalties polarized, money for interdenominational causes, such as the Lord's Day Alliance, disappeared.[47] Rochester left the Alliance to become editor of the *Presbyterian Record*. The *Lord's Day Advocate* folded.

The United Church, with T. A. Moore as secretary and George Pidgeon as moderator, welcomed a delegation from the Lord's Day Alliance, but its welcome was less warm than the one given Rochester by Presbyterians. The United Church was reevaluating its social concerns before going out to conquer Canada. On the one hand, the United Church *New Outlook* reported that there was some doubt whether the Jewish Sabbath commandment was a permanent Christian obligation. On the other hand, the Presbyterian Church reasserted "the profound importance of maintaining by precept and example the sacredness and integrity of the Lord's Day."[48] Rochester averaged one *Record* editorial a year dedicated to the Sunday question. There was no doubt in Presbyterian minds that the Sabbath was a permanent Christian obligation.

With the Depression, the Sabbath Committee disappeared into the Committee on Church Life and Work. This was no centralization, as before the First World War; this was the result of budget cuts. The Lord's Day Alliance met the same fate. Field secretaries were retired and George Mingie was forced out, taking the moribund Quebec branch with him. Quebec went its own way, directed by papal encyclicals, not the Shorter Catechism. In the hot, dusty days that followed, it was almost impossible to stop Sunday prairie baseball games, even those of black American teams. Musicians in Calgary had once called Sunday theatres the "thin edge of the wedge," but by 1932 job-hungry musicians were hammering in the wedge. Workers could be had seven days a week. William Aberhart crudely identified his Social Credit crusade with God's will and preached politics from his Sunday radio pulpit. The stronghold of Canadian sabbatarianism, Ontario, shook when Liberal Premier Hepburn suggested that the province might allow money-making excursion trains for ski parties. Walkathons in B.C., miniature golf on the Prairies, and late Saturday-night burlesque shows in Windsor seemed petty to governments worried about communism and anarchy.[49]

In 1938, on the fiftieth anniversary of the Lord's Day Alliance, a Presbyterian Church survey of Sunday conditions from east to west reported that the Maritimes generally respected Sunday, while B.C. did not. Quebec and Ontario were restless, while the Prairies were hostile to Sunday observance. The Maritimes were also relatively homogeneous in population and economically stagnant. British Columbia was too diverse, the Prairies too concerned with the Depression, and the distrust between Ontario and Quebec too great to build a consensus on a Canadian version of Christ's Kingdom.

Planning for the future was impossible; Hitler's armies marched, and the CBC aired news flashes all day Sunday. The CBC promised that its Sunday advertising would be in good taste, but what was good taste in a time of mass propaganda?[50] Radio stations eventually just cut much of their religious programming. The government suspended the federal Lord's Day Act to allow full-time munitions production. One by one, the field secretaries of the Alliance answered the call as war chaplains. Only the old and young were left. T. A. Moore died in 1940. Rochester fell on a Toronto street with a stroke. Then the government used the War Measures Act to suspend all provincial laws relating to Sunday, something that had not been done even during the First World War.[51]

The Second World War brought out new Sunday I.O.D.E. and Red Cross Patriotic Softball Tournaments and Concerts. Ski trains pulled out of Toronto in order to attract needed American tourist dollars. The film industry, led by Warner Brothers and Famous Players, gave its theatres for Sunday shows in the supposed hope that non-stop entertainment would stop the spread of venereal diseases among the enlisted men.[52] Faced with the onslaught, Presbyterians at first denounced the conscious paganizing of their Christian civilization.[53] But after church union, they were weak in numbers and in influence. Ottawa had become too big and impersonal to control. Then, when the nuclear age arrived, Sunday laws seemed almost annoyingly petty to governments and to an increasing number of people.[54]

In the post-war world, Presbyterians and the Presbyterian General Assembly deplored the secularization of Canadian life.[55] The president of the Lord's Day Alliance was Peter Dunn of St. Paul's Presbyterian Church, Hamilton. The new field secretary for eastern Ontario and English Quebec was the Presbyterian minister, A. B. Casselman. But unlike 1906, when the Alliance gathered in Hamilton in 1948 for its anniversary, all the key people were old. The identification with the Presbyterian Church was so strong the *Globe and Mail* called the Alliance General Secretary, Dr. George Webber, a Presbyterian.[56] He was a Methodist United Church minister; he was also seventy-two years old.

Once the soldiers had returned, Canada exploded into the pursuit of happiness. The *Financial Post* and *Globe and Mail* urged the government to demilitarize the country and to allow seven-day gas stations.[57] Although this undid some of the positive labour legislation from the war, it encouraged tourism and trucking. Bowling alleys, shooting galleries, and sidewalk hot dog stands opened. Since the National Hockey League decided not to move

Hockey Night in Canada from its traditional Saturday spot, originally chosen to avoid the Sunday law, baseball became Canada's unofficial national Sunday sport.

In 1950 Ontario passed its own Lord's Day Act, giving municipalities power over Sunday sports. All Canada watched to see what Toronto "the Good" would do next. Mayor Allan Lamport's multi-ethnic and religiously plural Toronto immediately voted for Sunday sports. Dr. C. L. Cowan, the former moderator of the Presbyterian Church and the minister of Hamilton's St. Andrew's Church, fought to keep Hamilton from following Toronto's example. In an interview with the *Hamilton Spectator*, he called Sunday sports "the thin edge of the wedge to eventually gain an open Sunday."[58] One would have thought that the butt of the wedge had already been shoved in. Canada followed Toronto, not Hamilton.

What was the Presbyterian influence on Canada's Sunday? Successful opposition between 1875 and 1900 to Sunday business and its railways came from ministers like John Charlton and William Caven in a newly united Presbyterian Church. From 1900 to 1925, the push for a united Christian Canada produced Shearer and Rochester, southwestern Ontario Presbyterian ministers, to wrestle successfully with Quebec, business, and the state. At church union, Presbyterians split into two weaker streams. War and depression and again war took the initiative out of Presbyterian hands. The War Measures Act, excursion acts, one day in seven acts, provincial acts, and municipal acts continued to place more power in government hands. By 1950 the death of the older, idealistic generation concerned with matters of church and state coincided with the rise of a new generation more concerned with the church and the world. Nuclear proliferation and economics were the pressing legacies of the Depression and the wars, but Caven, Shearer, and Rochester deserve the credit for the longevity of the Lord's Day Act, which remained in effect until 1985.

Presbyterian influence from 1875 to 1925, and to some extent to 1985, had been gained by southwestern Ontario Presbyterians of mainly Free Church background, who overlooked the 1875 Basis of Union guaranteeing "full liberty of conscience in matters of religion."[59] But the state finally solved that debate by deciding that it would not impose Presbyterian Sunday morality on Quebec or on any province or business; it was up to individuals to follow the fourth commandment in their own way. The Presbyterian Church, however, on petition from the Presbytery of Paris, in the Synod of Hamilton and London, worked between 1950 and 1954 on a declaration about the church and the nation.[60] With this new declaration, Presbyterians fought another round in the Sunday controversy until 1985 when the Charter of Rights made all religious legislation unconstitutional. For most southwestern Ontario Presbyterians, there could be no separation between church and state and no freedom of conscience when it came time to "Remember the Sabbath Day, to keep it holy."

NOTES

1. *Acts and Proceedings of the General Assembly of the Presbyterian Church in Canada*, 1875-85.

2. Papers of the Lord's Day Alliance of Canada, deposited in the Thomas Fisher Rare Book Library of the University of Toronto [LDA], Item 71, Minute Book 1888, March 21, 1889, 15.

3. *Acts and Proceedings* 1890. For an amusing celebration of secularism, see Christopher Armstrong and H. V. Nelles, *The Revenge of the Methodist Bicycle Company. Sunday Streetcars and Municipal Reform in Toronto, 1888-1897* (Toronto: Peter Martin Associates, 1977).

4. LDA 71, Minute Book 1888, August 8, 1899.

5. Richard Allen, *The Social Passion. Religion and Social Reform in Canada 1914-28* (Toronto: University of Toronto Press, 1971), 17. Sharon Patricia Meen, "The Battle for the Sabbath: The Sabbatarian Lobby in Canada, 1890-1912," Ph.D. thesis, University of British Columbia, 1979, 135, explicitly fitted Shearer into Allen's definition.

6. LDA 71, 111.

7. LDA 74, Minutes of the Executive Committee, 1901-18, 151.

8. Ontario Reform Commission 1970, *Report on Sunday Observance Legislation* (Toronto: Department of Justice, 1970), 35. Also George S. Holmsted, *The Sunday Law in Canada* (Toronto: Poole, 1912), 69-70. ·

9. *Acts and Proceedings* 1904, 267.

10. Meen, *Battle for the Sabbath*, 178.

11. LDA 5, Letterbrook 1905-1906, December 1905, Shearer to the Rev. P. L. Richardson.

12. LDA 5, December 14, 1905, Shearer to the Rev. Archdeacon Lloyd. For early Anglican social action, see Edward Pulker, *We Stand on Their Shoulders. The Growth of Social Concern in Canadian Anglicanism* (Toronto: Anglican Book Centre, 1986).

13. *Acts and Proceedings* 1893; *Lord's Day Advocate* [*Advocate*] 3 (May 1906).

14. For Roman Catholics, see Meen, *Battle for the Sabbath*, 187 and LDA 2, Letterbrook 1899-1902, December 21, 1900, Shearer to Mr. A. McKillop. For Baptists, see LDA 4, Letterbrook 1904-05, August 24, 1904, (Shearer) to Rev. S. C. Murray, and LDA 1, Letterbrook 1899-1900, February 22, 1900, Shearer to Rev. Thos. Wilson.

15. *Advocate*, 1 (April 1904), 2 (December 1904), and 2 (May 1905).

16. For petitions, see *Advocate* 1 (October 1903), 3 (December 1905) and 3 (January 1906), LDA 5, December 7, 1905, 291, Shearer to Mackenzie, etc. For the xenophobia and anti-semitism of the Alliance campaign, see LDA 5, July 20, 1905, Shearer to Rev. I. B. Colwell, LDA 5, June 8, 1905, Shearer to Funk & Wagnalls, Meen, *Battle for the Sabbath*, 207-8, and David Rome, ed., *On Sunday Observance, 1906*, National Archives of the Canadian Jewish Congress, Montreal, 1979.

17. *Official Report of the Debates of the House of Commons of the Dominion of Canada. Second Session—Tenth Parliament. 6 Edward VII. 1906* [HC], columns 19-20. For text of bill, see *Advocate* 3 (April 1906).

18. HC 5630 and 5769 for Bourassa, 5664 for Henderson and 5638 for Laurier.

19. *Debates of the Senate of the Dominion of Canada. 1906. Second Session—Tenth Parliament* [Senate], Ottawa, 1906, 1130-35, 1145-49.

20. LDA 5 (July 14, 1906), Shearer to J. B. Mitchell.

21. *Advocate* 3 (August-September 1906), LDA 6 (April 24, 1907), G. D. Bayne to Shearer, LDA 74 (July 4, 1907), Minutes of the Executive Board, Special Meeting.

22. *Advocate* 4 (March 1907).

23. *Advocate* 4 (October 1907), 6 (July-August 1909), 7 (March 1910), 7 (June 1910), 5 (July-August 1908), 8 (May 1912).

24. For Sunday slides, see the Toronto newspapers of 1912 and Patricia Meen's article, "Holy Day or Holiday? The Giddy Trolley and the Canadian Sunday, 1890-1914," *Urban History Review*, February 1980, 49-63. For Hamilton ice cream sales, look at *Hamilton Times*, July 8, and August 6, 1909. For American newspapers, Prime Minister Borden, and band concerts, see LDA 6, Correspondence 1902-13. Legal decisions and other matters are in the *Advocate*.

25. For Middleton's affiliation see Henry James Morgan, ed., *The Canadian Men and Women of the Time: A Handbook of Canadian Biography of Living Characters* (Toronto: William Briggs, 1912).

26. J. M. Bliss, "The Methodist Church and World War I," *Canadian Historical Review* 49 (September 1968): 213-33. For an example of the Anglicans, see LDA, Correspondence 1915 (L-Z), June 14, 1915, Rev. D. MacDonald to Rev. R. W. Ross.

27. LDA 8, Correspondence 1914 (S-Z) 1915 (A-K), August 15, 1914, George M. Wood to Rochester.

28. For shells and ammunition, see LDA 9, June 29, 1915, Joseph Waring to Rochester and November 12, 1915, Canada Crushed Stone Corp. to Rochester. For clothing and food, see LDA 7, November 15, 1915, Hugh A. Dougall to the Alliance and UCA *Advocate* 14 (April-May 1918). For smokes, alcohol, vaudeville, and musical instruments, 13 (October-November 1917), and LDA 10, Correspondence 1916 (A-S) March 29, 1916, Rev. D. W. Snider to Rev. J. D. Fitzpatrick. For the Red Cross involvement, one can read LDA 7, December 1, 1914, the Mayor of St. John, NB to Rochester.

29. For Halifax, see LDA 8, August 15, 1914, George M. Wood to Rochester. For New Brunswick, see LDA 7, Correspondence 1914 (A-R), December 3, 1914, Amon A. Wilson to Rochester.

30. LDA 10, January 3, 1916, E. H. Macklin, *The Manitoba Free Press*, to Rochester.

31. UCA *Advocate* 14 (October 1918). LDA 11, Correspondence 1916 (S-Z) - 1920, November 25, 1916, D. W. Snider to Rev. W. E. Prescott. Also, I am grateful to Mr. Lawlor Rochester for allowing me to consult the records compiled by his uncle, Lloyd B. Rochester, ed., *The John Rochester Family in Canada*, 4th ed. (Ottawa, 1976). Lloyd Rochester was Dr. Rochester's nephew.

32. LDA 11, November 21, 1916, Snider, citing the *Catholic Citizen*, to Hon. I. B. Lucas, Attorney General of Ontario. See also Public Archives of Ontario, Record Group 4-32, (Ministry of the Attorney General, Criminal and Civil Files) file 1915-740, May 13, 1915, Rochester to Hon. I. B. Lucas.

33. For example, *Montreal World*, October 13, 1918, "Montreal to Have Churchless Sunday." *Montreal News*, October 17, 1918, "Only One Service in City Churches Urged for Sunday."

34. *Toronto Star*, February 11, 1916, "Recruiting League Fears Meetings Have Lost Force." For Anti-Americanism, see LDA 7, June 8, 1914, Rev. Robt. Young to Snider, June 9, 1914, Miss Sarah Cairns to Mingie, and LDA 9, June 1, 1915, Rochester to the Prime Minister and Cabinet.

35. LDA 79, Ontario Branch Committees 1902-1921, Ontario Lord's Day Alliance Annual Report 1915. LDA 9, November 18, 1915, E. L. Pidgeon to Rochester.

36. UCA *Advocate* 15 (June 1919). And Privy Council Order 1537, September 7, 1925, reported in *Advocate* 21 (November 1925).

37. William M. Rochester, *Report of World Commission on the Christian Sabbath*. Read at the Third World's Christian Citizenship Conference. National Reform Association, Pittsburgh, Pennsylvania (1920?), 11 pp. For Presbyterians, *Acts and Proceedings* 1920, 22.

38. LDA 157, Scrapbook materials 1921-1924, May 2, 1924 *Saskatoon Phoenix*, *Advocate* 20 (August 1924).

39. LDA 160, Scrapbook 1925-26. *Albertan*, February 10, 1925.

40. *Advocate* 20 (July 1923).

41. LDA 152, Scrapbook 1921-24, *La Presse*, November 18, 1922. *Le Canard*, March 5, 1922.

42. LDA 154, Scrapbook 1921-24, June 10, 1922, *Toronto Star* and *Toronto Telegram*.

43. Advocate 19 (June 1923), 20 (June 1924), 19 (April 1923).

44. LDA 157, Scrapbook 1921-24, January 12, 1924.

45. John S. Moir, "J. G. Shearer. Crusader for Christ's Kingdom," *The Presbyterian Record* 99 (April 1975): 16-17.

46. LDA 13, Correspondence 1925, May 5, 1925, Mingie to Rochester.

47. LDA 13, May 9, 1925 and June 5, 1925, Mingie to Rochester.

48. *Advocate* 21 (July 1925) for Presbyterians and 22 (September 1926) for the United Church.

49. For the baseball games, LDA 17, Correspondence 1931-33, November 14, 1931, Regina, Saskatchewan. For musicians, LDA 161, Scrapbook 1926-27, February 2, 1926, *Calgary Herald* and LDA 17, November 19, 1932, F.C.C. Heathcote to Hon. R. H. Pooley, Attorney General of B.C. For Aberhart, LDA 18, Correspondence 1934-36, July 4, 1935, Reverend George Webber to the Hon. J. F. Lymburn, Attorney General of Alberta, June 12, 1936, Huestis to Webber. For Ontarion, LDA 17, December 11, 1931, Hon. William H. Price, Attorney General of Ontario to Heustis.

50. LDA 21, Correspondence 1939, September 8, 1939, Gladstone Murray, CBC General Manager to Rev. George Webber, and LDA 24, Correspondence 1942, May 1, 1943, Murray to Webber.

51. Privy Council Order 8535, November 4, 1943, *Canadian War Orders and Regulations 1943*, vol. 4, Ottawa, 1943.

52. The *Windsor Star*, January 2, 1942, and October 1, 1942, gives an example of boosting patriotic games and concerts. LDA 24, November 1942 holds a news release "From the National Executive Committee of the Imperial Order Daughters of the Empire." For ski trains, see LDA 169, Scrapbook 1939-42, *Toronto Daily Star*, November 29, 1940, and LDA 22, Correspondence 1940, October 25, 1940, "Press Release for Friday by G. D. Conant, Attorney General of Ontario." For the films, see LDA 25, Correspondence 1943-44, March 24, 1943, Ralph P. Bell, Director-General, Aircraft Production Branch, Department of Munitions and Supply to Webber. For an explicit and negative discussion of venereal diseases and films, see *Lord's Day Bulletin*, September 1944, "V.D. Control and Sunday Entertaining."

53. LDA 22, February 22, 1941, William Barclay, Moderator, signed a joint letter to the Legislature of Ontario.

54. LDA 29, Correspondence 1948, "Report of a Visit to Oshawa, January 28th and 29th, 1948 by the Rev. A. R. Skinner re Sunday Activities of Mayfair Lanes Bowling Alleys, and Oshawa Skating Rink."

55. *Acts and Proceedings*, "Resolution of the Board of Evangelism and Church Life and Work," 1946.

56. August 6, 1948.

57. The *Globe and Mail*, May 30, 1945, May 15, 1946. The *Financial Post*, May 25, 1946.

58. LDA 31, Correspondence 1950 (A-L), May 4, 1950, Rev. W. N. Byers to Webber.

59. *Acts and Proceedings* 1875, section 2, 5.

60. Gordon A. Peddie, *"The King of Kings." The Basis of Union of the Presbyterian Church in Canada and its relationship to the present need of the Church for a Confession of Faith in Jesus Christ as Lord of Church and State by Gordon A. Peddie, B.A., together with The Petition of a Memorial of the Presbytery of Paris to the General Assembly, 1942* (Toronto: Thorn Press, 1942).

III

PRESBYTERIANS AND
CANADIAN LITERATURE AND MUSIC

In his *A History of Canadian Literature*, W. H. New notes that "though Canada was a secular state, religion was everywhere in its history and language."[1] The pervasiveness of both Protestant and Roman Catholic religions has been one of the important factors in the growth and vitality of Canadian literature—literature which today commands international attention and respect. Anyone interested in the origins of Canadian literature needs to consider this religious context.

This section examines the contribution both of Presbyterian authors and of writers influenced by Presbyterian ideas. In "Ralph and Stephen and Hugh and Margaret: Canlit's View of Presbyterians," J. C. McLelland is primarily interested in what Canadian writers have said about Presbyterians. His is what he describes as "an irreverent look," which toys with the idea of "A Quest for the Historical Presbyterian, from Irving to Trevor" (i.e., Irving Layton and Trevor Ferguson). Before looking at Canlit's view of Presbyterians, Professor McLelland recounts the beginnings of our literary story epitomized in Susanna Moodie's *Roughing It in the Bush* and the homely practicality of the Reverend Thomas McCulloch's *Letters of Mephibosheth Stepsure*.

Professor McLelland believes that Calvinism was a grand attempt to justify God (theodicy), and that at the same time Calvinism proved a glorious failure, so we lament our unjustifiable God (threnody). It could be argued on the other side that John Calvin and most of his followers never sought to justify God. They asserted an absolute sovereign God who in the words of Robert Burns's Holy Willie's prayer, "Sends one to Heaven an' ten to Hell/a' for Thy Glory!" (quoted by J. C. McLelland, 121; Calvin's own estimate was two to heaven and eight to hell,[2] which was not much better and was biblically unwarranted). Calvin acknowledged that God's eternal decree of election and reprobation is a "horrible decree." When pressed to justify it, he appealed to the Apostle Paul's words,

"But who are you, a human being, to argue with God?" (Romans 9:20). As for Calvinism proving to be a glorious failure, scholars such as Michael Walzer,[3] Ernst Troeltsch,[4] Max Weber,[5] R.H. Tawney[6] and others, have shown that politically, economically, and socially, Calvinism was a considerable success in the sense of being a powerful shaping force in Western society. Theologically, the Calvinist system, though marked by inconsistencies and always in need of correction, has continued to be a vital force within Anglican, Baptist, Congregational, Presbyterian and Reformed churches. In the twentieth century it has experienced a revival, particularly through the theological renewal initiated by Karl Barth (1886-1968), a Swiss Reformed theologian.

Dr. McLelland offers four case studies in support of his thesis: Muscular Christians in the novels of Ralph Connor; Religious Romp in the humorous sketches of Stephen Leacock; A Dark Lord in the novels of Hugh MacLennan, and The Divine Jester in the work of Margaret Laurence. For McLelland, Laurence especially "was an honest and articulate voice in behalf of better answers, of openness between humans and a reformed religion" (120). Professor McLelland's conclusion is that Canadian literature presents Presbyterians under the long shadow of a strict sociotheology, symbolized by the names of Calvin and Knox. Its archetypal idea is the doctrine of predestination, indeed double predestination; its ethos includes a life of labour and thrift, paced by a humour both melancholic and ironic. The Presbyterian contribution, McLelland concludes, is a "pessimism about humanity wedded to an optimism about God's future" (121).

Jack Robinson's essay explores the theme of guilt in Margaret Laurence's Manawaka Tetralogy and Robertson Davies's Deptford trilogy. Both writers, according to Robinson, assume the Scottish Presbyterian background as a given and see the Presbyterian tradition as a testing ground for character. In their novels the strong do battle with the guilts induced by their Presbyterian heritage and they strive to find psychic peace and completion. For Margaret Laurence, the resolution of guilt is to be found in drawing upon the Elizabethan myth of four humours, while for Davies

wholeness or salvation it is to be discovered in the ideas or archetypes of the Swiss psychologist, Carl Jung.

Laurence's and Davies's judgment of the popular manfestations
of Calvinism in Canada, Robinson concludes, is that ultimately
pharisaism triumphed. Moral rigidity replaced grace; proper appearance was substituted for integrity. "Out of a proud people's
struggle to reclaim the social standing from which they were dispossessed in their forced migration to the new world," Robinson
says, "the Scots Presybterians have projected a God in their own
image, terribly conscious of 'proper appearances' and intent
upon keeping the conscience of humankind with an iron hand."
"A battered child among souls" is Davies's apt description of
Canada. Appropriately, Laurence's Rachel Cameron prays for
"God's pity on God."

Here two comments are in order. First, this critique is valid
and needs to be accepted with humility and contrition. A religious
tradition is as corruptible as any other human tradition, and since
"the corruption of the best produces the worst," the Presbyterian
tradition, as well as other religious traditions, stands in constant
need of reformation.

Second, the Calvinist tradition has produced not only a religious but also a social and moral deposit in Canada. In speaking of
the influence of Calvinism, Professor McGrath of Oxford University has offered this important insight:

> In understanding Calvinism as an historical force, which did so
> much to mould western European and North American culture,
> it is necessary to consider the moral and social deposit of faith
> which, although originally *shaped* by that faith, would remain
> behind after it departed. The cultural landscape of modern
> America is littered with such deposits, as a secular Calvinism—
> devoid of its original religious vitality, but retaining much of its
> moral and social worldview—began to emerge, eventually to
> gain the ascendancy.[7]

Allthough Professor McGrath has the United States mainly in
mind the same point can be made about Canada. The Calvinist or
Presbyterian character, although shaped by the beliefs and values

of Calvin and his followers, gradually became detached from its theological roots. As the "sea of faith" waned and the Calvinist God receded more and more into the background, faith and its social and moral deposit became separated. Christopher Lasch, the American social critic, has spoken of a Calvinism without a Calvinist theology, represented particularly by such thinkers as Thomas Carlyle and Ralph Waldo Emerson, who retained the moral realism of Calvinism but discarded its anthropomorphic view of God.[8]

The separation of the moral and social deposit from its theological base had serious consequences. We can see this in the whole experience of guilt divorced from its religious context. "Guilt, guilt and more guilt. But for the Children, even more than for the Parents, it is a guilt without final cause and therefore a guilt without final atonement or expiation. The further into the past the Calvinist God recedes, the more his legacy of guilt becomes separated from its objects: Children can feel guilty about *everything*" is Margaret Atwood's perceptive comment.[9] Hugh MacLennan's novel *Each Man's Son* is a fine illustration. Its main protagonist is a Dr. Ainslie who is riddled with a guilt instilled in him by his Calvinist father. Guilt is not something from which he could free himself: "Mackenzie had told him that although he might be an intellectual agnostic, he was an emotional child in thrall to his barbarous Presbyterian past. As he thought this, he felt guilty again. But why? Was there no end to the circle of Original Sin? Could a man never grow up and be free?"[10] A Presbyterian past becomes a great burden and is a source of shame. Yet both Davies and Laurence, Dr. Robinson notes, see not only the flaws but also the strengths of the Scottish Presbyterian tradition. The past, even if it is a flawed past, strengthens us in the present, and, properly understood and used, is a basis for hope for the future.

The two most popular Canadian novelists at the beginning of the century up to the First World War were both Presbyterians: Lucy Maud Montgomery and Ralph Connor. The Reverend Charles W. Gordon, a Presbyterian minister who wrote under the pseudonym Ralph Connor, became a household name in English Canada; more than five million copies of his first three novels were sold.

Barry Mack explores the Connor phenomenon in his essay, "Modernity Without Tears: The Mythic World of Ralph Connor."

Gordon wrote his popular novels at a critical time and addressed them to a society in the midst of transition. Among the major changes taking place were the emergence of industrial capitalism, the cult of efficiency, and the application of rational technique and business methods to society. Gordon did not take a critical attitude to these changes. He was, in George Grant's phrase, "a flatterer of modernity." Gordon, Dr. Mack says, fostered the illusion "that modernity could be embraced without significant costs and without tears."

Charles Gordon grew up in Glengarry in the 1860s where "unabashed Calvinism" has survived far longer than, for example, in New England. When he entered University College, Toronto, in 1881, Gordon had to struggle with the religious issues raised by the Darwinian revolution. His theological training at Knox College, Toronto, did not in any adequate way address this new challenge to the Christian faith. It was not until he took post-graduate studies at New College, Edinburgh, during which time he came under the influence of Scottish evangelist Henry Drummond, that he found what seemed to him to be a satisfactory answer. Drummond postulated a continuity between the natural and spiritual worlds and therefore a way of reconciling science, including Darwinian evolution, and the Christian faith. For Drummond the Darwinian "Struggle for Life" was followed by a new and higher "Struggle for the Life of Others." This latter struggle was tied to what Drummond called "the Mother Principle." Maternal self-sacrifice overcame male selfishness and was responsible for spiritual progress in a kind of "ascent of man." Dr. Mack believes that Drummond's theology laid the basis for the social gospel and that it was the rationale behind prohibition, public parks, and the urban reform movement. This may be claiming too much, although it was certainly an important influence in the social gospel movement in Canada. It was this "modernist theology" to which the Reverend Charles W. Gordon gave fictional expression, and in so doing achieved fame and fortune as Canada's most popular novelist.

Dr. Mack examines four Gordon/Connor novels to show how they promote the myth of evolutionary progress: *The Man from Glengarry* (1901), *The Foreigner, Corporal Cameron* (1911), and *The Patrol of the Sun Dance Trail* (1912). In conclusion, he assesses Ralph Connor's work both positively and negatively. On the positive side, his novels encouraged active engagement in the modern world, respect for traditional moral standards, and a certain beefy self-confidence. On the negative side, the novels acted as a kind of spiritual anaesthetic during the birth of modern Canada. They were, to use a phrase of Mark Twain's, "chloroform in print." After the First World War, Connor's readers awoke to discover that they had inherited not the Kingdom of God but the secular city. Still the novels are of interest to students of Canadian history because they enable us to see English Canada as it saw itself enter the modern world.

The final essay in this section by the late N. Keith Clifford focuses on "The Contribution of Alexander MacMillan to Canadian Hymnody." Alexander MacMillan, who edited the Presbyterian *Book of Praise* and the United Church *Hymnary*, also wrote a major commentary called *The Hymns of the Church: A Companion to the Hymnary of the United Church of Canada.* At the very outset, Professor Clifford sees the need to justify the topic of his essay. He notes that in most discussions of the relation of religion and culture, hymnody does not merit a significant place. Because of their elitist bias many historians do not regard hymnody as high culture. A shift has occurred, however, in recent years, and hymns and hymn writers have begun to receive some attention.

Alexander MacMillan, the father of Sir Ernest MacMillan, the great Canadian musician, was born and educated in Edinburgh. While a divinity student, he spent a summer in Fort Francis, fell in love with Canada, and returned after he graduated. He became secretary of the Church Hymnal Committee and later its convener. The Presbyterian *Book of Praise* was produced and approved by the General Assembly of the Church in 1918, largely as a result of his expert guidance. One of the distinctive features of the *Book of Praise* was its large selection of pre-Reformation hymns—the inclusion of some twenty-five translations of Greek and Latin hymns from Clement of Alexandria to Bernard of Clairvaux. MacMillan had been strongly influenced by the Oxford movement, and his later work contained an even greater emphasis on the catholic and liturgical dimensions of church praise.

Alexander MacMillan entered the United Church of Canada in 1925, and he was appointed to a committee which was set up to prepare a new hymn book for the new church. As a result of his leadership, the *Hymnary* was completed in 1931. In 1932, after the death of his wife, he resigned as full-time secretary of the Church Worship and Ritual Committee, and in 1935 published *Hymns of the Church: A companion to the Hymnary of the United Church of Canada.*

Dr. Clifford is critical of MacMillan for his rejection of the Moody and Sankey gospel hymns, of spirituals, and of such hymns as "The Old Rugged Cross." MacMillan and the various committees he worked with, Clifford believes, made a clear distinction between lower- and middle-class hymnody. The direction he took was clearly middle class, deeply liturgical, and more solidly rooted in the nineteenth than the twentieth century. This judgment is a little severe and may need some modification. An unfortunate implication is that common people or the "lower classes" have little or no appreciation of some of the great classical hymns of the church. It is of course a pity that Alexander MacMillan rejected Moody and Sankey hymns and spirituals. What is clear, however, is that until they were finally replaced by new hymn books in the 1970s, both the *Book of Praise* and the *Hymnary* shaped the piety, worship and outlook of The Presbyterian Church in Canada and the United Church of Canada.

NOTES

1. W. H. New, *A History of Canadian Literature.* Macmillan History of Literature (London: Macmillan Education, 1989), 1. George Woodcock notes that "an astonishing proportion of early Canadian fiction writers were clergymen of evangelical bent." "Possessing the Land" in *The Canadian Imagination*, ed. David Staines (Cambridge, MA: Harvard University Press, 1977), 75.

2. John Calvin, *Institutes of the Christian Religion*, 3.24.12.

3. Michael Walzer, *The Revolution of the Saints: A Study in the Origin of Radical Politics.* (Cambridge, MA: Harvard University Press, 1965).

4. Ernst Troeltsch, *The Social Teachings of the Christian Churches*, vol. 2 (London: Allen and Unwin, 1931). See also his article "Calvin and Calvinism," *Hibbert Journal* 8 (1909-10): 102-19.

5. Max Weber, *The Protestant Ethic and the Spirit of Capitalism* (New York: Scribner, 1958).

6. R. H. Tawney, *Religion and the Rise of Capitalism: A Historical Study* (Middlesex, England: Penguin, 1969).

7. Alister McGrath, *A Life of John Calvin* (Oxford: Basil Blackwell Ltd., 1990), 203-204.

8. Christopher Lasch, *The True and Only Heaven: Progress and its Critics* (New York: Norton, 1991), 15-16, chapter 6, especially 265.

9. Margaret Atwood, *Survival: A Thematic Guide to Canadian Literature* (Toronto: Anansi, 1972), 139.

10. Hugh MacLennan, *Each Man's Son* (Toronto: Macmillan, 1951), 64.

Ralph and Stephen and Hugh and Margaret: Canlit's View of Presbyterians

Joseph C. McLelland

An alternative title for this somewhat irreverent look at Canadian Presbyterians might be "The Quest for the Historical Presbyterian, from Irving to Trevor." Thus one might cite literary imagery in Irving Layton, "a man learning to forgive God," through to our own Trevor Ferguson, who enjoys both God and Presbyterians.[1] Layton laments effete Christianity, particularly Puritan ethos:

> What luck, what luck to be loved
> by the one girl
> in this Presbyterian
> country
> who knows how to give
> a man pleasure.[2]

Similarly, novelist M. T. Kelly states: "Everything felt like the worst Presbyterian Sunday."[3] American critic Edmund Wilson writes that Louis Dudek and Irving Layton perform "a very useful function by getting rid of Presbyterian inhibitions."[4] (If you prefer the obverse of this popular coinage, remember that the sweet heroine of the Mary Tyler Moore Show was a Presbyterian.)

Besides our research on the Reformers and on intellectual history, we need to listen to what Northrop Frye calls the social imagination. This explores and expresses "cultural history" which "has its own rhythms."[5] The literary artist plays many parts: entertainer (whether trivial or profound), lie-detector (to unmask hypocrisy, Tartuffery of all sorts), and seismograph (to record the fault in human beings, our weaknesses and convulsions). Religion is not only fair game but stands in constant need of such participant observers. "The corruption of the best is the worst."

Where Were We?

Literary Criticism, like sociology of knowledge, has helped us, in Robert Burns's words, "see ourselves as others see us." Northrop Frye in particular—both leading literary critic and erstwhile Reformed theologian—focuses the quest for context with the question "Where is here?" Thus "here" is Canada, from colonial outpost to industrial nation, or from Arcadian haunt to urban horror. In this light we can appreciate the beginnings of our literary story, epitomized in Susanna Moodie's *Roughing it in the Bush* and the homely practicality of Thomas McCulloch (founder of Pictou Academy) in his *Letters of Mephibosheth Stepsure*. Poems abound with titles like Snow, Frost, Bushed, Winter's Evening, Canoe-trip, Wilderness Gothic. In Grove's "Snow" a man is frozen to death in a blizzard; in Raddall's "Winter's Tale" the Halifax Explosion occurs on a winter's day. Ours is "an iron land" (Ralph Gustafson), "north of summer" (Al Purdy)—thirty acres of snow. Gilles Vigneault's song has become a symbol:

> Mon pays,
> ce n'est pas un pays
> c'est l'hiver.

Is Canadian theology by and large a winter theology? Does it, for instance, evidence the irony and satire of that seasonal modality? And is this wintry character the result of northern environment or of Scots Calvinist heredity, or both? D. G. Jones hears our poetry describing humans "burdened by a sense of guilt", and God, "if he appears, becomes a God of Vengeance rather than a God of Love."[6] The beautiful and positive poetry of Margaret Avison may be the exception that proves the rule.

One thesis to bear in mind is what Ronald Sutherland of Sherbrooke calls "the Calvinist-Jansenist Pantomime."[7] This is the notion that Quebec suffers from a seventeenth-century hangover, when Louis XIV saw fit to exchange what Voltaire dubbed "quelques arpents de neige." Canada (Frye again) began as an obstacle to the treasures of the East, continued as a colony (with garrison mentality), and then was cut adrift in quest of nationhood. The point is that we retain as a sort of frozen section much of that original context, including its language. This is the intellectual dimension of the "auld alliance" between France and Scotland, chief evidence for which lies in their sharing what is called "Common Sense philosophy." The influence of this on both Nova Scotia and Quebec in their formative years goes far to explain the common attitude to life, to work and to death.

Who are we? I submit that this should be changed to read, Where were we? Are we not, as the old joke says, displaced Scots who would rather have their debts forgiven than their trespasses? Over a period of some two hundred years they came, mostly forced by rapid social change, bringing their Scots dourness and pawky humour, as well as the Calvinist ethic. The likeness between *canadien* and Scot turns on a common attitude to the world as a vale of soul-making, hard and demanding: "purgatoire sur terre." The epic voice of E. J. Pratt, in what Frye calls "the greatest Canadian poem," shows the tension between the almighty deity of classical theology, the "great Panjandrum," and weak but stubborn human rebels.[8] The thesis of Margaret Atwood, that Canadians in general tend to assume the position of "victim" in face of their challenge to survive, is relevant, and her documentation reinforces that of Sutherland.[9] Also helpful is Atwood's distinction among the locations of coming of age in Europe ("what goes on in the bedroom"), the U.S.A. (the forest), and Canada (the coffin).

If the real question for Canadian Presbyterians is, "Where were we?" then Canlit helps us see how far our religion and theology have been a sort of threnody, a lament for lost homeland, its simple and stern ways, its heroic preachers and scholars. We suffer from what Herbert Butterfield calls the Whig interpretation of history. We are afflicted by hero worship, with Calvin and Knox as super-saints. Hugh MacLennan insists that "there is no group of people anywhere on the earth's surface that think more highly of their collective selves than the Scotch do."[10] Margaret Laurence agrees: "the Scots knew how to be almightier than anyone but God." (You know our favourite toast: "Here's tae us - wha's like us?")

This first point, concerning locale or geographical context, helps explain the emphasis on nature in early Canadian theology. It led James S. Thomson to say that natural theology seems indigenous to us,[11] a point Armour and Trott reinforce in their book on philosophy in Canada.[12] Let me phrase it like this: the natural theology of Canadians is natural theology. This includes both a theology of nature and a doctrine of natural knowledge that adapted Scottish Common Sense philosophy and later British Idealism to our Canadian universities. But that is another story.[13]

Scenes of Clerical Life

If locale was our first point, the role of the clergy is second. It is not surprising that the social imagination should take the clergy as archetypes of the religious life. This is as old as Chaucer and Boccaccio, as new as John Updike for the Lutherans and Peter De Vries for the Reformed. One thinks of the gentle irony of Trollope and Eliot concerning parsons, their foibles, intrigues, and pride. The drollery of the Barchester Chronicles is matched by Eliot's "Scenes of Clerical Life," where we find that most clergy are vain and bumbling innocents. They are "too high learnt to have much common-sense."[14] But turn to Scots literature and a sea-change occurs: a sentimental romanticism on the one hand, and on the other a dark sense of guilt and doom. A thesis has emerged in my research for this paper. The social imagination sees Presbyterians not so much as defenders of a classic theology stressing the sovereignty of God and the vocation of his people, but as burdened with an insoluble problem of evil; afflicted by the obvious injustice of things, yet stubbornly clinging to belief in a beneficent deity, they are restless and grieving. In search of a viable justification of God, a *theodicy*, they raise their lamentation, a *threnody*. I find this twin theme of theodicy and threnody the most telling in the material before us. My thesis is: Calvinism was a grand attempt at justifying God—theodicy; it proved a glorious failure, and so we lament our unjustifiable God—threnody.

Gavin Dishart of Thrums is James M. Barrie's "little minister"; for an Auld Licht preacher Dishart is incredibly naive. The plays of

James M. Bridie are better, while the writings of Ian MacLaren are worse. This genre belongs to the "Kailyard school," embodying that quality of "moral sentiment" characteristic of the Scottish Renaissance. We have been influenced by three waves from the old country. First was what Elizabeth Waterston calls a "cult of Burns," resulting in much Canadian poetry written in Braid Scots. Next came Walter Scott, imitated by John Galt. Robert Louis Stevenson was next, along with the Kailyard school.[15]

The influence of Robert Burns did contribute to a critical appreciation of Presbyterianism. But "the orthodox, wha' believe in John Knox" should be more disturbed by his fellow poet James Hogg, the Ettrick Shepherd. His novel *The Memoirs and Confessions of a Justified Sinner* explores the psychopathology of hyper-Calvinist ideas of predestination and perseverance. (Its antinomian hero provided the model for André Gide's *The Immoralist*, and perhaps for John Buchan's similar indictment of high Calvinism, *Witch Wood*.) Apologists will call this a caricature; and in part they are correct. But unless we listen to the voices of imagination, we become mere stooges in a comedy of errors. That is, we may think that we should be taken seriously, that it is self-evident how important to society is religion. To adapt the words of Mr. Thwackum, Tom Jones's tutor, by religion I mean Christianity, by that I mean Protestantism, and by that Presbyterianism, in fact the continuing Presbyterians in Canada, all 144,000 of them. But only a more detached opinion can verify or falsify such a claim. So let's listen.

Case Studies, or Who are we, really?

Muscular Christians – Ralph Connor

Charles W. Gordon is the G. A. Henty of Presbyterianism. Born in Glengarry, Ontario, in 1860, he suffers from two problems. One is a kind of posthumous excommunication by Presbyterians, since despite his lineage—Scottish minister for father, Knox College for alma mater—he played a notorious role as church union supporter. It was he who, at the stroke of midnight, June 10, 1925 instructed the General Assembly organist to play louder and still louder to drown out the summons to loyal Presbyterians to continue in sederunt even as the new United Church was officially born.

More important is the other problem: he is too good to be true. He joined the Kailyard tradition with moral idealism; three million copies of his thirty books were sold. His villains wore black, his heroes pure white. His theme was the heroics of, and the manly deeds on, the outposts of empire. Charles Sheldon's question, "What would Jesus do?"[16] symbolized the evangelical moralism of the time. Connor's experience as ordained missionary in Banff provided material for books featuring a courageous and visionary saver of souls, whose athletic ability (baseball or rugger or wrestling) turns the sceptical crowd his way.

Connor's first two books (*Black Rock: A Tale of the Selkirks* and *The Sky Pilot: A Tale of the Foothills*)[17] were written, he later said, "to awaken my church in eastern Canada to the splendour of the mighty religious adventure being attempted by the missionary pioneers in Canada beyond the Great Lakes." His preface to the second states that the pilot "came to them with firm purpose to play a brother's part, and by sheer love of them and by faith in them, win them to believe that life is priceless, and that it is good to be a man."

If this sounds thin as an evangelical creed, it was somewhat developed in the other pair of familiar works: *The Man from Glengarry*, 1901, and *Glengarry School Days*, 1902. Here the Christian virtues are clearly those of the Protestant or Puritan ethic. *The Man from Glengarry* has been called "his first real novel;" its hero is not a member of the clergy, indeed the inspiration for goodness comes from the minister's wife. Gordon's own mother, Margaret Robertson, was his model in this and other works. If his concept of "virtue" (literally "manliness") requires the feminine touch for its strength, is his doctrine of God more complex than it seems? The novel's treatment of the Communion season suggests so, with its delicate balance of law and gospel. Connor grasped the Presbyterian point, the dialectic of light and darkness. We look at each in turn.

Religious Romp - Stephen Leacock

Canadian letters may have begun with wintry poetry, but they soon found a summery voice. Stephen Leacock deserves a paragraph here. What teasing pen portraits he gives us! (Remember "the Awful Fate of Melpomenus Jones," the curate with a pathological shyness, who couldn't say goodbye while on a pastoral visit, became delirious, ill, and at last died?).[18] My favourite sketch concerns "The rival churches of St. Asaph and St. Osoph."[19] These Montreal Episcopal and Presbyterian congregations are shown in a dreadfully honest light. St. Osoph's, we are told, was so Presbyterian that it was no longer connected with any other church. "It seceded some forty years ago ... and later on, with three other churches, it seceded from the group of seceding congregations. Still later it fell into a difference with the three other churches on the question of eternal punishment, the word 'eternal' not appearing to the elders of St. Osoph's to designate a sufficiently long period." If this seems like exaggeration, remember that the subject of the duration of heaven and hell was a topic much discussed in Leacock's generation. For example, a symposium edited by William Cochrane of Montreal was entitled "Future Punishment: Or Does Death end Probation?" (1886), while the closest to a heresy trial our church has come concerned D. J. Macdonnell of St. Andrew's, Toronto whose sermon on universal salvation suggested that the "aeon" of punishment could bear a finite interpretation.

St. Osoph's minister, Dr. McTeague, also taught philosophy at the university, having spent fifty years trying to reconcile Hegel with St. Paul. His sermons were three parts Paul and one part Hegel, while his lectures were one part Paul to three Hegel. A reader of his book *McTeague's exposition of the Kantian Hypothesis* declared that "a man who could write that was capable of anything." His successor, the Reverend Uttermust Dumfarthing, provides stark contrast. His first sermon to St. Osoph's was on eternal punishment. He told them he was convinced that seventy per cent of them were destined for hell. "The congregation was so swelled next Sunday that the minister raised the percentage to eighty-five, and everybody went away delighted."[20]

We might add that such sketches of stern seceders are reinforced by Robertson Davies's profiles of "brass-bowelled Presbyterians." Davies is the serious person's Leacock, using his world of theatre, along with mythology, Jungian psychology, and even the occult to develop a wondrous typology of characters. He too sees us as guilt-ridden. In *Fifth Business*, first in the Deptford trilogy, Ramsay recalls that as a child "I was alone with my guilt, and it tortured me. I was a Presbyterian child and I knew a good deal about damnation." He meets a fitting partner in Liesl: "Calvinism? I am Swiss, Ramsay, and I know Calvinism as well as you do. It is a cruel way of life, even if you forget the religion and call it ethics or decent behavior or something else that pushes God out of it ... they want to show they can be Christians without Christ. Those are the worst; they have the cruelty of doctrine without the poetic grace of myth."[21]

Davies's eclectic "world of wonders" is donnish and elitist. His own perspective allows gnostic wisdom and mythology to mellow the hard dogma. Still, in a *Saturday Night* article he speaks well of our church: "The Presbyterians knew exactly where they stood; it was narrow ground, but it was firm ... They did not enter the union and are a strong, if small, denomination commonly called Continuing Presbyterians." And he is grateful that his own Presbyterian upbringing serves him well: "I have found the Shorter Catechism a rock at my back and a sword in my hand."[22]

A Dark Lord - Hugh MacLennan

From light to darkness: Apollo succumbs to Dionysus as we face the underside of our Reformed tradition: "Whenever I stop to think about it, the knowledge that I am three-quarters Scotch, and Highland at that, seems like a kind of doom from which I am too Scotch even to think of praying for deliverance." Again: the exiled Scots brought with them "that nameless haunting guilt they never understood, and the feeling of failure, and the loneliness."[23] It is this tragic sense of life that haunts MacLennan's Nova Scotia characters. His novel *Each Man's Son* (1951) provides the strongest case study.

The novel's protagonist, Dr. Dan Ainslie, is a childless man who seeks surrogate fatherhood by caring for the son of another. The title means that he remains his own father's son, as does the boy. Ainslie's father was a Presbyterian minister. As he wrestles with his sense of guilt, his friend MacKenzie observes: "'You may think you've rejected religion with your mind, but your personality has no more rejected it than dyed cloth rejects its original colour.' His voice became sonorous with irony as he tried to remember Calvin: 'Man, having through Adam's fall lost communion with God, abideth evermore under His wrath and curse except such as He hath, out of His loving-kindness and tender mercy, elected to eternal life through Jesus Christ—I'm a Christian, Dan, but Calvin wasn't one and neither was your father. It may sound ridiculous to say, in cold words, that you feel guilty merely because you are alive, but that's what you were taught to believe until you grew up.'" He pursues the point: "can you name any type in history more ridiculous than a Scotch Presbyterian? If you can't laugh at him, you'll be tempted to murder him." MacKenzie believes that the Highlanders enjoyed a simple, poetic faith; then "the Lowlanders with their Calvinism made us ashamed of living."[24]

MacLennan's preface to the book tells of the coming of the Highlanders to Cape Breton, bringing with them "an ancient curse, intensified by John Calvin and branded upon their souls by John Knox and his successors—the belief that man has inherited from Adam a nature so sinful there is no hope for him and that, furthermore, he lives and dies under the wrath of an arbitrary God who will forgive only a handful of His elect on the Day of Judgment." This prefatory note has a most significant story, told by Edmund Wilson. In a footnote he records a letter from MacLennan informing him that the novel "was not written to attack or even to emphasize Calvinism," while its preface was composed at the insistence of his Boston publishers, because "without it the underlying motivation would be incomprehensible to an American audience;" the preface is omitted in subsequent editions. Wilson notes how curious it is that "any such explanation should have been thought to be necessary—and, of all things, an explanation of

Calvinism in of all places, Boston."[25] Compare Herman Melville's comment on Nathanael Hawthorne's "touch of Puritanic gloom": "This great power of blackness in him derives its force from its appeal to that Calvinistic sense of Innate Depravity and Original Sin."[26]

MacLennan's most famous book, *Two Solitudes* (1945), scores the puritan ethic, translated into a means of power in the hands of Scots-Canadian Presbyterians. The familiar laws of Manchester school economics provide a mask of charity to hide self-serving. Huntly McQueen, for instance, makes a will (the year is 1934) leaving his entire fortune "to found and maintain a new Presbyterian theological college. It was to be located in the heart of the Ontario countryside, to have ample scholarships, and the chairs were to be so heavily endowed the trustees would be able to fill them with the ablest theologians they could import from Edinburgh and Aberdeen."[27]

Here, then, is a strong statement of the dark side of predestinarian Calvinism. If today we have mellowed, by ignoring or reinterpreting the doctrine of election, this insider's conscience insists that we face the tragic or pessimistic results in individual and societal instances.

Divine Jester - Margaret Laurence

After visiting Glengarry and Mariposa, Deptford and Cape Breton, we turn to Manawaka, Manitoba. This is Margaret Laurence country, as personalized as William Faulkner's Yoknapatawpha County, Mississippi. Her most memorable characters are women, often with Biblical names (Old Testament, of course), who are caught in social repression and inherited guilt. They rebel against injustice; they sacrifice, suffer, endure. Here are our two themes of theodicy and threnody. And since the test of a theodicy is whether it can justify not only God's ways but God himself, Laurence probes this wound of our faith most deeply. In the end God is a jester, a joker. What else can you say in face of the world's injustice, if you accept Calvinism's stress on divine will as almighty and incorrigible? In an interview Laurence had this to say about puritanism,

"You just absorb it through the pores. I come from a people who feel guilty at the drop of a hat, who reproach themselves for the slightest thing, and for whom virtue arises from work; if you're not working twenty-six hours a day, you just aren't virtuous."[28]

Manawaka is peopled with MacLeods and Camerons and fringe dwellers named Tonnerre. Margaret Laurence, besides her African books, has given us short stories featuring Vanessa MacLeod, who remembers "pictures of Jesus wearing a white sheet and surrounded by a whole lot of well-dressed kids whose mothers obviously had not suffered them to come unto Him until every face and ear was properly scrubbed." Her maternal grandmother lives by the MacInnes motto, "Pleasure Arises from Work." This means strict order and stern retribution. Laurence's women—especially Stacey and Rachel Cameron, daughters of Manawaka's undertaker (a fitting symbol for the wages of living)—endure the same bittersweet taste of hard grace. Stacey is the protagonist in The *Fire-Dwellers* (1969), meaning all of us who dwell in these purgatorial fires or are destined for hell. The novel opens with an epigraph from Carl Sandburg's poem "Losers." Stacey sees through the false fronts people wear to hide their fear, as she does herself. She keeps remembering the song:

> Ladybird, ladybird,
> Fly away home;
> Your house is on fire,
> Your children are gone.

Rachel Cameron (*A Jest of God*, 1966) is obsessed with the injustice of things. "If I believed, I would have to detest God for the brutal joker He would be if He existed." "My trouble, perhaps, is that I have expected justice." Here also is a reference to our Protestant iconography, a stained-glass window depicting "a pretty and clean-cut Jesus expiring gently and with absolutely no inconvenience, no gore, no pain, just this nice and slightly effeminate insurance salesman who, somewhat incongruously, happens to be clad in a toga." At the end she hopes for "God's mercy on reluctant jesters. God's grace on fools. God's pity on God."[29]

Hagar Shipley, in *The Stone Angel* (1964) resembles her Biblical namesake. She is in bondage and seeks her identity, her separate peace. The book opens with Dylan Thomas's lines, "Do not go gentle into that good night. / Rage, rage against the dying of the light." She is meditating; these are her last days. She has "often wondered why one discovers so many things too late. The jokes of God." In a moving and ironic passage we read of her being visited by Mr. Troy, the young minister, awkward with this stern old woman. She regards "God's little man" and tries to be gentle with him. He wants to pray (she lets him). She asks him to sing (he finally does, reluctantly but well). Her request is the Hundredth Psalm. All people that on earth and all that. She wonders why she has never been able to serve him with mirth, to find the Psalmist's joy. Nearing her end, she thinks: "If I could, I'd like to have a piper play a pibroch over my grave. *Flowers of the Forest.*"[30]

The pibroch is sometimes martial, often a dirge. The lament for Culloden, "Flowers of the Forest," turns up again in Margaret Laurence's last book, *The Diviners* (1975). Morag Gunn learns of her family heritage from her stepfather, Christie Logan. The Logan warcry is "The Ridge of Tears!" (*Druim-nan deur*). "A sad cry it is, for the sadness of my people. A cry heard at Culloden." And the Logan badge bears the sign of "a passion nail piercing a human heart, proper." Christie tells of the famous Piper Gunn, who led his clansmen on to the ship bound for the Red River during the Highland Clearances. He played "there on the shore, all the pibrochs he knew, 'Flowers of the Forest' and all them. And it would wrench the heart of any person whose heart was not dead as stone, to hear him."[31]

From theodicy to threnody: if you cannot explain Morag's experience of "the chaos of the outer world and the confusions of the inner," your rebellion becomes a lament for a lost meaning and a lost grace. Margaret Laurence was an honest and articulate voice on behalf of better answers, of openness between humans, and of a reformed religion.

Conclusion

Canadian Presbyterians, as CanLit sees us, stand under the long shadow of a strict sociotheology symbolized by the names Calvin and Knox. Its archetypal idea is the doctrine of election, understood in its strict sense of "double predestination"—God "Sends ane to Heaven an' ten to Hell, / A' for Thy glory!" according to Burns's Holy Willie. In its ethos such a creed includes a life of labour and thrift paced by a humour both melancholic and ironic, in short, pessimism about humanity wedded to optimism about God's future. Provided, that is, we are among the elect (and we are!). I submitted that theodicy and threnody are the two chief themes literature sees in Calvinism. Like all theology (I speak as philosopher), it offers little light on the problem of evil; perhaps it even signifies a darkening of the issue, or a celestial copout. But Calvinism does provide the keening lament of the Celts, afflicting us at last with a frightful demand and a profound protest: Is it nothing to you, who pass by?

NOTES

1. For example, *Onyx John* (Toronto: McLelland & Stewart, 1986).
2. "Look, The Lambs Are All Around Us!" in *The Love Poems of Irving Layton* (Toronto: McLelland & Stewart, 1980).
3. M. T. Kelly, *A Dream Like Mine* (Don Mills: Stoddart, 1987).
4. Edmund Wilson, *O Canada: An American's Notes on Canadian Culture* (New York: Noonday Press, 1964), 91.
5. Northrop Frye, "Conclusion," in *Literary History of Canada*, ed. Carl Klinck (Toronto: University of Toronto Press, 1965), 215ff.
6. George Woodcock, ed., *A Choice of Critics* (New York: Oxford University Press, 1966), 4.
7. Ronald Sutherland, *Second Image: Comparative Studies in Quebec/Canadian Literature* (Toronto: New Press, 1971), 60ff. Cf. Ronald Sutherland, *The New Hero: Essays in Comparative Quebec/Canadian Literature* (Toronto: New Press, 1971), 4, on Jonathan Edwards "harmonizing dark Calvinism with enlightened rationalism."
8. E. J. Pratt, "The Truant" (1943). *Selected Poems of E. J. Pratt* (Toronto: Macmillan, 1968).
9. Margaret Atwood, *Survival* (Toronto: Anansi, 1972), 36ff., 222.
10. See Donald Cameron, *Conversations with Canadian Novelists* (Toronto: Macmillan, 1973), 134.

11. Klinck, *Literary History*, 554.

12. L. Armour and E. Trott, *The Faces of Reason* (Waterloo: Wilfred Laurier University Press, 1981).

13. I develop this "Philosophy and Theology in Canada" in a forthcoming *Festschrift* for Douglas Jay.

14. "The Sad Fortunes of the Rev. Amos Barton," in *Scenes of Clerical Life*, 1856 (London: Macmillan, 1906), 59.

15. "The Lowland Tradition in Canadian Literature," in W. Stanford Reid, ed., *The Scottish Tradition in Canada* (Toronto: McClelland and Stewart, 1976), 203-31.

16. Charles M. Sheldon, *In His Steps* (New York: Grosset, 1896).

17. Ralph Connor, *Black Rock: A Tale of the Selkirks* (Toronto: Westminster, 1899), and *The Sky Pilot: A Tale of the Foothills* (Toronto: Westminster, 1899).

18. Stephen Leacock, *Literary Lapses* (Toronto: McClelland & Stewart, 1957), 12ff.

19. Stephen Leacock, *Arcadian Adventures With the Idle Rich* (Crowell, 1914; Toronto: McClelland & Stewart, 1959), 101ff.

20. "The Ministrations of the Rev. Uttermust Dumfarthing," in Stephen Leacock, *Arcadian Adventures*, 118ff.

21. Robertson Davies, *Fifth Business,* (Toronto: Macmillan, 1970), 226; cf. Brian Thorpe, "Discerning the Contemporary Gnostic Spirit in the Novels of Robertson Davies," Ph.D. diss., McGill University, 1989.

22. Robertson Davies, "Keeping the Faith" in *Saturday Night* 102 (January, 1987), 187ff.

23. Hugh MacLennan, *Scotchman's Return and Other Essays*, vol. 1 (Toronto: Macmillan, 1960), 8.

24. Hugh MacLennan, *Each Man's Son* (Toronto: McClelland & Stewart, 1951), 67, 69.

25. Edmund Wilson, *O Canada: An American's Notes on Canadian Culture.* (New York: Noonday, 1965), 71.

26. Philip Lee, *Against the Protestant Gnostics* (New York: Oxford University Press, 1987), 90.

27. Hugh MacLennan, *Two Solitudes* (Toronto: Collins, 1945), 353.

28. Quoted by Donald Cameron, *Conversations with Canadian Novelists* (Toronto: Macmillan, 1973), 100.

29. Margaret Laurence, *A Jest of God* (Toronto: McClelland & Stewart, 1966), 41f., 209.

30. Margaret Laurence, *The Stone Angel* (Toronto: McClelland & Stewart, 1982), 40ff.

31. Margaret Laurence, *The Diviners* (Toronto: McClelland & Stewart, 1976), 47-50.

Fleeing The Emptiness: Presbyterian Guilt in Laurence's Manawaka Tetralogy and Davies's Deptford Trilogy

Jack Robinson

In *The Knowledge of Man*, Martin Buber states, "Man is the creature who is capable of becoming guilty and is capable of illuminating his guilt."[1] The premise underlying Laurence's Manawaka tetralogy and Davies's Deptford trilogy is that the causes of guilt are not inscrutable. Unlike Kafka's fictions, wherein guilt is soul destroying precisely because its sources are so diffuse that they cannot be named, the novels of Laurence and Davies show clearly how guilt arises from a sense of sin rooted in specific religious and cultural myths. For both authors, the Presbyterian tradition provides a testing ground for character: the strong are able to do battle with the guilts induced by their religious heritage and to find their own paths toward psychic peace and completion. In defining such new directions, Laurence draws upon the Elizabethan myth of the four humours, while Davies employs Jungian archetype and symbol.

A useful introduction to the themes of the Manawaka tetralogy is found in Laurence's "fictionalized autobiography,"[2] *A Bird in the House* (1970). This fiction (which has been called a short story collection, but is more properly described as a novel) takes the imaginative budding writer Vanessa MacLeod, the prototype of her creator, from age ten to twenty in the decade from 1935 to war's end. Two extended-family homes symbolize Vanessa's Scots-Irish family background, paralleling the ancestral influences of Laurence herself.[3] In each of these homes Vanessa feels the captive bird's frantic need to escape.

In the first house the magic words of social harmony are "I'm sorry," suggesting the post-lapsarian sense of guilt of Vanessa's Scottish Presbyterian Grandmother MacLeod. The old matriarch implies in all she says and does that grace is to be achieved by good works, and that those works are to be of a definitely mercantile character. Her evidence for being among God's chosen consists of a demonstration of conspicuous consumption. She is of the tribe of God's elect because she and her husband have laboured to attain that position, whereas others are lesser and lower, dispossessed of God's grace. Vanessa intuits that these principles would isolate her from herself and others, and from the real world in all its mysterious disarray. Until Grandmother MacLeod's red brick house is sold and stuccoed and loses its essence of "stern dignity," Vanessa finds escape within it to her own private hiding places.

An equally intimidating structure is her Irish Grandfather Timothy Connor's "Brick House," described in the book's opening paragraph as "part dwelling place and part massive monument" and in the final story's title as "Jericho's Brick Battlements." At three, Vanessa thinks Timothy is God; at twelve, she hates the thought of moving into his house after her father's death, and wishes she could crumble its walls with a single cry, as Joshua's Christians brought down the heathen walls of Jericho. Timothy is a proud tough pioneer modelled on Laurence's own maternal grandfather. The wrathful authoritarian God of the Old Testament is the spiritual projection of a society led by such patriarchs.

Timothy's wife Agnes and daughter Beth are the peacemakers in the novel's microcosm of the human family; yet they occupy the narrative's background, while Timothy, its flawed and combative hero, is squarely in the foreground. In this dramatic tension we find proof of Laurence's deliberately ambivalent position in regard to the Old and New Testaments: she admires the quiet abiding love shown in the latter, but recognizes that the conquering spirit of the former is more central to the lives of our explorers and pioneers.

In the first novel of the Manawaka tetralogy, *The Stone Angel* of 1964, another all-controlling *paterfamilias* appears and is locked in dubious battle with his daughter, the novel's vital and raging heroine, Hagar Shipley. Like Timothy Connor, Jason Currie is a pioneering storekeeper whose life is one of emotional isolation and devotion to work. He is one of the founding fathers of Manawaka's new Presbyterian church, and revels in the minister's first sermon on toil, fortitude, temperance, and the ephemeral nature of earthly joys.[4] As a girl, Hagar takes literally his claim to be a "self-made man," and can scarcely believe her father to be one of God's creatures. As she grows up, however, she rails against his egotism and pride. Fulfilling the clan motto "Gainsay who Dare," which Jason has dinned into her, she derides his pioneering generation of "fledgling pharoahs in an uncouth land."

Hagar dares to disappoint her father's social ambitions for his only daughter by marrying the slovenly farmer Bram Shipley. While she is possessed by a sensual love for Bram, Presbyterian reticence silences her declarations of passion, and Hagar allows Bram to assume that his sexual needs are an affliction and an imposition. Finally she discovers that in his dissolute way Bram too wants his dynasty. She defies a second patriarch by leaving Bram, and in an inversion of her own youthful rebellion against the town's mean emphasis on social status, prevents her favourite son John from marrying the well-to-do Arlene Simmons; hence, she is partly responsible for their futile deaths in an accident caused by a drunken dare. The sin of proud daring is visited upon two generations.

Based upon the Hagar of Genesis, Laurence's heroine has a passionate marriage to Abraham; their son, the unemployable John, is an Ishmael figure, an outsider. After she has recalled her life story from the age of ninety, Hagar comes to understand that she has wandered in the wilderness, like her Biblical namesake; in this case, the wilderness is pride. In Laurence's fractured use of the Genesis story, Hagar realizes on her deathbed that her Jacob (grandson of Abraham and Hagar) has been her faithful son Marvin. It is Marvin and his wife Doris who have long supported and cared for the intractable old woman in her Vancouver home, where, ironically faithful to her father's avarice, she clings not to people but to her few worldly goods. Marvin pronounces a colloquial blessing upon his unregenerate mother when he speaks of her as a "a holy terror," reminding us that she gainsays God as well, playing secular rebel to Jason Currie's "God-fearing man."

In creating Hagar, Laurence must have had in mind St. Paul's reference to Abraham's two sons: the one born of a bondswoman representing the covenant to earthly bondage, symbolized by Agar or Mount Sinai; the other born of a free woman representing the true covenant, symbolized by Jerusalem above.[5] Hagar is earthbound: she represents humankind's tragically willful bondage to earth, flesh, the senses. Her symbol is *The Stone Angel*, the statue Jason Currie erected to the memory of his wife. To Hagar the doubly blind statue, its stone eyeballs blank, stands above the town "harking us to heaven without knowing who we [are] at all." In her sensuality, personal magnetism, and self-destructive pride, Hagar embodies the glory and tragedy of "who we are," and is Laurence's ironical justification of the ways of humanity to St. Paul.

By identifying Hagar with earth, Laurence draws upon a mythic pattern which dominates the Manawaka tetralogy. The Elizabethan myth of the four elements composing the universe, grounded in medieval medicine, divides human character into four humours corresponding to the elements of earth, air, fire, and water.[6]

The temperament associated with earth is choleric; thus, the essence of Hagar's defiant earthliness, by her alienating paternal birthright, is rage. Jason Currie passes on to his daughter not the Presbyterian's pride in his denial of self and worldly pleasures, but a proud and choleric reaction against this oppressive spiritual heritage. Only after Hagar admits her guilt in John's death, confesses her pride, and finds a brief peace can she transcend her earthbound nature, reaching in her dying moment for God's humble cup of grace, a glass of water.

Air is the element of Rachel Cameron, heroine of *A Jest of God* (1966); in accordance with the myth of the four humours, Rachel's character is phlegmatic. A thirty-four-year old spinster schoolteacher who has never escaped Manawaka, Rachel has the insubstantial and wavering qualities of air, but also its lightness and ability to move and change, and to feed fire. As the epigraph states, "The wind blows high, the wind blows low," and Rachel is wafted and buffeted by it. In her recurring nightmare, she is trapped in air, high on a gigantic ferris wheel, powerless to get off. The force

constraining her freedom is precisely the Presbyterian demon of
"proper appearances" which held Hagar in self-destructive rebellion against the social ambitions of her father.

The source of Rachel's extreme self-constraint is her repressive
mother, an aging hypochondriac whom Rachel lives with and cares
for. In her mother's prim white church, where Christ's death is
depicted as bloodless and painless, proprieties must be observed:
Rachel should attend because "it wouldn't be very nice not to,
" but her bright orange scarf is no more welcome than a mongoloid
boy who appears one Sunday. At home, Rachel is reminded that
her body and emotions are also unseemly, and that she should
think more of her mother. Mrs. Cameron, like Vanessa's Grandmother MacLeod, is the paradigm of the self-centred guilt-inducing
matriarch.

Change begins when Rachel acts upon her desires for sex and
love and children, and her fears of death and eccentricity. In so
doing, she becomes a fool so that, as the Pauline maxim has it, she
may become wise.[7] At her friend Calla's gaudy and expressive
Pentecostal tabernacle, Rachel is immersed in the waters and in-
flamed by the fires of spiritual inspiration. The growth toward self-
possession begins here and continues when she must rebuke Calla's
lesbian advances; when her love affair with Nick Kazlik ends in her
desertion and false pregnancy; when her maternal feelings for a
bright student lead her to slap the boy for hiding his talents; and
when the undertaker Hector Jonas points out that her father, former
undertaker Niall Cameron, had sought oblivion in alcohol and a
loveless marriage after his disillusionment in the First World War.

In the end, Rachel is able to own the strengths of her meekness
and to abandon the Biblical Rachel's "mourning for her children,"
the children she has wanted but never had. She realizes that her
dependant mother is the child now, and, having found a teaching
position in Vancouver, takes her "elderly child" to the city George
Bowering describes as a place "where fools may live in God's grace,
making their own traditions."[8] Rachel begins to slough off the skin
of guilts and fears inculcated by her Presbyterian heritage, and to
be reborn into the "golden city" of Jerusalem mentioned in the

novel's epigraph. Her hopes of residing in the heavenly city are expressed in images of flight: the bus carrying her and her mother from Manawaka "flies along, smooth and confident as a great owl through the darkness" toward Vancouver, where Rachel will be "light and straight as any feather."[9]

"Better to marry than to burn," wrote St. Paul, but this is little comfort to Stacey Cameron of *The Fire-Dwellers* (1969), who can only remark that "he didn't say what to do if you married *and* burned."[10] Stacey, Rachel's older sister, is a thirty-nine-year-old Vancouver housewife and mother of three, married to a salesman and lodged in a barely affordable middle-class home. Hers is the sanguine temperament corresponding to the element of fire. She burns with a fiery temper and smouldering desires, and with a sense of universal guilt for a chaotic and soulless world, which the epigraph compares to the decadent late Roman empire in which Nero "fiddled in a world of fire."

Alienation marks public and private life in Laurence's apocalyptic fictional vision. News events from the television or EVER OPEN EYE bombard Stacey's thoughts, memories, fantasies, and conversations, but late sixties images of Vietnam atrocities and mounting American domestic chaos blend with those of mundane television dramas to create a blur of unreality.[11] The supermarket is the modern temple, the tupperware saleswoman, the new oracle; gods and demons alike are marketing devices. In Stacey's personal life, people don't talk. An apparently happy neighbour tries to commit suicide. Frightful accidents threaten Stacey's children, but they want only to be left alone. Her husband, Mac MacAindra, though very unhappy in his job as salesman for a typical miracle-drug company and distraught at his best friend's suicide, wants only to maintain that everything is "all right."

Faced with an all-pervasive guilt, Stacey takes two actions. First, she has an affair with Luke, a young writer. Like the biblical Luke, he is a healer, momentarily releasing Stacey from the worries of her complex social roles, and allowing her to focus her vague guilts upon the affair. Second, she tries to break through the isolation of her children and her husband. She discovers that Mac's tight-lipped reserve stems from his father Matthew, a retired United Church minister who never admitted to his son that he had doubts or weaknesses. Matthew's model of perfection has had devastating effects, making Mac feel that to reach out for advice or encouragement is to fail.

Mac eventually tells Stacey about a boyhood incident in which he broke a window and his father made him pray for self-control. Mac would have preferred "any other whip," Stacey thinks. Her reflection reminds us that Rachel too wished that her mother had simply hit her rather than inflicting guilt by propitiating God's forgiveness for simple defects or errors. Mac, Rachel, and Stacey inherit a legacy of Calvinistic guilt by which not only pleasure but also fallibility is sinful. Stacey's personal hell-fire is the fear that she cannot be the perfect wife and mother. If God exists he will punish her through her children for her marital infidelity or some failure of maternal duty. Such anxiety cannot be resolved, but Stacey does learn to celebrate life in dance, and to dance in her mind—an expression of the desirous temperament which had prompted her youthful venture to the seedy glamour of Manawaka's Flamingo Dance Hall, where she met Mac and her adult life began.

While the earlier Manawaka fictions depict Presbyterian guilt and the desiccated emphasis upon personal infallibility and social appearance it fosters, *The Diviners* (1974) portrays some answers to these problems. Morag Gunn's element is water: she receives its melancholic humour from her Black Celt ancestry; moreover, she inherits "a portion of grace" from the water diviner, Royland, after life has taught her how to "look ahead into the past, and back into the future," like the river that seems, by the operation of an optical illusion, to flow both ways outside her Ontario home at McConnell's Landing.

Like Hagar Shipley, Morag is initially locked in battle with her father over the bonds of social status and ancestry. For a long time she hates Christie Logan for being the town scavenger and diviner of its garbage, and harbours the delusion that the source of her true nobility is to be found in Scotland, the origin of Christie's glorious tales of the heroic Piper Gunn. When she finds that Scotland offers her nothing, she returns to Manawaka in time to thank the elderly Christie for the affection and the cultural roots he did provide.

Morag lapses into the passivity of Rachel Cameron in her sterile marriage. She must outgrow her hopes that her husband, the English professor Brooke Skelton, will elevate her from Manawaka into a world of prestige and intellectual vitality. Condescending, insecure, and jealous of Morag's writing, Brooke reproduces in personal terms the power struggles of his family's colonial past in India. He attempts to colonize his wife, to eradicate the moodiness of the proud Black Celt and the inelegance of her Canadian colloquial speech. With great pain, Morag must recognize the folly of her hope to be reborn from her Manawaka self.

By coming to know and love men whose natures are identified with other elements, Morag becomes less bound by the limits of her own character. Brooke is a phlegmatic creature of air, afraid of bringing a child to the earth and of the earthly passions of men and women. Dan McRaith, Morag's painter-lover in London, is of earth: the human eyes in his paintings peer through landscape forms, expressing the choleric desperation of spirit held by earth.

The Métis Jules Tonnere, Morag's greatest love and the father of her child Pique, is fire, associated in memory with the terrible fire which figures in *A Bird in the House* and *The Fire-Dwellers*, in which his sister Piquette and her children burned to death in the family shack, an ironic Métis Gehenna outside the equally ironic Jerusalem of Manawaka. Since Morag has occupied a middle ground between the community leaders and the Métis in Manawaka's social strata, she is able to love and respect the sanguine Jules, who is not educated or articulate, and burns with the fires of self-destructive bitterness. Since fire and water are incompatible, Jules and Morag part, but not before she learns his tales of the heroic Métis past and makes them part of her present, and of the book she is writing (which is *The Diviners* itself).

Her quest repeatedly brings Morag home. The terrible isolation imposed by her Presbyterian heritage is finally less onerous for her than for Laurence's other Manawaka heroines. Hagar, Rachel, Stacey, and Morag demonstrate a progressive ability to repossess their alienating past and to carry it into the future with warmth and dignity. Through that repossession, Morag is able to divine from the course of her life an understanding of human existence, so that in literature her divining spirit can take flight like the symbolic great blue heron, which represents her vulnerable and awkwardly beautiful writing self.

* * *

The three novels of Robertson Davies's Deptford trilogy are romances with interlocking plots. *Fifth Business* (1970) is the best novel of the trilogy, because Dunstan Ramsay is its most vital and compelling narrator. *The Manticore* (1972), the story of David Staunton's protracted psychoanalysis, is more Jungian exegesis than fully realized fiction. *World of Wonders* (1975), the tale of Paul Dempster's youthful degradation and international acclaim as a brilliant magician, is too purely a romantic plotboiler, in which an invincible hero confronts adventure after adventure until the story ends.[12]

For a romance of the soul's completion which makes the Jungian way of individuation understandable as a lived reality, we must examine *Fifth Business*; hence I shall restrict my analysis to the first novel of the Deptford trilogy, which, by Davies's own admission, is his novel about guilt.[13] It is also his portrait of a Canadian hero who "has been shaped by Canada's unquestioned virtues, but also by its lack of spiritual self-recognition."[14] Both the guilt and the limiting virtues are of Presbyterian origin.

As Northrop Frye has observed, the childhood and youth of the romantic hero are often cruel: false domineering parents seek his destruction while his real ones are disguised.[15] Dunstan's spiritual journey begins when it becomes clear to him that his natural mother, or in Jungian theory his Eve figure, is a cruel and spiritually inadequate mother.[16] It becomes apparent that her maternal love is repressive when the thirteen-year-old Dunstan steals an egg from her kitchen to perform magic tricks. Mrs. Ramsay's Scottish reserve breaks down in a dionysian frenzy of possessiveness:

she whips the boy and forces him to beg "her—and secondarily God"—for forgiveness. Dunstan concludes from the incident that "nobody—not even my mother—was to be trusted in a strange world that showed very little of itself on the surface."[17]

Thus Dunstan begins the Jungian growth toward psychic wholeness by recognizing that his biological mother does not fulfill the needs of his soul for a mother archetype. He begins to know the feminine side of his soul, or the Anima, by seeking unconsciously for a second mother. In keeping with the Jungian principle that wisdom and wonder are to be found in the most unlikely and sordid places, Dunstan's discovery of his spiritual mother begins when Mary Dempster gives herself sexually to a tramp in the gravel pit outside Deptford.

The incident prompts Mrs. Ramsay to reveal the cruel consequences of her own sexual repression. In solidarity with the women of the town, she insists that Mary's husband must be dismissed as Baptist minister, and, in a very rare row with her husband (for there were no "scenes" in their Presbyterian household), she insists that any man who would speak up for Mary Dempster "associate[s] sex with pleasure" and is therefore a "filthy thinker." Agonized by his mother's hatred of "that woman," Dunstan enlists in the First World War, and feels only relief to learn that the "good, ignorant, confident" Mrs. Ramsay has died in the influenza epidemic of 1918.

Mary Dempster is the second archetype of Dunstan's Anima, or what Jung called the Mary figure. Jung's Mary is fully immersed in Eros or earthly love, but raises it to the height of spiritual devotion. Mary Dempster's extraordinary act of sexual healing reforms her tramp-seducer, Joel Surgeoner, and makes him an able social worker; moreover, Dunstan's feelings for Mary change from love to faith in her unconditional giving and saintly wisdom. After believing for a time that she is a saint, he comes to understand her central place in his personal mythology—though his lifelong support of her care in an asylum stems from his Presbyterian sense of guilt that he has precipitated Mary's madness, when, at age ten, he dodged a stone-filled snowball which struck Mary on the head and caused the premature birth of her son Paul.[18]

In his middle years, Dunstan becomes a respected hagiographer, a teacher with a Jungian interest in the mythic underpinnings of history, and finally the ghost-writer of an autobiography for his boyhood friend and magic student, Paul Dempster, who has become the world-famous magician Magnus Eisengrim. The fictitious volume is a hoax in the good cause of nourishing the sense of wonder or spiritual awe—the purpose of the Deptford trilogy itself. So long as Dunstan approaches the soul vicariously through books, however, he is the victim of his Presbyterian heritage, which elevates intellect above emotion and a socially proscriptive definition of virtue above the far less "proper" Jungian integration of the soul.

Only when he surrenders at age fifty to a schoolboy infatuation for the beautiful Faustine, who constitutes his Temptress, the Helen archetype and the third figure of his Anima, does Dunstan's own soul begin to awaken. It nears completion when he encounters the final part of his Anima, the Sapientia figure, representing a spiritual knowledge transcending the conventional understanding of good and evil. In a serio-comic bedroom scene in a Mexico City hotel, Dunstan battles and seduces Liesl Vitzliputzli, the grotesque but wise stage manager for Eisengrim's magical production. A Swiss, she speaks from experience in telling him that Calvinism has "the cruelty of doctrine without the poetic grace of myth," and that it has stunted him emotionally. Both Liesl and the eccentric Bollandist monk, Padre Blazon, who is Dunstan's Wise Old Man archetype, urge him to transcend Calvinist stoicism and become human by investigating his own place in myth. Liesl suggests that his role is that of "fifth business," the figure in opera who is not one of the four major characters, but who surreptitiously moves the action forward.

Dunstan plays that role when he brings together his two boyhood friends, Boy Staunton and Paul Dempster, and tells Paul the story of the stone in the snowball which drove Mary Dempster mad and caused Paul's youth to be one of hardship and depravity. In revenge against the thrower of the snowball, Paul either murders Boy or assists the despairing millionaire to achieve his wished-for suicide. Paul carries the stone, which Dunstan has kept throughout his life, from the meeting, and it is found in Boy's mouth the following morning when his body is dredged from the Toronto harbour.

Boy turns his back upon his spiritual self when he deliberately wipes from his memory the snowball incident and its implications, devoting himself to wealth, power, and his own youthful self-image. Jung found in many cultures the use of the stone as symbol of the soul.[19] In view of this symbol, Davies's message is clarified: Boy's soul is buried at first in snow, that most Canadian symbol of the existential void, and finally in his own flesh. While Boy's soul has been forgotten in the cultivation of the limiting social mask, or in Jungian terms the "persona," Dunstan achieves psychic wholeness by encountering his devil and integrating it into his spiritual being.

With symmetry typical of Davies, the Jungian "shadow" of Dunstan's unconscious, consisting of thoughts, motives, and feelings which the conscious mind represses because they are considered unworthy, is expressed when he judges Boy for being afraid to face the "shadow" of his narcissism. Dunstan's "shadow" is precisely his arrogance in sitting in judgment and in using Paul to punish Boy. He judges according to the new wisdom of his generation—the Jungian celebration of the entire soul, with its integration of spirit and flesh, sordid and noble, good and evil—but in doing so expresses the Calvinist impulse to judge and punish as the only way to keep humanity's innate evil in check.

In short, Dunstan acts in a manner very similar to that of his Presbyterian mother, when she exacted the traumatic punishment for his theft of the egg, ironically launching him on his Jungian quest for individuation. His judgment of Boy is diametrically opposed to the forgiving and redeeming love exemplified by Mary Dempster. Dunstan's putative saint is a model of the self-abnegation and charity that transcends conventional morality, but his Jungian "shadow," which asserts itself when he plays out his role of "fifth business," is the all-controlling and punitive Jehovah of the Old Testament.

In *Fifth Business* Davies dramatizes the tension between two definitions of the word "religion" in Canadian life.[20] The first derives from *religare*, meaning "to reconnect or link back," and in Davies's view is supported by Canada's Christian churches in their efforts to bind their members to particular forms of belief and conduct. The second definition is rooted in *relegere*, meaning "a careful observation and heedfulness toward the numinous— whatever inspires awe or reverence." The emphasis upon the numinous is central to Davies's extensive use of Jungian depth psychology in the Deptford trilogy, and to his use of the romance form in these novels, for the goal of romance is to inspire a sense of spiritual wonder.

Davies's statement that Canada's soul is "a battered child among souls" evokes thoughts of the beaten and repressed Dunstan. Both Davies and Laurence promote a religion of immanence and love in reaction to the Presbyterian stress upon obedience and post-lapsarian guilt. They find that in the popular manifestations of Calvinism in Canada, the Pharisees have dominated, with their association of grace with moral rigidity and social rank. Out of a proud people's struggle to reclaim the social standing from which they were dispossessed in their forced migration to the New World, the Scots Presbyterians have projected a God in their own image, terribly conscious of "proper appearances" and intent upon keeping the conscience of humankind with an iron hand. Such a humanly deformed God is pitiable; hence, Rachel Cameron's prayer for "God's pity on God."

Laurence and Davies urge Presbyterians and other Canadian Christians to recognize that cultural manifestations of religious ideals have left a legacy of guilt, inadequacy, and emptiness. They advise Canadians to emulate the heroines and heroes of their works by fleeing that emptiness in pursuit of more comprehensive and life-affirming definitions of love and the soul. Laurence's Manawaka tetralogy and Davies's Deptford trilogy imply that although guilt is not extirpated from the human psyche, through careful attention to the social myths which overlay and distort theology, its virulence can be significantly weakened.

NOTES

1.   Martin Buber, *The Knowledge of Man* (London: Allen & Unwin, 1965), 146.

2.   Clara Thomas, *The Manawaka World of Margaret Laurence* (Toronto: McClelland & Stewart, 1976), 96.

3.   For Laurence's statement on the connection between her fictional themes and her ancestral influences, see her "A Place to Stand On," in *Heart of a Stranger* (Toronto: McClelland & Stewart, 1976), 17.

4.   Margaret Laurence, *The Stone Angel* (Toronto: McClelland & Stewart, 1964), 89.

5.   This point is made by W. H. New in his Introduction to *The Stone Angel*, viii. The reference is to Galatians 4:22-27.

6.   George Woodcock, "The Human Elements: Margaret Laurence's Fiction," *The World of Canadian Writing: Critiques and Recollections* (Vancouver: Douglas & McIntyre, 1980), 56.

7.   Margaret Laurence, *A Jest of God* (Toronto: McClelland & Stewart, 1966), 135.

8.   George Bowering, "That Fool of a Fear: Notes on *A Jest of God*," in *A Place to Stand On: Essays by and about Margaret Laurence* (Edmonton: NeWest Press, 1983), 218.

9.   Laurence, *A Jest of God*, 201-2.

10. Margaret Laurence, *The Fire-Dwellers* (Toronto: McClelland & Stewart, 1969), 211.

11. Shortly before *The Fire-Dwellers* appeared, Laurence published an essay using some of these disturbing images and exploring the theme of television's distancing and alienating effects. She also addressed her own doubts about her roles as mother, author, and Christian in such a disorienting world, ultimately affirming them in the same tone of fearful and cautious optimism with which she chose to end her novel. See "Open Letter to the Mother of Joe Bass," *The New Romans: Candid Canadian Opinions of the U.S.* (Edmonton: Hurtig, 1968), 34-37.

12. For a full analysis of the trilogy as romance, see Ellen D. Warwick, "The Transformation of Robertson Davies," in *The Canadian Novel Here and Now*, ed. John Moss (Toronto: NC Press, 1978), 72-76.

13. Robertson Davies, "The Deptford Trilogy in retrospect," in *Studies in Robertson Davies' Deptford Trilogy*, ed. Robert G. Lawrence and Samuel L. Macey (Victoria: University of Victoria, 1980), 8. Davies tells how he made notes for a novel of revenge in 1960, but returned to those notes in 1968 to create from them *Fifth Business*, a novel about guilt: "During the intervening years, I had been occupied, in my few leisure hours, with problems of guilt. Where did it arise? At what age was a human creature capable of feeling and assuming the burden of guilt? Were the truly guilty always as burdened as were those whose upbringing and moral training disposed them to feel guilt and perhaps also to assume guilt which was not truly theirs? The novel, when I began to write it, was about guilt, and not revenge, though revenge played some part in it."

14. Davies, "Deptford Trilogy in Retrospect," 11-12.

15. Northrop Frye, *The Anatomy of Criticism* (Princeton: Princeton University Press, 1957), 186-88.

16. For a description of the four stages in the development of the Anima, see *Man and His Symbols*, ed. Carl G. Jung (London: Aldus Books, 1964), 195.

17. Robertson Davies, *Fifth Business* (London: Penguin Books, 1977), 36.

18. Elsewhere, Davies makes it clear that Mary is a madwoman: the question of her sainthood is important only for what it reveals about Dunstan: see Robertson Davies, *One Half of Robertson Davies* (Toronto: Macmillan, 1977), 176.

19. For explanation of the Jungian symbol of the soul, see Jung, *Man and His Symbols*, 221-22; for an explanation of Jung's definition of the symbol, see Gordon H. Roper, "Robertson Davies' *Fifth Business* and that Old Fanatical Duke of Dark Corners, C. G. Jung," in *The Canadian Novel Here and Now*, ed. John Moss (Toronto: NC Press, 1978), 60.

20. Robertson Davies, "Keeping the Faith," *Saturday Night* 102 (January, 1987): 187-90, 192.

Modernity Without Tears:
The Mythic World of Ralph Connor

D. Barry Mack

The years between the election of 1896 and the end of the First World War witnessed the birth of modern Canada. In one generation of rapid transition, Canada evolved from a string of largely isolated agricultural communities stretched out along the American border to a significantly urbanized and industrialized nation. These were the years of the Laurier boom, in which the National Policy of Sir John A. Macdonald and the Conservatives finally took hold, and Canada became "a nation transformed."[1] The integration of Canada's economy entailed an increased concentration of capital in central Canada, the rapid growth of labour unions, and a general growth in the complexity of all social institutions similar to that Britain and the United States had experienced decades earlier. Developments which had stretched over two or three generations in Britain and the United States, however, occurred in just one generation in Canada. Nor were the changes confined to economics. The settlement of the Canadian West entailed substantial immigration from Eastern Europe which was significantly to alter the ethnic balance of the country. Intellectually, there was a shift from Calvinist orthodoxy and a preoccupation with individual salvation to a more liberal interpretation of Christianity which emphasized social concern.

These were also the years in which the advertising industry was established in Canada.[2] The tricks that had been used to sell snake oil and circus tickets in the 1870s and 1880s began to be applied to a whole range of consumer goods. The Eaton's catalogue became as common a fixture in many households as the Bible had been in pioneer communities. This was also the generation in which English Canada briefly laid claim to a popular culture of its own, and experienced the exuberance of a shared national identity which culminated in Vimy Ridge and the paintings of the Group of Seven.

The dominant cultural institutions in English Canada were the Protestant churches and the public education system they had been instrumental in establishing. Between 1896 and 1921, the major Protestant churches, which had taken form in the decade after Confederation, began to function as national institutions with Toronto-based bureaucracies and to address themselves to the social issues provoked by rapid industrialization.[3] Of those Protestant churches, none played a more important role in shaping the institutions and culture of English Canada than the Presbyterians. Dalhousie, McGill, Queen's, Manitoba College, and the University of Saskatchewan all owed their existence to Presbyterian initiative, and it is no exaggeration to say that in those years English Canada was an intellectual colony of Scotland.[4] At a more popular level, Canada's favourite novelists were Presbyterians: Lucy Maud Montgomery and the Reverend Charles Gordon, better known to his readers as Ralph Connor.

Any study of popular culture in English Canada during the first two decades of this century must reckon with the Ralph Connor phenomenon. Accurate publishing figures are not readily available, partly because of numerous pirated editions, but in 1921, Gordon's publishers estimated combined sales of his first three novels *Black Rock* (1898), *The Sky Pilot* (1899) and *The Man From Glengarry* (1901) at five million copies.[5] In 1907, an ambitious young Canadian, George Doran, established his own publishing empire in New York by acquiring the American rights to *The Foreigner*.[6] *Corporal Cameron* (1911) and *Patrol of the Sun Dance Trail* (1912) played a major role in establishing the Canadian literary image of the Mountie.[7] Ralph Connor was a household name in English Canada. Whatever the exact number of books sold, Gordon made enough money from his royalties to build a substantial mansion on the banks of the Assiniboine River in Winnipeg and to ride the fastest horse in town.

The Connor novels and the popular response that they provoked have been analyzed in a variety of ways. They have been seen as evidence of an emerging sense of Western Canadian identity [8] or of a pan-Canadian nationalism.[9] The most striking feature of the Connor novels, however, is the advertisement for spiritual progress in the modern world that they represent. They were addressed to a society in the midst of transition and are the expression of a social mythology in relation to those changes. Unlike Catholic Quebec at the beginning of the twentieth century, Protestant English Canada welcomed modernity—industrial capitalism, the cult of efficiency, and the application of rational technique and business methods to society. There was very little religious or cultural resistance to the massive disruption it represented to traditional rural life. In fact, the transition into "modernity" was itself imbued with religious significance. The phenomenal popularity of the Connor novels is, I believe, largely attributable to the mythic assurance they provided to English-Canadian (and many American and British) readers as they marched into the modern world. Ralph Connor was, in George Grant's phrase, a "flatterer of modernity."

Rather than sensitively exploring the conflicts engendered by the transition into modernity and provoking reflection in relation to them, the Connor novels encouraged a sentimental evasion of those issues. The books both helped to smudge the magnitude of the transition that was taking place and encouraged the illusion that modernity could be embraced without significant costs and without tears. There was nothing to fear about the modern world and no hard choices to make. Everything that had been good in the old order could be preserved and enhanced in the new industrial and commercial society that was being born. In fact, the novels implied, the modern world was not far from the Kingdom of God.

Charles Gordon grew up in the backwoods of Glengarry in the 1860s, when it was a remote Gaelic-speaking agricultural settlement. It was a world still largely untouched by science or national politics, a world in which Westminster Confession Calvinism was expounded at great length on Sundays without apology by Gordon's Highland father. Unabashed Calvinism had survived far longer in the backwoods of Canada than it had in New England, for example. And the quasi-feudal customs of the Highland clans had survived longer in Canada than in Scotland.[10] This meant that the transition from traditional patterns of rural life to the modern commercial world and from Calvinism to liberalism—which was spread out over several generations in Britain and New England—was experienced by Gordon and his Canadian contemporaries in a few years.

Upon entering University College, Toronto, in 1881, Gordon was exposed to the aftershocks of the Darwinian revolution. The question of evolution became for him, as for many of his generation, the formative problem in his intellectual development. Unfortunately, his theological training at Knox College did not adequately meet that challenge. Not until his post-graduate year at New College, Edinburgh, did he find what seemed to him to be a satisfactory answer. It came not so much from the classroom of the distinguished Old Testament scholar A. B. Davidson as from a series of talks for Edinburgh medical students given by the most famous Scottish evangelist of his generation, Henry Drummond.[11]

Drummond, who preferred to present himself as a scientist rather than as a parson, was a clergyman who taught a course in natural science at the Free Church College in Glasgow. His fame in the Anglo-Saxon world dated from the publication of his first book *Natural Law in the Spiritual World* in 1882 in which he claimed a fundamental continuity between the natural and the spiritual worlds. The perceived conflict between science and Christian faith, he assured his readers, was mostly a problem of language that could be overcome by reformulating Christian doctrine in properly scientific terms. There were certain biological laws that applied to the spiritual world, so theology could be recast as science. This was nonsense, of course, but it is what the public wanted to hear and Drummond did have a graceful prose style. He was also a fastidious dresser and had a charismatic platform presence. Gordon's diary for 1889 is full of references to Drummond's mesmerizing appearance and captivating manner.

Drummond's attempt to reconcile science and theology by making theology "scientific" was quixotic mountebankery. What he eventually offered a gullible public instead was a poetic vision of cosmic spiritual evolution. According to Drummond, the Darwinian "Struggle for Life" was merely the first act of history.

A second factor, increasingly more important to evolutionary progress, was the "Struggle for the Life of Others." The Struggle for Life arose out of the biological imperatives of individual organisms for nutrition, but the advent of the family marked the beginning of the Struggle for the Life of Others and Christian civilization.

This Struggle for the Life of Others was tied to what Drummond called "the Mother Principle." Maternal self-sacrifice was the catalyst of spiritual progress in "the ascent of man." Male selfishness and egoism was gradually being overcome by civilized female concern for others. Patriarchal competition was being replaced by maternal co-operation. Thus, Drummond triumphantly assured his large audience, "The path of progress and the path of Altruism are one. Evolution is nothing but the involution of Love, the revelation of Infinite Spirit, the Eternal Life returning to itself."[12]

Drummond's "theology" emphasized the essential continuity of nature and grace. In fact, it was difficult for him to distinguish between the two. His notion of natural law in the spiritual world blended easily into a vague sense of spiritual law in the natural world. In Drummond, liberal evangelicalism converged on Marxist mysticism.[13] Discontinuities, like miracles, became problematic. Rather than see evil as something radical and intrinsic to human nature, he construed it as environmental. It was that which hindered true development in an organism, prevented "abundant life," and was therefore to be shunned. The doctrine of the Atonement, which was the very centre of Glengarry Calvinism, also became problematic, and Drummond replaced it with a general principle of individual self-sacrifice in the cause of cosmic spiritual progress. History was being drawn toward its divine telos by Christ's "law" of the sacrifice of self.

Drummond remained sufficiently evangelical to insist on the need for "conversion," and believed in a personal God to whom it made sense to pray, but the emphasis was on human spiritual development in a world which shimmered with the divine presence. Human spiritual development was a function of the environment—in which God was understood to be an active participant. The role of humans in a world in which God was immanent was to adapt perfectly to his divine environment and, according to the laws of spiritual biology and development, become godlike. The goal was divinisation through some sort of spiritual osmosis.

One important feature of such a theology was that it provided a link between individuals and the society of which they were a part, and thus laid the basis of a social gospel which was so obviously necessary in that generation. Human potential was wasted unless people found themselves in a suitable environment and began to develop. The various environments in which human beings found themselves at work and recreation were thus a key factor in shaping human spiritual growth. This was the theological rationale behind prohibition, public parks, and the urban reform movement in general. If the secular and sacred could not be neatly separated, and those with eyes to see in fact discovered the sacred in the midst of the secular, then theology had obvious social and political implications.

Drummond maintained that no environment was more important than the home, where character was first moulded under the potent influence of Mother Love. Here children first experienced the Struggle for the Life of Others and acquired a taste for Altruism. Mothers were the prime movers in the grand scheme of spiritual evolution.

> Run the eye for a moment up the scale of animal life. At the bottom are the first animals, the Protozoa. The Coelenterates follow, then in mixed array, the Echinoderms, Worms and Molluscs. Above these come the Pisces, then the Amphibia, then the Reptilia, then the Aves, then—What? The Mammilia, THE MOTHERS. There the series stops. Nature has never made anything since.[14]

It was from their mothers that children learned the true meaning of Otherism, Altruism, and Self-Sacrifice, which formed the *sine qua non* of spiritual progress and development.

This is the theology Charles Gordon took back to Canada with him in 1889, and nowhere in the English-speaking world was Drummond's impact greater than in Canada. Salem Bland, Mackenzie King, and Lord and Lady Aberdeen all read Drummond with appreciation,[15] as did the loggers and miners to whom Gordon ministered in the Rockies. In 1894, after the retirement of Sir William Dawson, Drummond was offered the principalship of McGill University.[16] What made Gordon unique among Drummond's many Canadian admirers is that he gave this "modernist" theology fictional expression, and in so doing achieved fame and fortune as Canada's most popular novelist. The Ralph Connor novels are a popular expression of Drummond's evolutionary creed. Collectively, they constitute a myth of spiritual progress which suited perfectly the mood in English Canada during the years of the Laurier boom. As *The Winnipeg Free Press* recalled, in summing up the life and work of "Canada's most famous citizen": "It was a period of optimism and enthusiasm in which everyone shared."[17]

The best known of the Connor novels, *The Man From Glengarry* was published in 1901. It recounts the spiritual development of Ranald Macdonald from proud Highland savage in the forests of Glengarry to responsible nation builder—one of the great men of a new Dominion which is itself imbued with growing spiritual significance. The metamorphosis is the work of Mrs. Murray, an incarnation of Drummond's Mother Principle. Because she humbly accepts the self-sacrificial role of Mother, she is the agent of spiritual progress.

Connor sets up an obvious contrast between the rigid Calvinism of the Reverend Mr. Murray and the patriarchal past, and the evangelical liberalism of his wife. The novel makes it abundantly clear that hers is the voice of wisdom; she is the real minister in Glengarry. The Great Revival is directly attributable to her quiet work in caring for the mortally wounded Macdonald Dubh rather than to the long-winded sermons that ultimately ruin her husband's health. In contrast with her husband's doctrinal sermons in which "all possible misapplications of the doctrine to practical life are guarded against," Mrs. Murray's approach to faith is "simple and real" and "practical." Hers, like Drummond's, is a natural Christianity. Her prayers breathe a heavenly simplicity; the absolute distinction between sacred and secular which was a prominent feature of Glengarry Calvinism disappears. Mr. Murray denounces

Ranald as "a savage and not fit for the company of decent folk" because he has been involved in a fight outside the church. Mrs. Murray sees in him "vast possibilities for good or ill," and resolves to influence that choice.

Effective evangelization for Mrs. Murray involves a process of spiritual nurture and education rather than threats of eternal damnation. A "conversion" of sorts is necessary—both Ranald and his father have to give up their savage Highland lust for revenge on the French Canadian villain, le Noir, and learn the lesson of civilized Christian forgiveness. But in the meantime, Mrs. Murray lends Ranald copies of *Rob Roy* and *Ivanhoe* to cultivate his imagination and his ideals. Literature and music, as well as nature, are imbued with the divine presence. Mrs. Murray plants the seeds of civilizing Christianity and carefully nurtures them. Clearly, the primeval forest of patriarchal Calvinism must give way to the new seedlings of maternal liberalism. The result, in Ranald's case, is a "muscular Christian." But significantly, his muscularity has nothing to do with his Christianity. In fact the two elements are diametrically opposed to each other. "Christianity" is construed solely as longsuffering maternal love, while "muscularity" is the residual influence of the savage/Calvinist past. But this tension is not explored in the novel, it is smudged. Mrs. Murray never contradicts her husband overtly— she silently points to a more excellent way in her actions. The novel implies that the new grows quietly and naturally out of the old; all that was good in the old will be preserved in the new. There is therefore no cause for tears or regret. Only what has been outgrown—like the savage patriarchal instinct for justice rather than undiscriminating maternal love—will be quietly put aside.

The other transition the novel describes is that from backwoods to city. Ranald Macdonald is not afraid of modernity. He has no desire to farm and realizes that the best prospects of a young man getting ahead lie in the city—which Drummond called the "storm centre" of the future. Armed with the physical strength and the Highland honour he has acquired in Glengarry, and the cherished memories of those at home, he resolves to "play the man" in the modern world.

Not only does Macdonald prosper financially, he develops spiritually in the process. There are certain tensions between the two objectives but never irresolvable conflict. When he resigns rather than stoop to deceit in working for his first employer, he is promptly offered a better job by the competition. Virtue pays.

Colonel Thorpe congratulates Mrs. Murray on the fact that she has "produced a rare article in the commercial world, and that is a man of honour," and eventually is persuaded that Ranald's Mackenzie Kingish methods in labour relations make good business sense. What was true on a small scale for Macdonald Bhain and his lumberjacks on the Ottawa River is no less true of the new industrial society. Macdonald Bhain "picked only the best men, fed them well, paid them the highest wages, cared for their comfort and held them in strictest discipline"—with the predictable result that "contracts began to come their way." By the end of the novel this has become Ranald's formula for successful management. It is clear that Ranald lives in a user-friendly universe which rewards those who act on the secret knowledge that the Struggle for Life is being superseded by the Struggle for the Life of Others. Christianity, properly understood and applied, is quite compatible with business profits.

Like the Macdonald clan chieftains of old, Ranald becomes feudal lord in the modern business world. He is a natural aristocrat and quickly attracts a large group of loyal vassals. He "picks men out of the gutter" and "binds them to his own interests." Sometimes he acquires tacksmen who bring with them followers of their own. Ranald's loyal subjects swear fealty and begin to adopt his mannerisms. The novel implies that there is no irresolvable conflict between Highland honour and the prudential ethics of the commercial world. The one grows naturally into the other. The old feudalism of the clan system could be carried into the modern world by natural aristocrats like Ranald. With a bit of team spirit, the new industrial order could be tamed and Christianized by the men from Glengarry, even as their fathers had subdued the wilderness.

The Man From Glengarry is not just about individuals. It is ultimately a celebration of Canada, and especially of life on the western frontier. Ranald's life is linked to the life and destiny of his country by the common denominator of spiritual growth. What is said about him is applicable, by implication, to his country. The reader is left with the impression that the leaven is at work and that the bread of the kingdom is rising. The ineluctable laws of biological growth have taken over and history is being drawn irresistibly up the corridors of time to the Kingdom of God with lots of money being made in the process.

This rosy view of the universe fits the mood of the Laurier years perfectly. Ralph Connor evidently told his audience what it wanted to hear. Eventually, however, the naivete of pioneer Canada gave way to farce when the heroic Highland lord who was to lead Canada into the modern world was revealed to be none other than Mackenzie King. After making his shrewd assessment of Hitler during a visit to Berlin in 1937, the great warrior chieftain lay down and slept the sleep of the just, wrapped in the Mackenzie tartan of his mythical ancestor, "Colin Dhu of old."[18]

Anthropologists have written much on the subject of myth in recent years. It has long been suggested that one of the functions of myth is pedagogical, and serves to promote certain role models and to perpetuate certain beliefs and practices. Claude Levi-Strauss has demonstrated at considerable length another typical use of myth: its use in obfuscating the unwelcome contradictions in a culture so as to make them palatable to its members. Myth smudges the inexplicable by associating it with the explicable, the unfamiliar with the familiar, the tabooed with the permissible. By obscuring the issue in question, irresolvable logical inconsistencies are lost sight of even when they are "openly" expressed.

The French literary critic Roland Barthes has developed this notion of myth in relation to literature. He notes that myth "resolves" cultural contradictions with narrative by "admitting" contradictions at a superficial level in order to disarm and ultimately dismiss them as insignificant. "Myth hides nothing; its function is to distort, not to make disappear." Myth serves to inoculate people from a serious struggle with the contradictions of their society.

> Myth does not deny things, on the contrary, its function is to talk about them; simply it purifies them, it makes them innocent, it gives them a natural and eternal justification, it gives them a clarity which is not that of an explanation but of a statement of fact ... it abolishes the complexity of human acts, it gives them the simplicity of essences, it does away with all dialectics, with any going back beyond what is immediately visible, it organizes a world which is without [serious] contradictions because it is without depth, a world wide open and wallowing in the evident, it establishes a blissful clarity: things appear to mean something by themselves.[19]

The Connor novels owed their enormous popularity to the fact that they resolved the unwelcome tensions English Canadians faced in an age of transition in the only easy way that they could be resolved—through narrative. The novels lent modernity an air of inevitability and stamped it with divine approval. The message was that the old Calvinist virtues of rural family life in the past could tame the new industrial order that might at first sight appear to imperil them. And a milder, more liberal creed, which stressed love and mercy rather than justice, represented a considerable advance in religious sophistication on the Calvinist of the past.

The Connor novels amount, then, to escapist romances that provided their readers with the comforts of sentimental evasion rather than a serious exploration of the issues of their day. In real life, the decision to leave Glengarry entailed real and sometimes tragic consequences. It is the task of serious fiction to open readers to an awareness of alternatives, alternatives which are sometimes radically incompatible. In the face of such either/or decisions, life and art assumes its depth. Instead, the Connor novels closed the world down and bathed it in an air of givenness and inevitability, gave it an "eternal justification" in which human choice, human struggle and ultimately human responsibility were dismissed. They promised a world of both/and, discouraged serious reflection, and blunted awareness of what was at stake in the transition into modernity. The decisions in Connor novels do not cost anything. They entail only happy consequences, they include no sense of loss in relation to foregone possibilities. In their essential triviality, they reflect the flabby anti-intellectualism of twentieth-century consumer culture[20]—in contrast to the tough-minded Calvinism of Thomas McCulloch's *Stepsure Letters* or the ironic clarity of Stephen Leacock's *Arcadian Adventures of the Idle Rich*.[21]

The Connor hero successfully manages to serve two masters without coming to grief, and in this respect no doubt provided much comfort to middle-class Protestant readers who were partici-pating with gusto in the great barbecue of the Laurier boom while experiencing twinges of nostalgia for a simpler and more virtuous past. The novels encouraged sentimental evasion of the contradic-tions which readers dimly sensed but preferred not to explore too deeply—at least until they were shaken from their complacency about the modern world by the First World War.

If *The Man from Glengarry* is about the transition from patriar-chal Highland Calvinism to maternal liberal modernism and from agrarian poverty to urban affluence, *The Foreigner* is about how a good-hearted but culturally backward Ukrainian boy becomes a modern Canadian. Structurally, it is the same novel as *The Man from Glengarry*. All that changes are the costumes and decor. Culturally backward Ukrainian immigrants are substituted for culturally backward Highland farmers.

The Connor novels reflect eighteenth-century Scottish rational-ist assumptions about social development. As in the novels of Sir Walter Scott, on which they are modelled, there is the idea that society has developed historically through distinct "stages." Each of these stages—hunting, pastoral, agricultural, commercial—has corresponding effects on all aspects of social life, from political institutions to "manners."[22] On the assumption that there is a core to human nature that cannot be fundamentally altered but only channeled and directed by social conditions, it is logical to posit both that there are a limited number of possible social arrange-ments and that all societies change and develop in the same way. The Connor novels reflect this uniformitarian assumption. High-lander, East European peasant, and native Indian are portrayed as fundamentally similar in their primitive state. This mitigates to some extent the charge of "racism" that has sometime been levelled against the Connor novels.

In Ralph Connor's world, Galicans turn out to be just like Highlanders except that they dress differently and speak another language. They are no more "foreign" than the parents of his Presbyterian readership. Kalman is in fact described as "a young Lochinvar" at one point. Connor admires the same thing in the Slavic community that he prizes in the Highlanders: physical strength, pride, passion, honour, hospitality, religiosity, and a sense of romance. What he dislikes in North Winnipeg—drunkenness, unmanly fighting, and filth—he also disapproved of in Glengarry. The only difference between Glengarry and North Winnipeg was a generation of spiritual development.

Kalman Kalmar is the same type as Ranald Macdonald. That one has Celtic roots and the other Slavic is minor. They have in common proud, passionate natures, less than ideal environments (in that their mothers have died), and fathers with causes to be avenged. They are both fearless fighters. Both men are noticed and rescued from evil by surrogate mothers. In Ranald's case, it is Mrs. Murray. In *The Foreigner*, Mrs. Jack French and the missionary, Mr. Brown, play the mother role. Both young heroes must be converted, and are given copies of *Ivanhoe* while they think about it. Ranald has to learn to master his fierce Highland passion to avenge his father's death and learn that vengeance belongs to God. Kalman must struggle against the "hereditary instincts of his Slavic blood," and must learn the same lesson in relation to Rosenblatt. Ranald becomes a successful lumberman; Kalman runs a mine. They both end up marrying girls from the same mold as their surrogate mothers. Both become great men, muscular Christians, leaders in their respective communities, and exemplary Canadians.

Like the Highland society that was crushed in 1745, the "Galicans" must learn respect for British justice and the traditions of parliamentary democracy, which Connor does not doubt represent a higher stage of political culture than the one they have known. Fortunately, the Canadian prairie is the ideal environment for inculcating such a lesson, partly because of the superiority of British institutions, partly because of the opportunities presented by the pristine land itself. Under such favourable conditions, the seeds of human potential germinate quickly and flourish. Margorie gushes ecstatically to Kalman at the end of the novel, "How wonderful the power of this country of yours to transform men!"

The message *The Foreigner* conveyed to its readers was that Galicans were promising immigrant material and would, with a bit of mothering, readily assimilate into the norms of modern liberal democratic Canadian society. Moreover, this transition is one that could be achieved with significant cost only to the mother figures who are the catalysts of change. All that is good about the Ukrainian past will be preserved in the Canada of the future. Kalman will continue to sing Hungarian love songs and speak Russian. No one has to make any difficult choices about language and tradition and identity. Assimilation costs nothing.

The Foreigner presents the same unambiguous endorsement of the modern world, the same linking of material and spiritual progress, and the same sense of a world without depth as *The Man from Glengarry* because ultimately it is a world without pain or even regret. It shares the same obfuscation of what is at issue in the destruction of traditional society in the modern world. Although Kalman plays the romantic Highland role of "young Lochinvar," his field of battle is a commercial one. Unlike his father, the fight in which he is engaged is not "a great cause," for which he "pays out his life." It is an ownership struggle over a coal mine. Kalman is invested with the romance of the Highland soldier and the Russian nihilist—while not ultimately forfeiting the profits of the businessman. He has it both ways.

The sentimental evasion of the costs of entering the modern world is most obvious in Connor's fictional treatment of the Riel rebellion in *Corporal Cameron* (1911) and *The Patrol of the Sun Dance Trail* (1912). The price of modernity in the settlement of the "the last best West" was the destruction of the Indian and Métis societies. But rather than explore this fact, and the tragic clash of cultures it implied, the Connor novels gloss over it in an ode of praise to the modern world and a celebration of the virtue of the North West Mounted Police. The Riel Rebellion is presented as the peaceful vindication of the peerless integrity of the North West Mounted Police and the sagacity of the Blackfoot leader Crowfoot, who sees the inevitability of spiritual and material evolution, refuses to allow his braves to join in the rebellion, and continues to place his faith in the providential care of the Great White Mother in London.

Unlike the lawless American "wild west," Connor assured his readers, Indians in Canada were given an alternative to violent rebellion. Defiance and revolt is the course urged by Copperhead, the Sioux instigator from across the line. But in the law-abiding land of the Union Jack, where the Mounties act as nurses and missionaries to the Indians, there was a better way. Copperhead was defeated, in the Ralph Connor edition of Canadian history, not by military force but by Christian charity and by his son, who chose to be loyal to his surrogate mother, Mandy Cameron, rather than to his father's cause. Copperhead's attempt to mount a revolt is thus ultimately checked by the Mother Principle.

In Canada, Connor says, the Indians under Crowfoot chose the way of acceptance and forgiveness. Despite the fact that they represented a formidable military threat, they did not avail themselves of the opportunity for revenge that presented itself to them. The Riel Rebellion did not fail because of overwhelming military superiority of one side over the other. The British military campaign was notably ineffective. Rather, the decisive factor was Crowfoot's realization that British justice could be trusted and his influence in restraining his braves from joining the revolt and tipping the military balance.

The Riel Rebellion fails for lack of a leader. *The Patrol of the Sun Dance Trail* implies that Crowfoot could have been such a leader, but that he understood the inevitability of historical progress, and like Ranald and Kalman overcame the primitive temptation for revenge. Crowfoot, too, opts for the Christian civilization of the Great White Mother. Patriarchal violence is extinguished by maternal love. The victory Connor celebrates is thus a moral rather than a military one. Crowfoot, too, decides to throw in his lot with the modern world in a way that must have soothed the consciences of Connor's readership—however squalid the living conditions of their Indian neighbours. Connor's comforting paradox in *The Patrol of the Sun Dance Trail* is that what appears to be armed conflict was really the triumph of peace. The Riel Rebellion, rather than being a result of injustice is, in fact, the vindication of British justice. On the subject of Indians, Connor told his readers, Canadians were entitled to feel a certain amount of smug self-righteousness.

The extinction of native society is portrayed as inevitable as the sunrise. It is not tragic, because there is no room for tragedy in Connor's world. Change is necessarily for the best because modernity is the best of all possible worlds. The difference between Ralph Connor and Sir Walter Scott is quite striking at this point. Scott had many deeply conservative instincts and was ambivalent about the changes he described. For him, change may be the inexorable result of economic forces, but it is by no means clear that it will bring a future which is ultimately preferable to what it replaces. The quality of stoic fatalism in Scott's novels is quite different from the cheery optimism that pervades the mythic world of Ralph Connor. In the Connor novels progress has a positive connotation and religious sanction that it does not have in Scott. There is no room for lament—because in the modern world "every tear will be wiped away." But to write this way of Indians in western Canada in the years immediately preceding the First World War involved an amazing amount of sentimental naiveté, or a willful blindness to the facts.

On the positive side, the Connor novels probably did help produce some solid Mounties and honest businessmen. They encouraged active engagement in the modern world, respect for traditional moral standards, and a certain beefy self-confidence. But the activity they inspired was unreflecting, to say the least. Attention to duty and muscular zeal in the fight against the forces of evil characterized the Connor hero, rather than any flair for penetrating analytical thought. These qualities made him a good foot soldier in the fight for prohibition and the war against the Hun.

But the war itself destroyed the illusion about the modern world that Ralph Connor had woven. By the 1920s readers were no longer willing to believe that the Great War represented the spiritual triumph of self-sacrifice and the Mother Principle over German barbarism.[23] The gap between fact and interpretation became too wide to sustain. Indian death rates could apparently be reconciled with the vision of spiritual progress, but it was harder to explain the casualties of the trenches. There was nothing in Henry Drummond's theology or in the Connor novels to account for the depth of suffering the war inflicted and no place for tragic lament. Gordon remembered, as a boy, the mournful majesty of his father pacing the manse floor in Zorra and playing a pibroch—but he himself could not play the pipes and did not understand what his father mourned. His own musical taste inclined to the guitar and quaint French Canadian songs around a campfire.[24]

After the war, his audience disappeared. The Connor novels had acted as a spiritual anesthetic during the birth of modern Canada—indeed Mark Twain's phrase about "chloroform in print" seems apt. During the 1920s Connor's readers awoke to discover that they had inherited not the Kingdom of God but the secular city. The artistic shortcomings of the Connor novels became embarrassingly obvious and people began to wonder how they had ever taken Charles Gordon seriously as a writer. Certainly, he was no longer taken seriously as a minister. When modern Canadians felt pain they increasingly turned to doctors and psychiatrists and salesmen rather than to ministers for a cure. Numbness could be more reliably achieved by other means than religious fiction.

The Connor novels have long lost their interest for most readers, but they are of abiding interest to students of Canadian history because they represent the old props and costumes of a conjuror's trick. They enable us to see English Canada as it saw itself enter the modern world.

NOTES

1. Robert Craig Brown and Ramsay Cook, *Canada 1896-1921: A Nation Transformed* (Toronto: McClelland & Stewart, 1974).

2. H. E. Stephenson and Carleton McNaught, *The Story of Advertising in Canada: A Chronicle of 50 Years* (Toronto: Ryerson, 1940).

3. See Brian Fraser, *The Social Uplifters: Presbyterian Progressives and the Social Gospel in Canada, 1875-1915* (Waterloo: Wilfred Laurier University Press, 1988).

4. See A. B. McKillop, *A Disciplined Intelligence* (Montreal: McGill-Queen's University Press, 1979); Leslie Armour and Elizabeth Trott, *The Faces of Reason: An Essay on Philosophy and Culture in English Canada, 1850-1950* (Waterloo: Wilfred Laurier University Press, 1981); S.E.D. Shortt, *The Search for an Ideal: Six Canadian Intellectuals and their Convictions in an Age of Transition 1890-1930* (Toronto: University of Toronto Press, 1976).

5. C. W. Gordon Papers, Gordon to George Adam Smith, September 21, 1936.

6. George H. Doran, *Chronicles of Barabbas* (New York: Harcourt, Brace, 1935), 36.

7. See Keith Walden, *Visions of Order* (Toronto: Butterworth, 1982), and Dick Harrison, ed., *Best Mounted Police Stories* (Edmonton: University of Alberta, 1978).

8. F. W. Watt, "Western Myth—The World of Ralph Connor," *Canadian Literature 1* (Summer 1959), 26-36; E. H. Wood, "Ralph Connor and the Canadian West," M.A. thesis, University of Saskatchewan, 1975.

9. Roy Daniells, "Glengarry Revisited," *Canadian Literature* 31 (Winter 1972), 45-53; J. L. and J. H. Thompson, "Ralph Connor and the Canadian Identity," *Queen's Quarterly* 79 (Summer 1972): 159-70; Susan Wood, "Ralph Connor and the Tamed West," in Lewis Merrill and L. L. Lee, eds., *The Westering Experience in American Literature: Bicentennial Essays* (Western Washington University, 1977).

10. J. M. Bumsted, *The People's Clearance* (Edinburgh: Edinburgh University Press, 1982).

11. See D. B. Mack, "Ralph Connor and the Progressive Vision" (M.A. thesis, Carleton University, 1986), chapters 2 and 3 for a discussion of Drummond's impact on Gordon.

12. Henry Drummond, *The Ascent of Man* (London: Hodder and Stoughton, 1894), 46.

13. James R. Moore, "Evangelicals and Evolution," *Scottish Journal of Theology* 38 (1985): 383-417.

14. Drummond, *Ascent*, 343.

15. See Richard Allen, *A Social Passion* (Toronto: University of Toronto Press, 1971), 9; PAC, King Diary, March 23, April 20, November 11, 1898, January 13, 15, 22, 23, 24, 1899; Lord and Lady Aberdeen, *"We Twa": reminiscences of Lord and Lady Aberdeen*, 2 vols. (London: W. Collins and Co., 1925).

16. George Adam Smith, *The Life of Henry Drummond* (Toronto: Fleming H. Revell, 1899), 425.

17. *Winnipeg Free Press*, Novovember 1, 1937.

18. King Diary, June 29, 1937, PAC. The tartan was a present from Lady Aberdeen whom he had just visited. Among other subjects they discussed Henry Drummond.

19. Roland Barthes, *Mythologies*, trans. Annette Lavers (London: Jonathan Cape, 1972), 143.

20. Ann Douglas, *The Feminization of American Culture* (New York: Alfred A. Knopf, 1977). The Connor novels also include a strong dose of muscular Christianity which probably explains their popularity in the U.S. at a time when Billy Sunday had become the leading evangelist. This does not amount to much more than macho posturing in the face of suspected effeminacy, and does not alter Douglas's judgment.

21. Ramsay Cook, "Stephen Leacock in the Age of Plutocracy 1903-1921," in John Moir, *Character and Circumstances: Essays in Honour of Donald Grant Creighton* (Toronto: MacMillan, 1970), 163-81.

22. Graham McMaster, *Scott and Society* (Cambridge: Cambridge University Press, 1981).

23. This is how the war is interpreted in Connor's *The Major* (1917) and *Sky Pilot in No Man's Land* (1919). See Mack, "Ralph Connor," 213-19.

24. Charles Gordon, *Postscript to Adventure*, rpt. (Toronto: McLelland & Stewart, 1975), xiii, 32-33.

The Contribution of Alexander Macmillan to Canadian Hymnody

N. Keith Clifford

In most discussions of the relationship between religion and culture, hymnody does not occupy a conspicuous place because the elitist bias of many historians has led them to focus exclusively on high culture. The recent interest of social historians in "popular culture" and "popular religion," however, has meant that hymns and hymn writers have begun to receive some attention.[1] Unfortunately those responsible for compiling and editing denominational hymn books have not shared in this revival of interest. Yet without understanding the criteria editors have used in selecting the hymns and tunes which will be available to church members, it is difficult to comprehend the social and cultural significance of denominational hymnody.[2] In this paper, therefore, I wish to focus on the work of Alexander MacMillan, who edited the Presbyterian *Book of Praise* and the United Church *Hymnary* and wrote a major commentary entitled *The Hymns of the Church: A Companion to the Hymnary of the United Church of Canada*, for these volumes have influenced the conception of hymnody to which three generations of Canadians were exposed, and they have defined the boundaries of hymnody, which remain intact today, in both the Presbyterian and United churches.

Alexander MacMillan (1864-1961) was born and educated in Edinburgh.[3] At the age of twenty-one, when he had completed his second year at the Divinity Hall of the United Presbyterian Church of Scotland, he was commissioned by the student missionary society of his college to survey Presbyterian mission fields in Manitoba and the Northwest which their society had adopted as a special project. When he arrived in Winnipeg, he presented a gift of £1,100 from the missionary society of his college, to Dr. James Robertson, the superintendent of Home Missions.[4] Then he accepted Robertson's suggestion that he spend the summer as a student missionary at Fort Frances, Ontario, where, in spite of mosquitoes, black flies, and his failure to master the birch bark canoe, he fell in love with Canada and resolved to return as soon as he had graduated.[5]

Having completed his studies in Scotland, MacMillan returned to Canada in 1887 and accepted a call to the Presbyterian church at Auburn, Ontario, a town some ten miles northeast of Goderich. In 1892, he moved to the Toronto lakeshore suburb of Mimico, and a few months later, the General Assembly appointed him to the hymnal committee which was revising the 1880 *Presbyterian Hymnal.* MacMillan became the secretary of the sub-committee on music which was chaired by the Reverend Daniel J. Macdonnell of St. Andrew's Church, Toronto.[6] He was pleased with this appointment, for he had received a thorough musical education, and during his theological studies he had specialized in church history and in particular the history of Christian worship. The hymnal committee, therefore, gave him an opportunity to pursue and develop his interests in both music and worship.

Shortly after work on *The Presbyterian Book of Praise* had begun, an invitation arrived from the Joint Committee of the Church of Scotland, the Free Church, and the United Presbyterian Church asking the Presbyterian Church in Canada to co-operate in producing a common hymnal for the English-speaking Presbyterian churches. In response to this invitation Daniel Macdonnell and Alexander MacMillan were appointed as the Canadian representatives, and they sailed for Scotland in the spring of 1894 to participate in these meetings. While there, Macdonnell became seriously ill and had to return to Toronto, leaving MacMillan to represent the Presbyterian Church in Canada. While Macdonnell's illness and early death from tuberculosis was a deeply felt loss to the hymnal committee and the Presbyterian Church in Canada, it served to move MacMillan very rapidly into a position of leadership. At the age of thirty, he represented the Presbyterian Church in Canada in discussions with all of the leading hymnologists in the Scottish church, and when he returned to Canada he replaced Macdonnell as the convener of the sub-committee on music.

The most important effect of MacMillan's contact with the joint committee in Scotland, however, was his exposure to the influence of the Oxford movement on Scottish hymnody. The hymns of the Evangelical revival had emphasized personal experience, but the hymns of the Oxford revival focused on the worshiping church and especially on the hymns of the pre-Reformation church. The United Presbyterian Church of Scotland, the denomination in which MacMillan was raised, was the first to respond to the liturgical hymnody of the Oxford revival, and in their 1877 hymnal "the Anglican influences were most marked."[7] Moreover, the United Presbyterians were also the moving force behind the movement for a common Presbyterian hymnal, and it was in the discussions of the joint committee that MacMillan became aware of the full extent of the influence of the Oxford revival on Scottish hymnody. Its influence on him can be seen in the inclusion of some twenty-five translations of Greek and Latin hymns from Clement of Alexandria to Bernard of Clairvaux in the first edition of *The Presbyterian Book of Praise*, and in his subsequent work there was an even greater emphasis on the catholic and liturgical dimensions of church praise.

Initially it appeared as if the Canadian church would accept the *Joint Hymnal*. But when the first draft appeared, the Canadian committee discovered that it did not contain any selections from the paraphrases nor any evangelistic hymns which the Canadian church considered essential. When negotiations failed to secure the inclusion of these hymns, the Presbyterian Church in Canada decided to go ahead with the publication of its own hymn book.[8] On July 1, 1896 tenders were called for the publication of *The Presbyterian Book of Praise*, and on September 4, the offer of Oxford University Press was accepted. At a subsequent meeting on October 19, Alexander MacMillan and John Somerville were appointed to proceed to England to supervise the revision of the proofs and to prepare the indexes of hymns, tunes, and authors.[9] Here again MacMillan had an opportunity to work with many of the most skilled and experienced crafts people in the production of hymn books. Thus by the time he returned to Canada in March of 1897, he had accumulated more experience in these matters than anyone else in Canada.

From 1896 to 1914 MacMillan traveled widely in connection with the promotion of church praise in the Presbyterian Church. Indeed, he found that his work for the Committee on Church Praise occupied so much of his time that a decision had to be made as to whether he would continue in congregational work or devote himself full time to the work of the committee. Finally in 1914 he resigned from his pastoral charge and became the full-time secretary of the Committee on Church Praise, a post which he held until 1925. The year before MacMillan's appointment, the General Assembly had authorized a revision of *The Presbyterian Book of Praise.*[10] Thus the majority of time between 1914 and 1918 was spent on the revision of the church's hymn book.

When the revision was first recommended by the General Assembly, the church union negotiations were temporarily on hold following the 1912 vote. But since the Presbyterian Church intended to proceed with these negotiations, the General Assembly instructed its committee to consult with the Methodists, who were also in the process of revising their hymnal. When the two committees met, however, they discovered that their views as to what was essential in a hymnal were so at variance that it was impossible to move forward toward a joint hymnal. In its 1915 report to the General Assembly, the committee summarized the differences as follows:

> In comparing the work of the two committees, we found that the Presbyterian Book of Praise would contain over one hundred psalms and the Methodist Hymn Book less than ten. The Methodist book would have over eighty of Wesley's hymns—ours between twenty and thirty.[11]

Three hundred and fifty-seven hymns were common to both books but in spite of this large degree of overlap the committee concluded that "should a united church be the result of the present negotiations it will require a number of years of interchange and development of church life before one common book representing the whole people could be prepared."[12] Thus it recommended that the Presbyterian Church in Canada should proceed with the publication of its own revised *Book of Praise.*

Some people, such as Charles S. Thompson of Chalmers Church, Vancouver, opposed this decision because they believed that the costs involved were unwarranted in wartime.[13] Others found it difficult to believe that the Methodists had turned down the opportunity to issue a joint hymnal. Archibald Mitchell of Coaldale, Alberta, was particularly upset because, as he explained, he belonged to one of "the sawn-off districts" that had resulted from the comity arrangements between Methodists and Presbyterians in western Canada. He wanted a union hymnal because he missed singing the Psalms. "The singing for us Scots folk," he said, "is mair than half o' the service and it is bad enough condemning us to be Methodists without robbing us for ever of the Psalms o' oor ain kirk. The Psalms o' Dauvit hae a meaning to us no Methodist can understand. They are woven in the warp and woof of our history."[14]

Still others opposed moving ahead because they were not convinced that the revision had been thorough enough. Some thought this was especially apparent in regard to the tunes which the committee had selected for the hymns. One, who identified himself as "Presbyterian," said he was opposed to all "tunes of a jiggy, jerky character for such music often provokes a desire in young thoughtless folk to accompany their singing with giggling and dancing." Therefore, he recommended that "at least a score of jingling tunes with dance rhythms" be struck off the present list. When some, such as J. G. Brown of Victoria, agreed with "Presbyterian" and suggested that it was impossible to expect much better from "a committee composed of fifteen or sixteen ministers, none of whom claims to have any special qualifications for a work of such vast importance to our church," Robert Haddow, the editor of the *Presbyterian*, pointed out in an editorial that since praise was an integral part of the worship service, it was entirely appropriate to appoint ministers to the committee, especially when many of them had years of experience in this area of the church's life and work. Moreover, Haddow continued, since the committee had been instructed to prepare a book which would be of use not only in Sabbath services, but also for Sunday schools, prayer meetings and religious gatherings of all kinds in pioneer settlements and mission fields as well as city churches, a measure of compromise was necessary in accommodating musical tastes that were not as highly cultivated and unerring as those of the individual who signed himself, "Presbyterian."[15]

While it was fairly easy to deal with these criticisms, World War I was creating problems of a different order. As Oxford University Press pointed out, paper was rationed and many of their most skilled employees were in the armed forces. In view of these difficulties the General Assembly in 1915 and 1916 agreed to postpone publication, but these delays created a number of other dilemmas. Among the more important of these was that as soon as the congregations became aware that a new edition would be forthcoming, sales of the first edition fell off sharply even though in many congregations the existing hymn books were beginning to fall apart. Consequently, in 1917 Alexander MacMillan was instructed to proceed to England, as he had done twenty years earlier, to begin the process of producing the plates, correcting the proofs and preparing the indexes of the revised edition of the *Book of Praise*.[16] A year later he returned in time to present to the General Assembly of 1918 an advance copy of the new hymnal.

In the preface of this revised edition of the *Book of Praise* his colleagues on the committee acknowledged MacMillan's contribution in the following tribute:

> The Reverend Alexander MacMillan has acted as Secretary to the Committee throughout the period of revision and his colleagues desire to acknowledge in the warmest terms their own and the Church's indebtedness to him. Without Mr. MacMillan's expert guidance and unstinted labours from first to last, The Book of Praise could not have been made so excellent a gift to the Church as the committee believes it to be.

MacMillan's contribution to the first edition had been acknowledged by the General Assembly, but this more formal acknowledgment was appropriate because his influence was especially apparent in the 1918 revision. The addition of a whole section of "Ancient Hymns and Canticles" designed for a highly liturgical service of worship was a MacMillan touch. Such services, of course, were not common in Canadian Presbyterianism at the time, but this was obviously a goal toward which MacMillan was attempting to move the church. Had it not been for church union, the *Book of Praise* might have been the only hymn book that MacMillan had an opportunity to edit. But when he entered the United Church in 1925 further possibilities opened up for his special skills.

A year after the United Church came into existence, the General Council instructed its Committee on Church Worship and Ritual "to survey the whole field of hymnody, and to make such preparation for a new book as may be necessary."[17] The man responsible for these preparations was Alexander MacMillan, secretary of the committee, who was recognized by this point as one of the most outstanding authorities on church music in Canada. Some people, however, were less than enthusiastic about a former Presbyterian being in charge of this enterprise, especially when the Methodists believed that the "ministry of song" was one of the major gifts they had taken with them into the United Church of Canada. MacMillan consequently faced a number of problems in preparing *The Hymnary* for publication.

The members of the Church Worship and Ritual Committee had complete confidence in MacMillan because they wanted a hymn book which would demonstrate to the world that the United Church ought to be taken seriously, and they believed that MacMillan's high standards and experience would help them achieve this goal. Some, however, felt that the committee was less than representative of the new church. Reflecting these misgivings, one correspondent wrote that "if a certain group in that committee has its way, particularly Dr. MacMillan, the book will be what we speak of as highbrow! This will make it utterly impossible as a book to be used by small churches throughout the country."[18] Perhaps the most biting criticism, however, was that MacMillan and the committee were sacramentarians. W. H. Raney of St. Mary's Ontario, for example, believed that some of the communion hymns contained in the 1928 draft of the hymn book, contained "a subtle" suggestion of salvation by a semi-physical process."[19] Walter J. Phelps of Montreal agreed, and declared that "there must be some

Anglo-Catholic of great influence on this Committee of Worship."[20] Though never explicitly stated, it was nevertheless implied that the man responsible for this Anglo-Catholic sacramentarianism was Alexander MacMillan.

Firmer grounds for the suspicion that the *Hymnary* would be similar to the *Book of Praise* lay in the fact that MacMillan was the editor of both volumes. That the suspicion of similarities became clear when the first draft of the hymn book was presented to the general council in 1928 and the committee indicated in its "Prefatory Statement" that sixty metrical psalms would be "placed at the beginning of the book."[21] Had this proposal been given final approval, the two books would have been virtually indistinguishable in their structure. Placing a separate section of metrical psalms in the new hymnal raised a fundamental question about the nature of organic union. Was the Presbyterian tradition of psalmody to be kept separate from the Methodist and Congregational traditions of hymnody or were these three traditions to be blended and mixed together under an appropriate topical arrangement? The failure to resolve this issue earlier had prevented the Methodists and Presbyterians from issuing a common hymn book prior to 1925.[22] Consequently, when the first draft of the new United Church hymn book appeared in 1928 with the suggestion that there would be a separate section of sixty psalms at the beginning of the book, there were some angry reactions.

The first to protest against the separation of the metrical psalms and the hymns was R. Lorne McTavish of Saskatoon. He reminded the committee that they were charged with the duty of "preparing a Book of Praise not for Scotland nor for Presbyterianism or Methodism or Congregationalism but for the United Church of Canada." He had no objection to having psalms in the new book, he said, but "let them appear, as all other selections, under their proper subject classification."[23] Former Presbyterians like Alexander Wilson of St. John, New Brunswick, however, countered by saying that "too great prominence can hardly be given the Psalms which have so enriched the spiritual life of many who are now members of the United Church of Canada."[24] But it was

J. R. Patterson who cut the ground from under both the committee and other former Presbyterians when he pointed out that the 1927 edition of *The Church Hymnary*, which was authorized for public worship by the Presbyterian churches in Scotland, Ireland, England, Australia, New Zealand and South Africa, did not contain a separate psalter.[25] Given this fact it appeared as if former Presbyterians had no basis for insisting on a separation of psalms and hymns in the new United Church hymn book, but the pressure was so great that the committee included a separate section of metrical psalms at the end of the book, instead of at the beginning.

Among those who were alarmed by this public discussion of the first draft of *The Hymnary* in the *New Outlook* was the most prominent Methodist member of the committee, Dr. Samuel P. Rose, the Professor of English Bible and Practical Theology at United Theological College in Montreal.[26] He was apprehensive about the division which seemed to be emerging between former Methodists and Presbyterians over the question of the psalter. He disliked the "tendency to abuse the experts" which was apparent in many of the letters, and he was angry with Dr. S. W. Fallis, the secretary of the Board of Publication, for initiating the discussion in the *New Outlook* with an editorial.[27] Therefore, Rose used his personal authority to shut down any further discussion of the hymn book in the *New Outlook*, and he recommended that any further comments should be sent to Alexander MacMillan.[28]

W. B. Creighton, the editor of the *New Outlook*, was not happy with this interference in the affairs of the church paper. Therefore, after noting that the 1928 draft was an interim report "intended to discover the mind of the church," he went on to observe that "apparently Dr. Rose had not thought the discussion in our columns was 'revealing the mind of the church.'" In defence of the *New Outlook*, Creighton said:

> We do not wish to support foolish or unwarranted statements, but we are fully satisfied, in our own mind, that the letters which have appeared in our paper ... represent ... the mind of a very large majority of our people. We cannot speak for the cultured few, the musical elite, but we think we can speak for the churches

at the crossroads, and the great mass of our members who do the singing in our churches both Sunday and week days. These people may be inarticulate, so far as the committee is concerned, but they have needs which the new hymnary must meet or else fail to function as a book for the whole church.29

While this reply emphasized the tensions which had emerged between the "experts" and the "rank and file," of even more concern to Rose was the tension which had arisen between the Church Worship and Ritual Committee and the Board of Publication.

All of the Canadian Methodist hymn books had been published in Canada, but the Presbyterian *Book of Praise* had been published in England by Oxford University Press.30 In preparing the 1897 edition and the 1918 revision of the *Book of Praise*, MacMillan had worked closely with the Oxford University Press staff. As a result, it was assumed that MacMillan would favour having Oxford publish the new United Church hymn book. Former Methodists, however, were determined that this hymn book, like their own Methodist hymnals, would be published in Canada. Therefore, when the draft was sent to a sessional committee at the 1928 General Council, the committee recommended that when the new book had received final approval, it "shall be published and sold by our own Publishing House."31 The General Council passed this recommendation with very little thought or discussion about what the decision might mean. Rose was among those who thought that the Council had made a mistake, and in a letter to Alexander MacMillan in September 1928, he said, "If Dr. Fallis can do as good and cheap work as Oxford, why was there valid reason against his showing so by tender? The question is, can he?" "It seems to me," Rose concluded, "that even yet the committee should require some evidence that he can before we finally hand over our work to him."32

In focusing on MacMillan's previous relations with Oxford University Press, everyone seemed to ignore that publication of hymn and service books for a variety of denominations represented the press's bread and butter and it was prepared to fight in order to defend its interests in this matter. In the Canadian market no other type of book sold as well as hymn books. For example, in 1913, the year before World War I, 97,898 copies of the 1897 edition of the

Book of Praise were sold in Canada, 11,556 more than in the preceding year.[33] These sales figures, which were more or less guaranteed for the life of the hymn book, were too large for any press to ignore. Consequently, for reasons other than cordial relations with Alexander MacMillan, Oxford University Press was determined to do some hard bargaining in order to get at least a part interest in the publication and distribution of the United Church's new hymn book. Dr. Samuel W. Fallis, however, refused to allow Oxford any part of the contract for either publication or distribution. Relying on an extremely rigid interpretation of the General Council's motion he said, "I did not at the time and do not now see any reason why we should not undertake the matter entirely ourselves. Reasons of course have been suggested, but none of them impress me at all, while the arguments on the other side are quite conclusive."[34] Oxford's trump card, however, was that if the United Church was unprepared to co-operate, Oxford would refuse permission to use any of the hymns and tunes to which they held the copyright.[35]

Fallis bitterly complained that the granting of permission on copyright "is customary courtesy between publishing houses, and so far as we know has never been refused, certainly never upon such grounds."[36] S. B. Gundy, Oxford's representative in Toronto, however, stood firm and replied, "Surely the principle of 'what we have we hold' is not the prerogative of one party only."[37] Seeing no way out of this dilemma, the executive of the Board of Publication unanimously passed a motion proposed by Elmer Davis and H. J. Pritchard that if negotiations with Oxford University Press failed "we recommend the publication of the book without these hymns and tunes."[38] To pass such a motion unilaterally in an effort to get themselves off the hook, however, placed the Board of Publication not only in conflict with Oxford University Press but also with the Committee on Church Worship and Ritual, who had been charged with selecting the hymns for the new hymn book. Consequently, a few months before the general council meetings in 1930, it began to appear as if the whole project was going to blow up in their faces.

It was at this point that Richard Roberts, the minister of Sherbourne Street Church, Toronto, and a member of Church Worship and Ritual Committee, decided to take up the matter with Dr. Fallis, who was a member of his congregation.[39] Roberts was convinced they were drifting into a "catastrophe" for three reasons. First, the hymn book committee would not consent to the issuing of the book without the Oxford hymns and tunes. Second, the executive of the General Council had given its *imprimatur* to the 1928 draft and it was not in the power of any other committee "to alter the draft in a single particular." Third, "the world would gape at the appearance of the hymn book of a great church" which was without these hymns, and many congregations would "refuse to accept a book so impoverished."[40] As a result, Roberts made it clear that if the Board of Publication insisted on publishing the book without the Oxford hymns, they would have to do it without the help of the hymn book committee, for he believed they would not be prepared "to father a defective book." He recommended, therefore, that Dr. Fallis take the initiative in resolving the whole affair as soon as possible.[41]

It was not Fallis, however, who took the initiative, but S. B. Gundy who outlined a new proposal. The price of Oxford's co-operation was that they be given an opportunity to sell the leather-bound edition at a special discount which would be in addition to the lowest trade rate. The hymn book committee eagerly accepted this compromise, but again it was Fallis who dug in his heels and refused to give Gundy 15 percent below the lowest jobbers' rate.[42] Richard Roberts and Harold Young, therefore, had to work out a further compromise. They recommended that Oxford be given the regular 30 percent discount plus an additional jobbing discount of 10 percent which Fallis was prepared to grant. In addition, however, they recommended that Oxford be given a further 5 percent discount for granting the use of their copyrights.[43] Much to everyone's relief, all concerned finally accepted this compromise, and it was then possible to print a special edition of the *Hymnary* for use at the 1930 General Council. Although this edition had no indexes, prose psalms, canticles, Apostles' Creed, or prayers, and it had only a temporary binding, it was sufficient to win Council approval.[44] On May 1, 1931 the *Hymnary* in its final form was ready for congregational use.[45]

After all the tension and arguments the production of the book had generated, the Board of Publication decided to placate everyone by hosting a special dinner on April 16, 1931 at the Royal York Hotel, Toronto, to mark the publication of the *Hymnary* and to honour Alexander MacMillan for his contribution to the book. On this occasion Dr. MacMillan was presented with a gold watch, his wife received a bouquet of spring flowers, and it was generally agreed "that the book came as near to being ideal as human productions could possibly be, and was destined to play a very great part in the developing life of the church." It was Dr. Trevor Davies who captured its full significance when he said that the new *Hymnary* "was bound to be one of the strongest forces making for unification within the church."[46] These sentiments were echoed throughout the church when, for example, Saskatchewan Conference noted with satisfaction the completion of the new hymnary and gave thanks "for this unifying and enriching influence in the life and work of the church."[47]

*   *   *

The receipt of a gold watch, however, did not mark the end of Alexander MacMillan's contribution to Canadian hymnody, for he was determined that, like all the other great hymn books in the Anglican, Methodist, and Presbyterian traditions, the *Hymnary* would have a companion volume which provided background on the authors and composers of every hymn.[48] Closer to home there had been precedents for such a companion volume in the Presbyterian Church in Canada because in 1880 a brief pamphlet entitled *Our Hymn Writers* had been published in connection with the *Presbyterian Hymnal*, and in 1899 MacMillan himself had published a pamphlet entitled *Helps to the Use of the Presbyterian Book of Praise* which was designed as an aid to the first edition of *The Presbyterian Book of Praise*.[49] Following the 1918 revision of the *Book of Praise* and the completion of the *Hymnary*, however, MacMillan was ready to tackle a much more comprehensive type of companion than had ever been produced in Canada. After MacMillan's wife died in 1932, he resigned as the full-time secretary of the Church Worship and Ritual Committee and began to devote his attention to this task which was completed and published in 1935 under the title *Hymns of the Church: A Companion to the Hymnary of the United Church of Canada*.[50] The importance of this book is that it gives further insight into what Richard Roberts referred to as MacMillan's "encyclopedic knowledge of the subject" and into many of the presuppositions which governed his work on both the *Book of Praise* and the *Hymnary*.[51]

Books of this genre typically comment on each hymn in the sequence in which they appear in the hymn book. But MacMillan's volume was historically conceived, and as a result it moves through the history of church praise from the Biblical period to the twentieth century placing the hymns of the church in their appropriate historical context. The volume, therefore, is a history of church praise as well as a commentary on the authors of individual hymns in the *Hymnary*. This aspect of *Hymns of the Church* throws some light on the "Preface" to the *Hymnary* which speaks of a "link with our fathers of generations past."[52] The organization of the book, then, clearly pointed to MacMillan's catholic understanding of the church's hymnody and his life-long attempts to make certain that the hymn books of the Presbyterian and United Churches reflected the full range and richness of that hymnody in all its aspects.

Although the United Church of Canada was a bold new experiment in ecumenicity, MacMillan with his historic sense of the church's tradition believed that the worship and praise of this new church had to be deeply rooted not only in the traditions of the three uniting churches but also in the hymnody of the universal church. This belief reflected not just his historic awareness of the riches of that tradition of praise but also his conception of the unity of the church. In the conclusion to *Hymns of the Church*, he tied together his conception of the communion of the saints and the church's historic unity with church praise when he said:

> Hymns have been a most effective witness to that unity of the church which underlies all diversities. As Christian people sing the psalms, ancient canticles, early and medieval hymns translated from the Greek and Latin together with songs of Reformation times, and modern hymns which have come out of many Communions, they are brought into communion of worship with the Church of the past, and with all who today call upon the name of the Lord Jesus, their Lord and ours.[53]

While such a conception of the unity of the church was not prominent in the discussion of union prior to 1925, it is fortunate that the person responsible for compiling the first major text the United Church of Canada produced was inspired by such a view, for it was exactly what the church needed.

Yet while MacMillan's historical awareness enabled him to touch base with all periods of the church's history, there were nevertheless certain limitations to his conception of the universal church and the types of sacred song appropriate for the *Hymnary*. One of these limitations was the type of gospel hymn which had been made popular by the Moody and Sankey evangelistic campaigns in Britain and the United States. MacMillan was familiar with this development because in *Hymns of the Church* he quotes at some length from Ira S. Sankey's *My Life and Sacred Songs*.[54] But it was his opinion that "the hymns used by them [Moody and Sankey] and to a large extent prepared for them were simple and unadorned and made no pretension to be regarded as part of the permanent literature of the time." The same was true of the melodies to which these hymns were set, for they "were not intended to be set in place with the lasting music of past and present times."[55] Furthermore, as MacMillan makes clear, "'gospel hymns' are to be regarded as by no means restricted to hymns of any one time or country or place. The hymns that proclaim and commend the gospel of our Lord and Saviour Jesus Christ are to be sought and found in abundance within the wide circumference of the hymns of the Christian Church of many ages and many lands."[56]

Although MacMillan accepted a number of gospel hymns by Fanny Crosby and others, it is clear that he had many reservations about them and that the boundaries he defined for the *Book of Praise* and the *Hymnary* excluded many of these hymns because he thought they were inappropriate for worship in the Presbyterian and United churches. Many on the committee shared MacMillan's opinion and supported this boundary for, as Richard Roberts put it, "many parts of the church [the United Church] are already too sympathetic with the inferior type of book."[57] What specific American books Roberts had in mind is not exactly clear because he did not elaborate. But what is clear is that the North American revivalist and camp meeting tradition was not one with which many of the most important members of the Church Worship and Ritual Committee were familiar. Richard Roberts, for example, was a Welsh Calvinistic Methodist, MacMillan and Professor R. E. Welsh were Scots Presbyterians, and Dean David L. Ritchie was a Scots Congregationalist. Professor S. P. Rose, who had edited the 1917 *Methodist Hymn and Tune Book*, would have been more familiar with this tradition of sacred song, but since he had spent most of his career in the pulpits of the major urban Methodist churches in Canada, he was not particularly anxious to perpetuate the more exuberant aspects of Methodism's frontier past. Consequently, there were many on the committee who shared MacMillan's reservations about "gospel hymns."

This boundary, however, had its roots not only in an aversion to the revivalist tradition, but also in a conception of worship which was centred in the Word rather than the Spirit.[58] In a service of the Word, the reading and exposition of Scripture in the sermon is the focal point of the worship service, and the emphasis is placed on God's coming to people rather than on their response. In such a service, therefore, toe-tapping, hand-clapping, and swaying to the music were inappropriate because the object is not Spirit-filled ecstasy but rather thoughtful meditation on God's glory and the wonders of his grace. The fact that the task of producing a United Church hymn book was placed in the hands of the Committee on Worship and Ritual emphasized the point that the church's hymnody was subordinate to the demands of its worship, and the presence of

Professor Richard Davidson, editor of the United Church's *Book of Common Order*, and W. D. Maxwell, who would later be recognized as a major authority on the history of worship, further underlined the committee's intention to keep the church's hymnody within the bounds of the Reformed tradition of worship.

However, this boundary was not simply a musical and textual boundary, it was also a class boundary, for MacMillan and the various committees he worked with made a very clear distinction between lower- and middle-class hymnody.[59] For example, MacMillan would have dismissed any suggestion that he include in his hymn books the popular Salvation Army chorus:

> There may be some on me and you
> But there ain't no flies on Jesus.[60]

Moreover, he would have rejected William Booth's arguments in favour of singing "catchy gospel songs" to attract the unchurched working classes, because his hymn books were designed for the use of the churched rather than the unchurched masses.

It was, however, not only Salvation Army choruses that were ruled out, but also black and white spirituals and most forms of contemporary sacred song which had deep roots in popular culture. For example, such well-known white spirituals as "You Got to Cross that Lonesome Valley," and black spirituals such as "Nobody Knows the Trouble I've Seen," as well as more modern black gospel songs like "Didn't it Rain," and "You Better Run, God Knows You Better Run," find no place in the hymnals of the Presbyterian and United churches. Again, not only spirituals and gospel songs were ruled out. Such well-known favourites as "The Old Rugged Cross," "The Church in the Wildwood," and "Count your Blessings, Name Them One by One" were also placed outside the pale of acceptable hymnody in these churches. However, because these songs are part of a wider popular culture and because congregations love to sing them, a whole host of gospel song books have sprung up along side the official hymn books of the Presbyterian and United churches, and they are still to be found in almost every congregation.

The establishment of a boundary on the right wing of Presbyterian and United Church hymnody inevitably led to the establishment of a boundary on the left wing. The social gospel, as has been recently shown, had an impact on the agenda of the Presbyterian Church in Canada, and it has been seen as a formative influence in the establishment of the United Church of Canada.[61] Indeed it was the emphasis of this movement on social rather than individual salvation which helped to strengthen the resistance to the gospel song in these churches. But the extent and influence of this movement on the hymnody of these churches has been negligible. Henry S. Coffin's *Hymns of the Kingdom of God* (1910) and *The Pilgrim Hymnal* (1904), of which Washington Gladden was the associate editor, appear to have had very little impact on either the Presbyterian or United Church committees.[62] In fact, MacMillan did not even mention Gladden's association with this hymn book in *Hymns of the Church*, and only one of Gladden's hymns found its way into the Presbyterian and United Church hymn books. *The Pilgrim Hymnal* of 1904 was published by the American Congregational Sunday School and Publishing Society and was therefore clearly within the Congregational tradition of hymnody, but its liberal theological presuppositions, its emphasis on the immanence of God, its pronounced humanitarianism, its stress on this world rather than on the next, and its non-ecclesiastical tone placed it outside the left-wing boundaries which MacMillan established for acceptable hymnody within the Presbyterian and United churches. The same was true of the one hundred hymns published in a special 1914 issue of *The Survey* on the "Social Hymn." The compilers of this volume wanted hymns that could be sung by Jew and Gentile, Protestant and Catholic alike. Moreover, they wanted hymns, as Louis Benson has put it, that dealt "not with the individual, but with humanity in the mass, not with spiritual experience but with social living, not with salvation of the soul, but with the uplift of society. Thus "no hymns of atonement, sin, and sacrifice" were included.[63] These criteria were obviously unacceptable to MacMillan. Both the *Book of Praise* and the *Hymnary*, therefore, charted a course through the church's hymnody which was anything but radical; it was clearly middle class, deeply liturgical and more solidly rooted in the nine-teenth than in the twentieth century.

In spite of these limitations, however, both the *Book of Praise* and the *Hymnary* quickly won a place for themselves within the Presbyterian and United churches, and they shaped the piety, wor-ship, and outlook of these churches until they were finally replaced by new hymn books in the 1970s. Any text which is in constant use for several generations, which is used wherever a group gathers for worship, is bound to shape that group's culture. Moreover, because hymn singing is a group activity in which congregations continu-ally give voice to their faith, it tends to have a very lasting effect on those who participate in it. This is especially true on those occasions when a congregation sings its old favourites, for it is in these mo-ments that they can experience what Victor Turner refers to as "communitas," that is, one of those liminal moments when all so-cial distinctions and community differences suddenly dissolve and people experience a profound sense of unity and group solidarity.[64] These moments are not easily forgotten by those who experience them, for they bond the individual to the group and they confirm one's sense of personal identity. Thus hymn singing is an impor-tant cultural medium for shaping thought and behaviour, and those individuals, like Alexander MacMillan, who compile and select the hymns which are available to members of a denomination have to be seen as important figures in the definition of these cultures.

NOTES

1. Sandra S. Sizer, *Gospel Hymns and Social Religion: The Rhetoric of Nineteenth-Century Revivalism* (Philadelphia: Temple University Press, 1978), and Susan S. Tamke, *Make a Joyful Noise unto the Lord: Hymns as a Reflection of Victorian Social Attitudes* (Athens: Ohio University Press, 1978). For recent Canadian scholarship on hymnody see George A. Rawlyk, ed., *New Light Letters and Songs* (Hansport, NS: Lancelot Press, 1983); Lionel Adey, *Hymns and the Christian Myth* (Vancouver: University of British Columbia Press, 1986), and *Class and Idol in the English Hymn* (Vancouver: University of British Columbia Press, 1988); Hugh D. McKellar, "150 Years of Presbyterian Hymnody in Canada," *Papers of the Canadian Presbyterian Church Historical Society*, 1986, 1-13. For Britain see Horton Davies, *Worship and Theology in England*, vol. 4 (1850-1900), and vol. 5 (1900-1965) (Princeton, NJ: Princeton University Press, 1965). See also Eric Routley, *Christian Hymns Observed* (London: A. R. Mowbray, 1983).

2. See Erik Routley, *Hymns Today and Tomorrow* (Nashville, TN: Abingdon Press, 1964), especially chapter 7, "On editing Hymnals."

3. For biographical information on Alexander MacMillan (1864-1961) see his obituary in *The United Church Observer*, April 1, 1961, 27 and the Toronto *Globe and Mail*, March 6, 1961, 10. See also references in note 5.

4. C. W. Gordon, *The Life of James Robertson* (Toronto: Westminster, 1908).

5. See Alexander MacMillan, *Looking Back: Reminiscences of the Reverend Alexander MacMillan, D.D., Mus.D, from 1864 to 1945* (Toronto, unpublished manuscript, 1945). I am indebted to Keith MacMillan of Ottawa for access to this manuscript of his grandfather's reminiscences and a typescript of a conversation between the Reverend Alexander MacMillan and Dr. George Kilpatrick that was broadcast on CBC radio September 23, 1957, in recognition of Dr. MacMillan's seventieth year in the ministry.

6. J. F. McCurdy, ed., *Life and Work of D. J. Macdonnell* (Toronto: William Briggs, 1897). See in particular Robert Murray's assessment of Macdonnell's work on the 1884 *Presbyterian Hymnal* in chapter 19 and his early work on *The Presbyterian Book of Praise* in chapter 35.

7. See Louis F. Benson, *The English Hymn: Its Development and Use* (Richmond, VA: John Knox Press, 1962), 531.

8. For details on these negotiations see W. Barclay McMurrich, *Historical Sketch of the Hymnal Committee of the Presbyterian Church in Canada* (London: Henry Frowde, 1905).

9. See John Somerville, "The Making of a Hymnal," *The Westminster*, May 1897, 209-10.

10. Alexander MacMillan, "Book of Praise Revision," *The Presbyterian*, April 22, 1915, 417.

11. See *Acts and Proceedings* 1915, 253. See also the "Report of the Committee on New Hymn and Tune Book," *Journal of the Methodist General Conference*, 1914, 192-94.

12. *Acts and Proceedings* 1915, 253.

13. Letter to the editor, *The Presbyterian*, February 4, 1915, 116. See the reply to this letter by W. J. Dey, the chairman of the Committee on Church Praise, *The Presbyterian*, February 18, 1915, 191.

14. Letter to the editor, *The Presbyterian*, March 4, 1915, 246.

15. "The Tunes in the Book of Praise," *The Presbyterian*, July 8, 1915 and July 15, 1915.

16. "Report on Church Praise," *Acts and Proceedings* 1917, 42-43, 222ff. As Hugh McKellar has noted in "150 Years," "Because the copyright on a British collection edited by Roundell, Lord Selborne and entitled *The Book of Praise* had expired, that title was available, as it had not been in 1897."

17. See *Record of Proceedings* 1926, pp. 79 and 90.

18. Unsigned letter to R. Lorne McTavish dated Toronto, October 31, 1928, UC Board of Publication Box 16a, file 1. UCA.

19. *New Outlook*, January 9, 1929, 72.

20. *New Outlook*, January 9, 1929, 72.

21. "Prefatory Statement" to *Draft of a Hymnary Submitted to the Third General Council of the United Church of Canada* (pamphlet dated September 1928). See also *United Church (UC) Year Book* 1928, 416ff.

22. *Acts and Proceedings* 1915, 253.

23. *New Outlook*, November 21, 1928.

24. *New Outlook*, January 2, 1929. For MacMillan's views on the Psalms, see Alexander MacMillan, "Church Praise in the United Church of Canada: The Presbyterian Contribution," *New Outlook*, June 24, 1925, 14.

25. *New Outlook*, January 12, 1929.

26. For biographical information on Samuel P. Rose (1853-1936) see H. J. Morgan, *The Canadian Men and Women of the Time* (Toronto: William Briggs, 1912), 967-68, and his obituary in the Montreal Ottawa Conference *Minutes 1937*. See also S. P. Rose, "The Making of a Hymn Book," *Canadian Journal of Religious Thought* (1930), 308-13. It should be noted that Rose was the editor of the 1917 revision of the *Methodist Hymn and Tune Book*.

27. S. P. Rose to A. MacMillan, November 26, 1928, U.C. Church Worship and Ritual Committee, Box 2, file 11, UCA. See also *New Outlook*, November 21, 1928, 4.

28. *New Outlook*, February 20, 1929, 210.

29. *New Outlook*, February 20, 1929, 200.

30. See *The Methodist Hymn and Tune Book* (Toronto: Methodist Book and Publishing House, 1894). In 1896 the Methodist Publishing House put in a bid to publish the *Book of Praise* but the Presbyterians accepted the bid of Oxford University Press. See UC Board of Publication Box 8, file 195. UCA.

31. *Year Book 1928*, 87.

32. S. P. Rose to MacMillan, September 25, 1928, U.C. Committee on Church Worship and Ritual Box 2, file 10. UCA.

33. *Acts and Proceedings* 1914, 277.

34. Fallis to Gundy, March 22, 1929, UC Board of Publication Box 16a, file 1. UCA.

35. S. B. Gundy to E. W. Wallser, January 17, 1929, U.C. Board of Publication Box 16a, file 1. UCA.

36. Fallis to Gundy.

37. S. B. Gundy to W. T. Gunn, March 1, 1930, U.C. Board of Publication Box 16a, file 1. UCA. The struggle between Fallis and Gundy was something of a family feud because Gundy had been an employee of the Methodist Publishing House for eleven years prior to becoming the Canadian representative of Oxford University press in Toronto. See Gundy's letter of resignation addressed to William Briggs, January 8, 1904, U.C. Board of Publication Box 10, file 6. UCA.

38. Minutes of the Executive of the Board of Publication, February 25, 1930. UCA.

39. For biographical information on Richard Roberts, see Gwen R. P. Norman, *Richard Roberts* (Toronto, typescript, 1966). UCA.

40. Richard Roberts to S. W. Fallis (no date), U.C. Board of Publication Box 16a, file 1. UCA.

41. Roberts to Fallis.

42. Gundy to Fallis, March 13, 1930, U.C. Board of Publication Box 16a, file 1. UCA.

43. Harold Young to Fallis, April 5, 1930, U.C. Board of Publication Box 16a, file 1. UCA.

44. *New Outlook*, October 1, 1930.

45. *UC Yearbook 1931*, 78.

46. Toronto *Globe*, April 17, 1931, 14, and the *New Outlook*, April 29, 1931.

47. *New Outlook*, April 29, 1931.

48. See Keith C. Clark, "A Biography of Handbooks and Companions to Hymnals: American, Canadian and English," *The Hymn* 30 (July-October 1979), Part 1, 205-10; Part 2, 269-72; 31 (January-April 1980), Part 3, 41-47; Part 4, 120-26.

49. *Our Hymn Writers, being biographical notices of the authors of the hymns selected by the Hymn Book Committee of the Presbyterian Church in Canada* (Toronto: James Campbell & Son, 1880) and Alexander MacMillan, *Helps to the use of the Presbyterian Book of Praise, prepared under the Music Committee of the Presbyterian Church in Canada* (Toronto: 1899). MacMillan's fifteen-page pamphlet was a very specialized aid for organists, choirmasters, and ministers which recommended the tempo at which every psalm and hymn in *The Presbyterian Book of Praise* ought to be sung by indicating first, the "metronome tempo," and second, "the number of seconds which would be occupied in singing the tune from beginning to end in strict time."

50. Alexander MacMillan, *Hymns of the Church: A Companion to the Hymnary of the United Church of Canada* (Toronto: The United Church Publishing House, 1935). The Only reference to this book that I have found is a notice in "Letters in Canada: 1935," *University of Toronto Quarterly* 5 (April 1936): 451.

51. Richard Roberts wrote the Foreword to MacMillan's *Hymns of the Church*.

52. *The Hymnary* (Toronto: The United Church Publishing House, 1930), iii.

53. MacMillan, *Hymns of the Church*, 309.

54. MacMillan, *Hymns of the Church*, 275.

55. MacMillan, *Hymns of the Church*, 295.

56. MacMillan, *Hymns of the Church*, 297.

57. Roberts to Fallis.

58. For MacMillan's conception of worship and the role of the church praise within worship, see Alexander MacMillan, "Worship Song in the Congregation," *The Pathfinder* (1923), Part 1 (253-54), Part 2 (293-94), Part 3 (371-72), and Part 4 (413-14). See also Alexander MacMillan, "The Place of Worship in our Lives," *East and West* (March 7, 1925); Alexander MacMillan, "Young People and Worship Song," *The Presbyterian*, February 14, 1915, 122; and Alexander MacMillan, "Worship Song at the Front," *The Presbyterian*, January 20, 1915, 58. Unfortunately, the last two articles do not represent MacMillan at his best.

59. Lionel Adey in *Class and Idol in the English Hymn* has dealt with the question of social class and hymnody comparatively. Utilizing Hugh McLeod's seven-class system (*Class and Religion in the Late Victorian City*, 1974) and Charles Booth's observations concerning the classes from which the various denominations drew their support (*Life and Labour of the People of London*, 1902). Adey puts Congregationalists near the top of the scale and Primitive Methodists at the bottom and on this basis compares their hymnody. Unfortunately, there is no comprehensive study of religion and social class in Canada. John Porter's *The Vertical Mosaic* (1965) is the only work which seriously addresses this question and he is concerned not with the classes from which the denominations draw their support but with denominational representation in Canada's elites. On this scale (which was formulated prior to the emergence in 1971 of Roman Catholic demographic dominance in Canada), French Roman Catholics are dramatically under represented; Anglicans and Presbyterians are greatly over represented; while the Baptists and United Church are slightly under represented. Such a scale, however, is not finely tuned enough to establish a framework for the comparative analysis of hymnody and social class in Canada. Until a more extensive treatment of religion and social class in Canada becomes available, therefore, the class boundaries of Canadian hymnody will remain impressionistic.

60. Cited in Tamke, *Make a Joyful Noise*, 6.

61. See Brian J. Fraser, *The Social Uplifters: Presbyterian Progressives and the Social Gospel in Canada, 1875-1915* (Waterloo: Wilfred Laurier University Press, 1988), and Richard Allen, *The Social Passion: Religion and Social Reform in Canada 1914-1928* (Toronto: University of Toronto Press, 1971).

62. See Benson, *The English Hymn*, 580, 582, 584.

63. See Benson, *The English Hymn*, 586.

64. For an illuminating discussion of Turner's conception of "communitas" in relation to worship, see J. Randall Nichols, "Worship as Anti-structure: The Contribution of Victor Turner," *Theology Today* 41 (January 1985): 401-9. See also Victor Turner, "Passages, Margins, and Poverty: Religious Symbols of Communitas," Part 1, *Worship* 46 (August-September 1972), 390-412, and Part 2, *Worship* 46 (October 1972), 482-94. These essays have been reprinted in Victor Turner, *Dramas, Fields, Metaphors: Symbolic Action in Human Society* (Ithaca, NY: Cornell University Press, 1974), chapter 6. Other dimensions of this concept are explored in Victor Turner, "Luminality and the Performative Genres," in *Rite, Drama, Festival, Spectacle: Rehearsals Toward a Theory of Cultural Performance*, ed. John J. MacAloon (Philadelphia: Institute for the Study of Human Issues, 1984), 19-41, and the papers from the Jerusalem Seminary on Comparative Luminality published in *Religion* 15 (1985).

IV

Presbyterians and Canadian Theology

Presbyterianism represents a particular way of believing and practising the Christian faith. The Reformation in Zürich under Huldrych Zwingli, in Geneva under John Calvin, in Basel under John Oecolampadius, in Strasbourg under Martin Bucer, and in Edinburgh under John Knox developed in ways that distinguished Presbyterianism from Lutheranism on the right, on which it was strongly dependent, and from the Anabaptist and Spiritualist movement, by which it was also influenced on the left. The Reformation spread through France, along the Rhine to the Low countries, to Hungary, Czechoslovakia and Poland, and to England and Scotland.

The term "Reformed" was the common designation for this particular type of theology and practice. Accordingly, Queen Elizabeth I spoke of it as "more reformed" than Lutheranism.[1] "Presbyterian," was another description of its distinctive form of church government by "presbyters" or elders—teaching elders (ministers) and ruling elders (lay)—and because of its hierarchy of church courts ascending from the local session or consistoire, to presbytery, synod and/or General Assembly, each (except for session) with an equal representation of ministers and lay elders.

One of the great strengths of the Reformed or Presbyterian tradition, some would even say its greatest strength, is its emphasis on theology. Huldrych Zwingli, John Calvin, Heinrich Bullinger, Martin Bucer, Peter Martyr Vermigli, and John Knox were major theological thinkers as well as excellent leaders and administrators. They laboured and struggled for a far-reaching reform that encompassed the whole of life, both private and public. Reforms were initiated not only at the level of individual faith and conduct but also at the public level which included the main institutions of church and state, their governing structures and bases of power. The result was nothing less than revolutionary, as Michael Walzer has demonstrated in his important work, *The Revolution of the Saints*.[2]

The chief source of this revolutionary ferment was the theology of John Calvin,[3] who was known in his day as "the theologian." Albrecht Ritschl, the well-known nineteenth century theologian, described Calvin's major work, *The Institutes of the Christian Religion*, as "the masterpiece of Protestant theology." Although his theology does not lend itself to easy characterization, it is comprised, as Alexandre Ganoczy has said, of three main theological principles: "glory to God alone," "Scripture alone," and the principle, or rather, confession of "Christ alone."[4]

In the first place, theology begins and ends in the apprehension of the majesty of God, knowledge of whom and obedience to whom, Calvin declared, is the sum of human wisdom. Second, his theology took its source from Scripture, the written Word of God, which, through the internal witness of the Spirit, is the ultimate standard of Christian faith and life. Third, Calvin's theology was centred on Christ, who by the whole course of his obedience in life and death and by his resurrection achieved redemption for humanity, a salvation which is received by faith alone. The doctrine of predestination, with which Calvin's name is usually associated, was simply the ascription of the whole of salvation to God. Yet in his zeal to ascribe all to God, Calvin mistakenly located not only election but also reprobation (the destiny of the majority) in the eternal, inscrutable will of God. Nevertheless, for Calvin predestination was not a speculative philosophy but a comforting doctrine that emphasized the Christian's calling to a holy and exemplary life. Moreover, Calvin directed the troubled conscience, in seeking the assurance of salvation, to Word and Sacrament and not to predestination.

Calvin's theological ideas were fashioned, as Alister McGrath stated, "into one of the most potent intellectual forces history has known, directly comparable in its influence and pervasiveness to the more recent rise of Marxism."[5] One other authority can be cited. Ernst Troeltsch, the German philosopher and sociologist of religion, believed that Christianity decisively transformed human culture and civilisation at only two points: during the Middle Ages through the scholastic synthesis of Thomas Aquinas and in the early modern period through Calvinism.[6] It was one of those rare moments in modern history when "Christianity moulded, rather than accommodated, itself to society."[7]

With the death of John Calvin in 1564, Calvinism[8] severed some of its links with Geneva and assumed an important international place and role. By the third quarter of the sixteenth century, Calvinism had established itself not only on the Continent but also in the British Isles. It sought, as Menna Prestwich has said, "not to adapt itself to society but to cast society into a new mould."[9]

Although Calvin's final words to the Geneva ministers were, "Ne changer rien, ne innover," changes were made and innovations introduced. Calvinism proved to be sufficiently malleable, accommodating itself to new local and historical contexts.[10] To begin with, there was a continuing doctrinal refinement, particularly in the doctrine of predestination, which led to the controversy between the Calvinists and Arminians, and which was resolved at the Synod of Dort (1618-19) with its rather severe restatement of Calvinism in the form of TULIP theology (total depravity, unconditional election, limited atonement, irresistible grace, and perseverance of the saints).[11]

Another attempt to modify the severity of double predestination was made by Moyse Amyraut of the Saumur school, who put forward a doctrine of hypothetical universalism.[12] In the seventeenth and eighteenth centuries, the concept of the covenant became a regulative principle of Reformed orthodoxy.[13] It not only mitigated the harshness of double predestination but was also an important influence, in the form of federal theology, on the civil polity of the government in the United States. The Westminster Confession of Faith and Catechisms (1643-47), which incorporated a mild form of federal theology, became the major statement of Reformed theology in the English-speaking world. In Scotland, it replaced the Scots Confession, and as Calvinism was transplanted to the United States and British North America, the Westminster Confession became the dominant doctrinal standard of Presbyterian churches.

Scottish Presbyterianism was an heir of this Calvinist theological tradition, which was transmitted to the Scottish Church in the sixteenth century by John Knox, who described Calvin's Geneva as "the most perfect school of Christ on earth," and Andrew Melville, who had studied on the continent and was a committed Calvinist. In the following century, Scottish Calvinist theologians such as Robert Baillie and Samuel Rutherford served as the Scottish commissioners to the Westminster Assembly. Yet the Church of Scotland not only received the theological legacy of Calvinism but added to it in the development of a distinctively Scottish theology. During the period of the Scottish Enlightenment and in the nineteenth century, Calvinism came under increasing attack. Scottish Evangelicals and even some of the Moderates, such as Principal George Hill of St. Mary's College, St. Andrew's, defended it. It was this Scottish Calvinist theology which was exported to those lands where Scottish immigrants settled. One of those places was British North America, and it should be noted that the one theological work, apart from his two anti-Roman Catholic polemical treatises, which Thomas McCulloch wrote in Nova Scotia was entitled *Calvinism, the Doctrine of the Scriptures, or A Scriptural Account of the Ruin and Recovery of Fallen Man, and A Review of the Principal Objections Which Have Been Advanced Against the Calvinist System* (1848).

In the first essay in this section, "History of Presbyterian Theology in Canada to 1875," I attempt a brief survey. I raise at the outset the important question whether there is a theology in the Canadian idiom as there was and is theology in the German, Scottish or American idiom, a Canadian theology with a degree of cohesion and thematic continuity.

To answer this question, I investigate Canadian Presbyterian theology during three different periods: the early period of settlement, the period when Scottish Common Sense was the dominant philosophical influence in North American theology, and, rather briefly, the period beginning in the 1870s and extending to the First World War when theology came under the strong influence of German idealist thought. This third period was a crucial one in Canadian Presbyterian theology; it merits a separate essay which I hope to present to a future symposium.

In the first period, the focus of the discussion is on Henry Alline, revivalist and anti-traditionalist, and on Thomas McCulloch, anti-revivalist and traditionalist. Henry Alline's theology represented a rebellion against the harsher elements of New England and Nova Scotian Calvinism. Thomas McCulloch, educator, theologian, amateur scientist, and literary figure, was a vigorous exponent of Calvinism, which was under attack in his day. As an heir of the Calvinist theological tradition, he asserted the primacy of Scripture, Reformed covenant theology, the doctrines of predestination and of sin, and its remedy in the work of Christ's atonement.

In the second period Scottish Common Sense, the characteristic flowering of the Scottish Enlightenment, was the dominant philosophical influence. It was exported to British North America and became the philosophical and theological orthodoxy among Presbyterians, Congregationalists, Methodists, Anglicans, and Unitarians. Among its proponents in Canada were Henry Esson, the first professor of mental and moral philosophy at Knox College, and George Paxton Young, his successor who later became professor of philosophy at the University of Toronto and espoused the idealism of T. H. Green. The outstanding Canadian Presbyterian theologian of this period was Dr. Michael Willis, a staunch Calvinist who was also known for his anti-slavery stance.

In the third period, Scottish Common Sense vanished, "leaving not a rack behind." Theological educators came under the influence of German idealism and turned with enthusiasm to evolutionary ideas, the social gospel and the religion of feeling. The conclusion to which this discussion points is that although Canadian theologians did not seek the deliberate cultivation of a distinct Canadian Presbyterian theology, they produced a theology "with a local habitation and a name" worthy of respect and attention, which constitutes a distinctive and significant contribution to Canadian life and culture.

In the next essay, "Canadian Presbyterians and Princeton Seminary, 1850-1900," Richard W. Vaudry explores the relationship between Canadian and American Calvinism. He observes that Princeton College and Seminary were built on some of the same

Scottish foundations as was Canadian Presbyterianism. From John Witherspoon to James McCosh, Scottish influences at Princeton were as readily apparent as they were in Canada from Thomas McCulloch to Michael Willis.

Princeton was the largest and arguably the most influential Presbyterian seminary in nineteenth-century America. Founded in 1812, by the 1930s it had graduated about 6,500 students. A number of Canadian students studied at Princeton Seminary, and in the period between 1861 and 1865, because of dissatisfaction with Knox College, a larger than average number of Canadians went there. Among the most prominent Canadian graduates were George Leslie Mackay, missionary to Formosa, James Robertson, superintendent of Western Missions, the Reverend William Cochrane of Brantford, Louis Henry Jordan of Queen's University and James Frederick McCurdy of University College, Toronto. In addition, Principal William Caven and Professor William MacLaren of Knox College, Sir William Dawson, principal of McGill, and Donald MacVicar, principal of Presbyterian College, Montreal, all had Princeton connections. These connections were mainly with Charles Hodge, the major American Presbyterian theologian of his day, and Dr. James McCosh, president of Princeton College. Dr. Vaudry argues that in an age of theological change and uncertainty, many Canadian Presbyterians looked south to Princeton for clear directions on Scripture, the Westminster Confession of Faith, and the defence of the Calvinist faith. This is not surprising since Charles Hodge boasted that no new doctrines had been introduced during his tenure at Princeton, indeed, that Princeton "had never brought forth a single original thought."[14] Hodge paid little attention to the challenge of Enlightenment philosophy and criticism.

The major theological figure in the Presbyterian Church in Canada after 1925, Professor W. W. Bryden, is the subject of John A Vissers's paper: "Recovering the Reformation Conception of Revelation: The Theological Contribution of Walter Williamson Bryden to Post-Union Canadian Presbyterianism." Echoing the judgments of professors J. C. McLelland and James D. Smart, both of whom were Bryden's students, Vissers argues that it is not possible to understand the development of the Presbyterian Church in Canada after 1925, including its contribution to Canadian life and culture, apart from understanding the significance of W. W. Bryden's life, ministry, and theology. He taught a generation of ministers how to think theologically and thereby contributed to a theological awakening in the Church.

W. W. Bryden has usually been labelled a "Barthian." Professor Vissers's essay seeks to demonstrate that Bryden's theology, while certainly influenced by Karl Barth, was also shaped by Scottish liberal evangelical Calvinism of the nineteenth and early twentieth centuries. An equally strong influence was Calvin's doctrine of the knowledge of God. Professor Vissers believes that W. W. Bryden's neo-Reformation view of revelation and the knowledge of God emerged as the theological rationale for the post-union Presbyterian Church in Canada, providing it with a firm theological basis for its continuing existence in Canadian society.

The final essay in the collection, on "The Role of Women in the Preservation of The Presbyterian Church in Canada: 1921-28," by the Reverend Roberta Clare, while not strictly on theology, is included in this section because of the importance of its subject matter. Regrettably, there have been few studies of the role of women in the Presbyterian Church in Canada. Ms. Clare seeks to remedy this lack. Through a careful study and analysis of primary sources, she argues that during the crisis years, 1921-25, Presbyterian women acquired unprecedented influence over church affairs, and that in 1925 they made a major contribution to the rebuilding of the church through Women's Associations and the Women's Missionary Society.

Presbyterian women became actively involved in the church union controversy with the establishment of the Women's League in 1922. This anti-union women's organization, parallel to the men's Presbyterian Church Association, was formed when many women realized that "without their being consulted, all the funds and property of their churches would pass into the United Church of Canada." Better organized and less cautious than the men's association, the Women's League contributed finances and literature to the anti-union campaign and afterwards worked with the Women's Missionary Society to refinance, rebuild, and refurbish Presbyterian Churches.

Roberta Clare questions why The Presbyterian Church in Canada took so long to ordain women to the ministry of Word and Sacrament. Many of the supporters of women's ordination entered union and were instrumental in passing legislation in the 1930s to ordain women. The Presbyterian Church was so preoccupied with sheer survival that it could not afford to revive a potentially divisive issue. It was not until 1966 that the General Assembly, employing the Barrier Act procedure which requires a majority of the presbyteries to approve an action, passed legislation to permit women to be ordained to the eldership and the ministry of Word and Sacrament.

NOTES

1. Philip Schaff, ed. *The Creeds of Christendom*, vol. 2 (New York: Harper & Brothers, 1877), 389-90, quoted by William Stacy Johnson and John H. Leith, eds., *Reformed Reader: A Sourcebook in Christian Theology*, vol. 1 (Louisville, KY: Westminster/John Knox Press, 1993), xx. This volume and its companion, vol. 2, ed. George Stroup, offer a fine collection of primary texts central to the history of the Reformed faith. See also John H. Leith, *Introduction to the Reformed Tradition* (Atlanta: John Knox Press, 1977).

2. Michael Walzer, *Revolution of the Saints* (Cambridge, MA: Harvard University Press, 1965).

3. The literature on Calvin is vast. Reference may be made to the recent biography by William Bouwsma, *John Calvin: A Sixteenth-Century Portrait* (New York: Oxford University Press, 1988); E. J. Furcha, ed., *In Honor of John Calvin 1509-1564: Papers from the 1986 International Calvin Symposium, McGill University* (Montreal: Faculty of Religious Studies, McGill University, 1987); A. Ganoczy, *The Young Calvin*, trans. David Foxgrover and Wade Proyo (Philadelphia: Westminster, 1987); Wilhelm Niesel, *The Theology of Calvin*, trans. H. Knight (Philadelphia: Westminster, 1956); and F. Wendel, *Calvin: Origins and Development of His Religious Thought*, trans. Philip Maret (New York: Harper & Row, 1963).

4. Ganoczy, *The Young Calvin*, 188-94.

5. Alister E. McGrath, *A Life of John Calvin* (Oxford: Blackwell, 1990), xii.

6. Ernst Troeltsch, *The Social Teachings of the Christian Churches*, vol. 2 (London: Allen and Unwin, 1931). See also his article "Calvin and Calvinism," *Hibbert Journal* 8 (1909 -10): 102-19.

7. Alister E. McGrath, *Life of John Calvin*, xii.

8. "Calvinism" was originally a term of abuse used by Calvin's Lutheran and Roman Catholic opponents to describe his theological system, and in particular his view of the Lord's Supper. Calvin repudiated the term (cf. his Dedicatory Epistle in his Commentary on Jeremiah). The term is ambiguous and it should be used with considerable care. It may refer: (1) to the teachings of Calvin; (2) to the teaching of Reformed churches; (3) to the TULIP theology of the Synod of Dort; (4) to the set of ideas, theological, ethical, social, and political, which have left their mark on western civilization. Moreover, there are different forms of Calvinism, and as mentioned earlier, a Calvinism without a Calvinist theology.

9. Menna Prestwich, ed., *International Calvinism 1541-1715* (Oxford: Clarendon, 1985), 7. See also Alister McGrath, *A Life of John Calvin*, 196ff.

10. Edward Farley has argued that Calvinism is modifiable. The genius of the Presbyterian heritage, Farley thinks, is its "critical modernism," by which he means a willingness to reconcile an eternal gospel with current realities. While this is true, it is not the whole truth. Many Reformed theologians also recognized that one embraces the modern world at some cost and that there is always the danger of giving up one's heritage for a mess of pottage. There is, therefore, a limit to modifiability. Farley speaks of selectively accepting categories presented by the modern world, but he fails to indicate by which norm or norms this selection is to be made. Reformed theology sought to apply the Scriptural principle as the ultimate norm in all matters of Christian faith and life. Cf. Edward Farley, "The Presbyterian Heritage as Modernism: Reaffirming a Forgotten Past in Hard Times," in Milton J. Coalter, John M. Mulder, and Louis B. Weeks, *The Presbyterian Predicament* (Louisville, KY: Westminster/John Knox Press, 1990), 49-66.

11. See Carl Bangs, *Arminius: A Study in the Dutch Reformation* (Nashville: Abingdon, 1971), and Alan P. F. Sell, *The Great Debate: Calvinism, Arminianism and Salvation* (Grand Rapids, MI: Baker, 1983).

12. Cf. Brian G. Armstrong, *Calvinism and the Amyraut Heresy: Protestant Scholasticism and Humanism in Seventeenth-Century France* (Madison: University of Wisconsin Press, 1969).

13. Cf. William Klempa, "The Concept of the Covenant in Seventeenth and Eighteenth Century Continental and British Reformed Theology," in Donald K. McKim, *Major Themes in the Reformed Tradition* (Grand Rapids, MI: Eerdmans, 1992), 94-107.

14. Mark A. Noll, "The Princeton Theology," in David Wells, ed., *Reformed Theology in America* (Grand Rapids, MI: Eerdmans, 1985), 17.

History of Presbyterian Theology in Canada to 1875

William Klempa

The aim of this essay is to trace the history of one strand of Protestant theology in Canada up to 1875. Yet, can we speak without cant[1] of a history of theology in Canada and thus of a history of Presbyterian theology? From early days, Canadians established places of theological education, taught the body of knowledge known as theology, and to a greater or lesser degree used and communicated this theology in their preaching, teaching, and practice. The issue is whether there is something that can properly be designated as theology in the Canadian idiom—as there was and is theology in the German, Scottish, or American idiom—with a degree of coherence, substance, and thematic continuity.

The question is usually answered negatively. In an important study of sermon literature in 1979, S. F. Wise observed (but he grants that he is understating the matter) that really no connected history of formal thought in Canada is possible.[2] The stock of ideas has been imported and replenished mainly from other places such as Europe, the British Isles and the United States. Accordingly, the Canadian intellectual historian must be concerned primarily with the inter-relationship between ideas and actions: the intellectual commonplaces of the age, its root notions, assumptions, and images. These, Wise believes, will be of more significance to the historian than the study of coherent bodies of abstract thought.[3]

Gerald R. Cragg earlier made a similar judgment with respect to a history of theology. In a lead article in the first issue of the *Canadian Journal of Theology*, in April, 1955, Professor Cragg noted that prominent among the forces that have shaped our Canadian history "has been a kind of theological 'colonialism'—a dependent spirit which has persistently looked elsewhere for leadership. Ideas and those who inculcated them could carry little weight unless they clearly bore the *imprimatur* of some foreign origin. It was tacitly assumed that no good thing could come out of a Nazareth as remote as ours from the fountain-heads of truth."[4]

A number of Canadian intellectual historians, including Leslie Armour and Elizabeth Trott in their *The Faces of Reason*,[5] Ramsay Cook in *The Regenerators*,[6] and A. Brian McKillop in his *Disciplined Intelligence* and *Contours of Canadian Thought*,[7] have more recently made us aware of the intellectual vitality and substantial nature of Canadian thought in philosophy, historical writing, theology, and literature. Ramsay Cook notes that Canadian thinkers talked freely about all sorts of problems, but he adds that "they almost never alluded to the cultivation of a national sentiment."[8] That is, they did not set out to produce a distinctively Canadian philosophy, theology, social and political thought, or even Canadian literature. Their discussions were carried on at a high level, and the literature that was produced ranks favourably with British and American literature on these subjects. This is particularly the case with theological works. While Canada has had no theologian of the stature of the Scot, John McLeod Campbell, or the American, Charles Hodge, James MacGregor, Henry Alline, Thomas McCulloch, William Lyall, George Paxton Young, John Clark Murray, Michael Willis, William MacLaren, George M. Grant, and John Watson were far from being intellectual pygmies. In fact they can take their place worthily along with their British or American theological counterparts. Our lack of familiarity with these names and their work has impoverished our appreciation of our heritage. This paper is a small effort to retrieve our past and assess the contribution those thinkers made.

This study is divided into three parts. It was said of Alexander MacLaren, the great English non-conformist preacher, that he had a magic silver hammer with which he struck Biblical texts and they always divided into three equal parts. No such magic hammer is at hand but it appears that the history of Presbyterian theology in Canada from its beginnings to the present century falls neatly into three main periods: first, the early days of settlement; second, the period from the first part of the nineteenth century to roughly 1870 when Scottish Common Sense realism was the dominant philosophical influence in theology; and third, the period beginning in the 1870s and extending into the twentieth century which witnessed the "romantic religious revolution,"[9] when theology came under the strong influence of German idealist thought. This essay will concentrate on the first two periods with only brief reference to the third. I am indebted to Sydney Ahlstrom, the Yale historian, for this threefold schema. His two important essays, "The Scottish Philosophy and American Theology" of 1955,[10] and his presidential address to the American Society of Church History in 1975, "The Romantic Religious Revolution and the Dilemmas of Religious History,"[11] describe not only the American but also the Canadian scene. In Canada as in the United States, Scottish realism became the servant of theology, functioning as an apologetic tool for Calvinist orthodoxy. This philosophy, as Ahlstrom says, was "free enough from subtlety to be communicable in sermons and tracts. It came to exist in America, therefore, as a vast subterranean influence, a sort of water-table nourishing dogmatics in an age of increasing doubt."[12] But then a kind of rationalistic *rigor mortis* set in and a new theological turn became virtually inevitable.

The Early Period of Settlement

Armour and Trott have observed that the Scots were a sermonizing people for whom religion was primarily a matter of doctrine rather than of feeling (surely for many of them it was both!) and that they brought this tradition of public reasoning with them when they came to Canada. They were largely responsible for the development of colleges and universities in general, and of academic philosophy and theology in particular.[13] In this early period the outstanding figure is Thomas McCulloch, one of the most prominent educators and theologians in the Maritimes. But first, brief reference must be made to one of the most fascinating figures of the end of the eighteenth century, Henry Alline, also a Maritimer.

Henry Alline (1748-1784)

Henry Alline adhered to no particular church, had no formal education, and attended no theological seminary (a matter of considerable pride to him), yet he was responsible for "The Great Awakening of Nova Scotia," one of the most significant movements in the history of the colony.[14] He merits a place in this discussion because of his Calvinistic roots and his rebellion against the harsher elements of New England and Nova Scotian Calvinism.

E. M. Saunders, in his *History of the Baptists in the Maritime Provinces*, has asserted that what Joseph Howe was to the state, Henry Alline was "in the realm of religion and church life;" and although that is perhaps an exaggeration it points to Alline's significance.[15] Similarly, George Rawlyk of Queen's University in *Ravished by the Spirit*, considers Alline's *Journal* to be "one of the two or three most illuminating, honest, introspective accounts available concerning the spiritual travails of any eighteenth-century North American mystical evangelical." Rawlyk adds: "Alline's Alline may confidently be located in the mainstream of North American religious history,"[16] which is indeed a bold claim considering the fact that Alline understood himself as an anti-traditionalist and outsider.

Henry Alline was born in Newport, Rhode Island, in 1748, the child of a strict Calvinist household. He relates in his *Journal* that the fear of hell haunted him from earliest years (at the age of eight he cried in bed at the awful prospect of eternal damnation). Young Alline conceived of God as "a hard hearted and cruel being, [and] that there was a need of praying a great deal, to get him pleased, and get his favour."[17] When he was twelve, Alline's family moved to a farm near Falmouth, Nova Scotia, at which point his formal schooling ceased. His religious struggles continued. As a young man, however, he turned his mind to what were then if not forbidden at least frowned-upon pleasures. He became a leader in organizing the card parties and frolics of the neighbourhood. One evening on the way to one of these parties, God came to him in a dramatic way, and Henry Alline was converted. His conversion, recorded vividly in his *Journal*, found a place in William James's *Varieties of Religious Experience*. James viewed Alline's religious experience as a "classic example" of the "curing of a 'sick soul.'"[18]

With his conversion came a call to preach. Alline hesitated because of his lack of formal education, but this did not finally deter him. After an unsuccessful attempt to return to New England to study theology he decided in 1776 to become a "new-light" revivalist preacher. When confronted at Cornwallis by two Presbyterian ministers who asked him about his right to preach, he replied that his "authority was from heaven." True to their Presbyterian convictions the ministers criticized him for being "without a license from a society of ministers," which they prided themselves in possessing, and for "breaking through all order," a particularly heinous sin in their eyes. Alline gave tit for tat. If he lacked a licence to preach, they lacked something more important—conversion. Alline attacked them and other unconverted ministers for the great harm they had caused. "I have found them in my travels," he said, "more inveterate against the power of religion than the open profane."[19] Two years later Alline remedied his defect. (It is not known whether the Presbyterian ministers remedied theirs.) He was ordained near Cornwallis "in a large barn" as an itinerant minister by the imposition of hands by nine delegates. From 1776 to 1783, he travelled the length and breadth of the settled areas of the Maritime Provinces on horseback and in all kinds of weather, often preaching several times a day. On his way to Boston in 1784 he took ill at the home of a Congregational minister at Northhampton, New Hampshire, where he died, literally worn out from his revivalist labours, at the age of thirty-five. On his gravestone are these words: "He was a burning and a shining light and justly esteemed the Apostle of Nova Scotia."[20]

James MacGregor, the pioneer of Presbyterianism in the Maritimes, described Alline's theology as "a mixture of Calvinism, Antinomianism and Enthusiasm."[21] Alline combined certain mystical tendencies from his reading of such writers as William Law (1686-1761), John William Fletcher ("the Shropshire Saint"), and Edward Young. At the heart of Alline's theology is the conviction that God must be lovable, just, and good. In line with the revivalist tradition Alline emphasized the necessity of a decision for Christ. Christ is the "Heavenly Charmer," one's "Lover" and "Redeemer." Conversion is marriage to Christ, "the most beautiful creature that I ever beheld." As Rawlyk has noted, Alline was obsessed with the word "ravish," and he used it repeatedly to describe the moment of his conversion. The sexual imagery is unmistakeable, the ravishing of the soul followed by deep satisfaction, a kind of "religious orgasm."[22]

There was also a highly speculative element in Alline's theology that testified to his daring and novelty. He spoke of an "Out-birth" of the universe rather than a creation out of nothing. This "Out-birth" is a kind of emanation from God, and here Alline was indebted to neo-Platonism, the mystical theology of William Law, and the cabala of Jewish mysticism.[23] Alline also subscribed to the theory of the pre-existence of souls. Not only Adam but all humanity existed in a pre-material spiritual state, and there was no sexual differentiation: "Adam himself was a Male and Female being when he was as he came from God."[24] The Fall occurred because Adam had freedom of will and instead of choosing good chose evil, consequently plunging the spiritual world into destruction. All humans participated in the fall and therefore, all are guilty and tainted by original sin. The reason we cannot remember this pre-existent state is that we have been in a "deep sleep" ever since the fall, held by a loving and merciful God until each has been tried and given another opportunity to choose the good.[25]

Alline put forward an equally speculative view of the origin of the physical universe. The physical world is a result of an "interposition" on the part of God. Sexual differentiation is also the result of this suppressive activity of God. Alline seems to suggest that woman was created after the Fall and is part of God's providential plan for the redemption of the race. Salvation does not depend upon any outward act of the human being (*à la* Arminianism), or any decree of God (*à la* Calvinism) but upon "the union of the inner man to" and "the turning of the inmost soul after God." Alline denied a physical resurrection. The resurrection is spiritual; the immortal body which fell now rises again. With regard to eschatology, Alline believed that heaven and hell are not places but eternal conditions of the soul, and that every day is judgment day. In what

Maurice W. Armstrong calls the first Canadian metaphysics, Alline wrote: "It is as inconsistent to go back to before the beginning of Time, to talk of God's *electing* or reprobating the Children of Men, as for a Man to go round upon a Ring all his Days to find an End; for it is in pursuit of a period that was never known, even to God Himself."[26]

All of this has a certain fascination. Nevertheless, we should note what one well-known contemporary revivalist thought of Alline's theology. In a July 13, 1783 letter to William Black, John Wesley, the founder of Methodism, said: "He [Alline] is very far from being a man of sound understanding; but he has been dabbling in Mystical writers, in matters which are too high for him, far above his comprehension. I dare not waste my time upon such miserable jargon."[27]

Alline's teaching did not long survive his death. Still, other groups took up his emphasis on feeling and experience, which became an important element in religious life in Canada.[28] Not unlike the proto-romantic Jonathan Edwards, with his emphasis on the religious affections, Alline represents an early form of romanticism in Canada, predating its revolutionary influence by almost a century.

Thomas McCulloch (1776-1843)

If Alline saw himself as an anti-traditionalist, Thomas McCulloch was the very epitome of all that was traditional in theology. He was suspicious of revivalism, and though he was staid in comparison with Alline, McCulloch's work and influence were of a more enduring character.

Thomas McCulloch was an outstanding educator, theologian, and amateur scientist and the author of two polemical works, *Popery Condemned by Scripture and the Fathers* and *Popery Again Condemned* and of the *Stepsure Letters*—and as *Stepsure* author he was, according to Northrop Frye, "the founder of genuine Canadian humour, that is, of the humour which is based on a vision of society and is not merely a series of wisecracks on a single theme."[29] Born in Renfrewshire, Scotland, in 1776, he studied both arts and medicine at the University of Glasgow and proved to be such an excellent student of oriental languages that at the age of twenty he was conducting a private tutorial class in Hebrew. His theological studies were taken at the Secession Divinity Hall at Whitburn near Edinburgh where he studied under a sharp and satirical theologian, Professor Archibald Bruce, who wrote *The Catechism Modernized* in 1791, a cutting satire on lay patronage and its effects in the form of a parody on the Shorter Catechism.[30] In 1803, after a four-year pastorate in Scotland, McCulloch responded to an appeal to come to Canada as a missionary. Prevented by bad weather from going to Prince Edward Island, he remained in Nova Scotia where he served for the next forty years as a parish minister and educator.

Along with associates from the Antiburgher Secessionist Church, McCulloch established Pictou Academy, an institution which numbered among its distinguished graduates Sir T. D. Archibald, baron of the English Court of Exchequer, Sir Hugh Hoyles, Chief Justice of Nova Scotia, Sir William Dawson, Principal of McGill College, Judge Ritchie of the Supreme Court of Canada, and such ministers of the gospel as John Geddie, the great missionary to the New Hebrides, and George Patterson, author of *The History of the County of Pictou* and *The Doctrine of the Trinity*. Although called an academy, Pictou was in reality a college teaching a wide range of courses including logic, moral philosophy, science, Hebrew, and theology. The quality of its teaching was recognized by the University of Glasgow which conferred the degree of M.A., after the usual examinations, on three of its first graduates. Yet the Academy had a brief career. McCulloch was perennially thwarted by vested religious interests in his efforts to secure degree-granting powers, and the Academy was reduced by 1838 to the status of a grammar school. This did not prevent him from realizing a second great educational ambition—the establishment of a divinity hall in connection with the Academy for the theological education of a Presbyterian ministry on Canadian soil. This seminary became the precursor of Pine Hill Divinity Hall. After thirty-five years as a parish minister and educator in Pictou, Thomas McCulloch accepted the principalship of Dalhousie University in 1838, a position which he held until his death in 1843.

McCulloch was a vigorous apologist for Calvinism. His theological lectures were published posthumously in 1848 by a Glasgow publisher under the title, *Calvinism, The Doctrine of the Scriptures*, or "A Scriptural Account of the Ruin and Recovery of Fallen Man, and A Review of the Principal Objections Which Have Been Advanced Against the Calvinistic System."[31] McCulloch's brand of Calvinism is largely informed by the works of Jonathan Edwards, the great American puritan theologian, Benedict Pictet, an eighteenth-century Swiss Reformed theologian, and Principal George Hill of St. Mary's College, St. Andrew's, leader of the moderate party in the Church of Scotland and author of the three-volume *Lectures in Divinity*. Curiously, although perhaps not all that curiously, since it is typical of nineteenth-century Scottish Calvinist writers, there is not a single reference to Calvin's writings in McCulloch's work.

According to McCulloch, Calvinism is a system which is not congenial to the views and tendencies of human nature and has consequently been reviled and rejected for a variety of reasons—all, of course in his opinion, ill-founded. First, Calvinism has been put on the shelf because even in religion fashions change and the unwary are beguiled, because its principles are not always known, and because its friends have held mistaken and unguarded views. Furthermore, opponents have frequently directed attacks against distorted views of its doctrines and tenets.

McCulloch's two main antagonists are Dr. John Taylor,[32] an eighteenth-century convert from Presbyterianism to Unitarianism and author of *The Scripture Doctrine of Original Sin* (1767), which provoked the famous reply of Jonathan Edwards, and Dr. Daniel Whitby,[33] an eighteenth-century polemical Anglican divine who wrote an anti-Calvinist volume, *A Discourse Concerning ... Election and Reprobation* (1710). Against Taylor and Whitby, McCulloch contends that Calvinism is the true theological system because it alone provides a Biblical account of the "ruin and recovery" of fallen humanity.

The popular song tells us that "a spoonful of sugar helps the medicine go down." McCulloch wrote winsomely and well, but there is little sugar coating and what he presents is straight Calvinist medicine in six chapters.

McCulloch's book begins in a typically Calvinist fashion by asserting the normative character of the Bible or what is known as the Scriptural Principle: Scripture rather than reason is the test of divine truth. Accordingly, McCulloch criticizes Dr. Whitby for his view that if Scripture does not "coincide with the common reason of mankind, it ought to be rejected." The phrase "common reason" is a slippery one. "Every age," McCulloch notes, "has had its tastes in religion, which, however diversified, human reason has approved in succession."[34] Reason is imperfect in knowledge and is also so variable that it cannot constitute itself the test of divine truth. Scripture alone suffices as an indispensable criterion. At the same time, McCulloch held to a view of progressive illumination, insisted that the Scriptures should be read in their original languages, and stressed the importance of a historical understanding of the biblical text.

In setting forth the Calvinist system, McCulloch makes use of the schema and insights of covenant or federal theology, the dominant theological movement in reformed circles in the seventeenth and eighteenth centuries. According to this view, God enters into a twofold covenant or agreement with humanity. The first covenant, known as a covenant of works, is made with Adam.[35] When Adam disobeys and the covenant is broken, God establishes a new covenant of grace which is fulfilled in Christ, the second Adam and representative of a new humanity. While this view made possible a dynamic interpretation of history, it seems wrong on at least one important count that McCulloch did not acknowledge. It suggests that God deals with humanity in two entirely different ways: by works under the dispensation of the law and by grace under the dispensation of grace. It implies, therefore, two ways of salvation: one without Christ and the other through Christ, one the way of works and the other the way of grace. This federal covenant theology distinguishes itself from Calvin who spoke of only one covenant, a covenant of grace, with two modes of administration, old and new.

The doctrine of predestination figures prominently in McCulloch's discussion of Calvinism. It is understood in the usual Reformed sense "that one is taken, and another left."[36] Not everyone is saved. For McCulloch, Calvinism can be most clearly set forth by contrasting it with Arminianism. In the Calvinist system election does not depend upon the faith and good works of the elected. "In the system of redemption, human conduct, as a condition or co-operating cause, is completely excluded."[37] Faith does not procure salvation but simply receives the gift of grace. Moreover, there is no inconsistency between freedom of the will and an absolute decree. The human mind at its present stage may not comprehend how freedom of the will and absolute decree coincide; but that they completely harmonise, the Scriptures exhibit to faith's satisfaction.

In McCulloch's view, the notion of universal redemption cannot be supported by the Bible. Armour and Trott state that McCulloch "meticulously locates every scriptural passage which *favours* the doctrine he is attacking. By the time he has made the universalist case, his own position seems feeble by contrast."[38] On the contrary, McCulloch is largely successful in showing that the words "all" and "world" do not necessarily mean every single individual, as universalists insist, but may mean "from every group or nation," an interpretation that the main exegetical tradition favours.

Few Biblical exegetes today, however, would concur with his view of a double decree and a doctrine of limited atonement. Like most Calvinists, McCulloch claimed to know too much about the mystery of the divine will in the same way as too many Arminians claimed to know too much about the mystery of the human will. McCulloch does grant that we lack perfect knowledge and that there are difficulties which must remain unsolved until the mystery of God is revealed. That there is mystery is true but it must be located in the proper place. McCulloch's God, like Calvin's, is a God of the horrible decree. It would have been preferable had McCulloch seen election in closer connection with Christ, interpreted it in more dynamic terms as God's purpose for humankind, and thus proclaimed it as a message of hope and comfort. But perhaps this is too much to expect from a mind that had been shaped by the strict double-decree schema of scholastic Calvinism.

Yet McCulloch's discussion is not without some moderating features. In one place he deals with Whitby's objection that Calvinism is less accordant than Arminianism with divine benevolence since it holds that the vast majority of humanity is damned. Calvinists, McCulloch says, acknowledge the redeemed to be a great multitude which no man can number. The fact that some Calvinists have represented the elect as comparatively few constitutes no part of the Calvinist system. Yet the chief point at issue between Calvinist and Arminian is not whether those elected are few or many, "but whether a part of the human race are unconditionally chosen, or the whole included in a conditional decree."[39] While Arminianism may appear more benign than Calvinism, its doctrine that God elected those whom he foreknew would respond is equally if not more harsh. It devolves upon the Arminian, McCulloch says, "to explain how a God of perfect benevolence, foreseeing that any would reject the offer of his mercy, could yet, consistently with his own nature, call them into existence."[40] McCulloch adds the comment that the benevolence of God has to do with the happiness of those toward whom it is exercised; therefore, "to measure the extent of salvation solely by the benevolence of God, is, in other words, to render misery and salvation of equal extent."[41] Be that as it may, both Calvinism and Arminianism, employing the faulty model of a static decree, ended in insuperable difficulties.

McCulloch concludes his discussion by admitting that Scripture does not provide Calvinism with replies to every objection but he takes heart in the fact that other systems are liable to objections equally formidable. During the present state of human existence, the Scriptures do not disclose the whole counsel of God. Human knowledge remains imperfect. The Christian must be content to walk by faith "and, without unprofitable prying into what God has concealed, to say with an apostle, "O the depth of the riches both of the wisdom and knowledge of God! how unsearchable are his judgments and his ways past finding out! (Rom. 11:33)."[42]

Theology Under the Influence of Scottish Realism

We turn our attention next to the period after the early days of settlement to approximately 1870, during which time Scottish Common Sense realism came to be the prevailing philosophical influence.

Scottish realism was a characteristic flowering of the Scottish Enlightenment. Its founder and most creative contributor was Thomas Reid (1710-96), regent at King's College, Aberdeen, an active member of the Aberdeen Philosophical Society from 1758 to 1764, and thereafter successor to Adam Smith in the chair of moral philosophy at Glasgow. While a parish minister at New Machar, he was drawn from Berkeley to Hume when he read Hume's *Treatise on Human Nature* (1739). Reid's *An Inquiry into the Human Mind on the Principles of Common Sense*, an effort to combat Hume's philosophical scepticism, was published in 1764. Alasdair MacIntyre has stated that part of Reid's originality lay in challenging Hume by appealing against Hume's philosophy to the principles of just those plain, unphilosophical persons who were so highly valued by Hume himself.[43] Against Hume he argued that certain truths are evident to almost every human being, a fact denied only by those who are either of unsound mind or in the grip of some unsound philosophical theory. Our awareness of these truths is elicited by but not derived from experience.

The other members of this school of philosophy included Dugald Stewart (1753-1828), who taught moral philosophy at the University of Edinburgh from 1785 to 1810, and Sir William Hamilton (1788-1856), professor of history and philosophy at Edinburgh who tried to combine common sense with notions obtained from Kant. In the Scottish universities the role of the professor of mental and moral philosophy was a crucial one. He was the official defender of the rational foundations of Christian theology, of morals, and of law.[44] The same understanding and practice came to obtain in Canada.

Since the Moderate party in the Church of Scotland was the authentic religious expression of the Scottish philosophy, it is proper to speak of the Moderate-Common Sense synthesis.[45]

The Moderate theological position has been described by J. H. S. Burleigh as "ostensibly if tepidly orthodox."[46] According to Sydney Ahlstrom, its great weakness was its "benign and optimistic anthropology,"[47] which struck at the very heart of the Christian faith. Thomas Chalmers compared a Moderate sermon to a winter's day. It was "short and clear and cold."[48]

Moderatism had its impact on Presbyterianism in Canada. James H. Lambert credits Alexander Spark, who ministered in St. Andrew's Church, Quebec City, from 1794 to 1819, with introducing Presbyterian Moderatism to Lower Canada. Spark had studied under Professor George Campbell, a leading Moderate and close associate of Thomas Reid in the Aberdeen Philosophical Society and author of *Dissertation on Miracles* (1762). Spark's theology can be summed up in the following statement in a sermon preached on January 10, 1799, the day appointed for a general thanksgiving: "Piety, morality, and public faith must go hand in hand. Religion corrects the irregular propensities of the heart—gives strength and stability to virtuous purposes, and cherishes those dispositions, and that temper of mind which are most friendly to peace, order, and good government."[49] Spark questioned the doctrine of justification by faith alone and spoke of election and orginal sin as both unworthy of God's justice and inconsistent with human moral agency.

Scottish realism was exported to North America and it became dominant for longer or shorter periods among Presbyterians, Congregationalists, Methodists, Anglicans, and also Unitarians. Sydney Ahlstrom has noted that it had an "overwhelming attraction across nearly the entire spectrum of American Protestantism, from the most liberal champions of Boston Unitarianism to the archdefenders of Reformed orthodoxy at Princeton Seminary, and including those intermediate forms of 'New School' revivalism being fostered at Andover, Gettysburg, and Yale."[50] Combined with natural theology, it was a useful apologetic tool. Charles Hodge at Princeton was influenced as much by realism as by the theology of Francis Turretin. In Canada the same pattern prevailed.

At Knox College in Toronto, the first permanent professor appointed to the faculty, Henry Esson, was strongly influenced by

Scottish Realism. Born in 1793, Henry Esson studied for the ministry at Marischal College, Aberdeen, graduating in 1811. In 1817 he went to Montreal as an assistant to James Somerville of St. Gabriel's. Esson's life was marked by tragedy and conflict. His twenty-four-year-old wife died in 1826, and his two sons died in childhood. In 1822 an evangelical group unhappy with Esson called another minister, Edward Black. A vicious struggle ensued between the two ministers. During this unholy quarrel Esson was accused of fornication, but was cleared of this charge by a court of law. A synodical committee decreed that he remain at St. Gabriel's and Black go elsewhere. Whether as a result of this struggle or some conversion experience, Esson's moderate theological views changed and he began to preach with evangelical fervor. In 1844 he sided with the Free Church cause, and later that year accepted a position to teach literature, history, and philosophy at the Free Church college in Toronto, later known as Knox College. He came to occupy the mental and moral philosophy chair, and in 1851 he applied for the new chair of civil and English history at the University of Toronto but died before an appointment was made.

Upon Esson's death, George Paxton Young, a Scot who was minister of Knox Church, Hamilton from 1849 to 1853, was appointed Professor of Mental and Moral Philosophy at Knox College. In 1864 he resigned his chair, perhaps because he could no longer subscribe to the Westminster Confession of Faith, and accepted the position of inspector of grammar schools for the province. In 1868 he again accepted a position in Knox College and took charge of the Preparatory Department in Mental Philosophy and Classics. This department he conducted until his appointment to the chair of mental and moral philosophy in University College in 1871. During the eighteen years of his professorship in University College he taught philosophy with an ability, enthusiasm, and success which have probably never been surpassed. His death in 1889 was marked by a large issue of the student newspaper, the *Varsity*, with tribute after tribute. Educated in the school of Scottish realism he became increasingly critical of it and adopted a position close to the idealism of T. H. Green.

The outstanding and most productive Presbyterian theologian of this period was Michael Willis, described by D. C. Masters as "a scholar of some eminence." Born in Greenock, Scotland in 1798, he studied Latin and Greek at the University of Glasgow and showed such promise that he was nominated for the professorship of Greek at the University of St. Andrews, an appointment he did not receive. Willis studied theology at the Divinity Hall of the Old Light Burghers at Perth, and in 1821 he was ordained minister of Renfield Street Church, Glasgow. While a parish minister he also taught theology and became recognized as one of the leading theological scholars of his day. In 1839 he received an honorary doctor of divinity degree from Glasgow University. That same year the Secessionists reunited with the Church of Scotland, but in 1843 he left along with Thomas Chalmers and 400 other ministers over the question of patronage, the cause of the original secession. A speech Willis made at the 1845 Free Church Assembly against a minister charged with teaching semi-pelagian doctrines brought him to the notice of the entire church. This address was regarded by many as an eloquent defence of Presbyterian teaching.

During the last two years of his ministry in Glasgow, Willis was outspoken on the subject of slavery. He believed that money donated by American slaves to the Free Church cause ought to be returned. This brought him into conflict with his fellow ministers and may have been the reason he was passed over for the vacant position of Professor of Divinity in the Free Church College. Willis also opposed the illustrious Thomas Chalmers who argued against state provision for the poor.

The whole problem of the poor, Willis contended, could not be solved by acts of individuals or even by the co-operative action of the churches. Governments should organize relief on a national scale: "a direct responsibility lies on the body politic for the care of its destitute members; a responsibility which it may not wisely nor righteously devolve on sectional Churches, or ecclesiastical functionaries."[51]

In 1845 Willis was sent as a deputy of the Free Church to Canada, and two years later accepted an appointment as Professor of Theology at Knox College. He became principal in 1857, and in 1863 he received an honorary Doctor of Laws degree from Queen's University at a convocation at which John A. Macdonald was similarly honoured. Willis continued to teach until his retirement in 1870 when he returned with his wife to Britain to live in London. He died in 1879.

Michael Willis lectured in systematic theology, Biblical criticism, church history, and pastoral theology. He was well read in Reformation and post-Reformation theology, the *Institutes* of Calvin in Latin, and the works of Maestricht, Francis Turretin, William Ames, and Hermann Witsius. One of the texts he used in his course was the three-volume set of George Hill's *Lectures in Divinity*. Among the books which he donated to Knox College Library when he retired were Schleiermacher's *Brief Outline of the Study of Theology*, Neander's *Church History*, James McCosh's *The Method of the Divine Government*, and Sir William Hamilton's edition of Thomas Reid's works. Although he was undoubtedly familiar with Scottish Common Sense Realism, it does not figure prominently in his theological writing.

Willis had a special interest in patristics. Principal William Caven noted in his obituary notice in the *Knox College Monthly*, "His knowledge of Patristic Literature far surpassed that of most Presbyterian divines," and was not equalled by many others.[52] In 1865 he published a *Collectanea graeca et latine: selections from the Greek and Latin Fathers: with notes, biographical and illustrative for classroom use*, an earlier version of which had been used in the 1850s. Willis believed that every theological student ought to have some acquaintance with patristic literature in the original language "to test the references so often made to the authority of the fathers, both in historic questions and questions of doctrine and interpretation."[53] In his collection each selection from patristic literature is prefaced by a short introduction which demonstrates Willis's familiarity with the secondary literature.

In his theology, Willis was a staunch Calvinist with a polemical but not narrow bent of mind, and on the whole he was charitable to those who conscientiously differed from him.[54] Like most Calvinists he adhered to the scriptural principle, that is, the affirmation of the final authority of Scripture in matters of faith and life. He held that the Bible should be read in the original languages "critically and exegetically." In his class on biblical criticism, he covered such topics as manuscripts and versions and introduced his students to the principles of hermeneutics, employing as the text Thomas Hartwell Horne's *Introduction to the Critical Study and Knowledge of the Holy Scriptures*. Willis stressed the importance of hermeneutics and there are striking similarities with contemporary emphases. In an 1860 closing term lecture "New Testament Ethics: Questions Solved," which dealt with the issue of slavery and attempts by some to support it from the New Testament writings, Willis said: "The men who seek to serve their cause by such a reading of the Bible as coincides with their selfish interests care little for your hermeneutics; but it is all important that the public teacher should know how to save the sacred page from being a shelter to the extortioner."[55] Willis showed a familiarity with German scholarship yet he was noticeably cautious about it because of its "spirit of lax speculation on the canon of scripture and its inspired authority."[56] For Willis, the importance of Scripture was its witness to Christ. In a sermon on the passage, "Come to me all you who are weary," he said, "We may come to the Bible, come to church, and to the sacramental table, and not, after all, have come to Christ. What does He say? He does not say, Come to the Bible, though He invites us to 'search the Scriptures,' but He says, 'Come unto Me, all ye that labour and are heavy laden, and I will give you rest.'"[57]

Willis embraced the main features of Reformed covenant theology. The holy and sovereign God was pleased to deal with humanity by means of covenant. God made a covenant of works with humankind, and the breach of that covenant had universal effects. In Adam all sin; therefore, in Adam all die. Christ is appointed the mediator of a new covenant and he fulfills its condition. He renders the obedience which Adam failed to render and achieves righteousness for us. In a sermon on "Adam and Christ," Willis states that we may not question the wisdom or equity of the arrangement by which one was constituted the representative of many. We know that the judge of all the earth must needs do right.[58] Then Willis turns "to the brighter side of the picture." The covenant of redemption in Christ more than retrieves our loss. Each representative head affects the whole body of the represented: "The entire seed of Adam in one case, so death has come on the all: the entire seed of Christ in the other, so the all inherit eternal life."[59] Willis is even prepared to suggest that "the finally saved *may be* more in number than the finally lost," but he immediately adds that there is no ground in the passage for the assertion that the whole human race is redeemed by the second Adam. Still Christ's obedience avails to a far greater effect than simply retrieving our loss, investing every pardoned one with a title to eternal life. Salvation is sovereign:

> emanating from no necessity in the Divine nature, but according to the purpose of His own will. Grace chose the persons; grace found the Surety; grace applies the redemption as well as devised it; not only proffering the gift, but moving the soul to accept it; and no less securing to its objects the end of their faith in the complete salvation of their souls, than working in them to will and to do of God's good pleasure.[60]

Willis emphasizes that human activity is not dispensed with or superseded by grace. One takes hold of the covenant of grace by faith, and faith unites one to Christ.[61]

In Willis's views of election, one can detect a subtle shift especially compared with Thomas McCulloch's views. Willis's language is more moderate, the tone softer, and the emphasis on election rather than reprobation. The doctrine of election appears to have become less and less a subject of preaching, for Willis complains that preachers who are evangelical give little or no place to the doctrine of sovereign grace. Christ, he states, preached eternal electing love and the Apostles embraced this doctrine, but it appears to be judged inexpedient to follow these precedents. Of those who are thus minded, Willis asks: "May not your philosophy, as well as your theology, be at fault?"[62] As he wrote elsewhere, election may be denied on earth, but it is confessed in heaven.[63]

In his discussion of election, Willis indicates a preference for a middle position or at least what he regards as the middle. He says that we must guard against extremes. On the one hand we are required to set forth the Gospel message in terms as encouraging as truth will permit, declaring the good news to every creature and not wantonly limiting universal terms; on the other hand, we must neither hide any part of the counsel of God nor mutilate the scheme of grace by adapting the revelation of divine sovereignty to human prejudices.

Willis holds that much error on the subject of election arises from confounding the free self-determining will of God with arbitrary and capricious acting. God's will, however, Willis says, is never exercised except in full harmony with all his moral perfections, as Ephesians 1:5 states: "He has predestinated us according to the good pleasure of his will."[64] Yet it is a presumption to suppose that God must be merciful to all; that is, merciful in pardoning and saving every sinful creature. Yet Willis is quick to add that we must make a distinction between the ground of the condemnation of a sinner and the ground of election. It is not sovereignty that is the cause of condemnation, though election is the cause of salvation. No reason can be given for the salvation of sinners but that so it has pleased God. But it is not so with those who perish; the ground of their condemnation is their sin.[65]

Like McCulloch, Willis criticizes those who adopt a doctrine of universal redemption, but again there is a subtle shift. He poses two questions: (1) Does Scripture warrant us to say that Christ has atoned for all, the believing and unbelieving alike? (2) Does our declaring this, either in the sense in which those who deny election explain the design of the Atonement, or that of those who hold a special election along with an indefinite atonement, give us any advantage in addressing sinners? For Willis the first question resolves itself into a question of exegesis. There can be no dispute that Christ in some sense of the expression gave himself "a ransom for all." Yet these words do not mean that Christ has died to make salvation sure to all. Phrases such as the above are not to be taken in the sense of absolute universality. Along with Professor Moses

Stuart, Willis says that "all" means Jews and Gentiles alike, people of all nations. Christ, Willis states, lives for all, in that sense in which he died for all, for people of all nations, of all conditions, of all characters. Yet we would be false comforters were we to say that all shall be effectually drawn to the Saviour.

Lest one is left with the impression that Willis was an academic Calvinist intellectual, his anti-slavery activity is worth noting. In May 1851 he represented the Anti-Slavery Society at the annual meeting of the Foreign Anti-Slavery Society held in New York, speaking with such notable ministers as Henry Ward Beecher. (Beecher took up most of the three hours. At one point in the meeting, Beecher asked the rhetorical question, "Who would send a slave back?" Apparently someone shouted, "I would." Beecher then rephrased his question, "Would anyone in his right senses send him back?" This was greeted with loud cheers.) Willis lamented the aloofness of the Episcopalian, Presbyterian, and Baptist ministers to the abolition cause. He himself helped Mr. William King who ministered to the Buxton charge near Chatham and conducted the first Communion service among the black people. Three young men from this charge later attended Knox College and one of them, John R. Riley, graduated in theology in 1867.[66]

Theology After 1870

Perry Miller has spoken of the radical revolution which took place in the American mind in the two or three decades after the Civil War: "Scottish Realism vanished from the American colleges, leaving not a rack behind."[67]

The disappearance of Scottish realism was less complete in Canada, but it was dramatic enough. Why this sudden change? Fashions do change, or as A. N. Whitehead put it: a philosophy is never refuted, it is only abandoned to be taken up later in another form. Yet the reasons are surely deeper. It became increasingly clear that this school of philosophy could not withstand the barrage of questions posed by the age of Darwin and Huxley. Professor Tracy in an article, "The Scottish Philosophy" in 1895 in the *University of Toronto Quarterly* noted: "However sincere their purpose, and however great their ability, they have not succeeded in … solving the epistemological enigma which has puzzled all modern philosophy. The question: How does mind know its object? and what is the relation in which mind stands to the material world? are almost left where they were before."[68] Common Sense philosophy had made theology static and lifeless so that a new theological turn was virtually inevitable. It is perhaps no mystery then that at the end of the century teachers of philosophy and theology turned with such enthusiasm to evolutionary idealism, the social gospel and the "religion of feeling."[69] As with any movement there are pluses and minuses. The major minus was what has been rather barbarously labelled "immanentism," the view that the world can be understood from within itself, and not from any being or principle supposed to operate from without. Immanentism became the prevailing view in philosophy and theology.

In 1872 John Watson, a student of Edward Caird, arrived in Kingston to teach philosophy at Queen's; he continued in this position for fifty years, retiring in 1922. John Clark Murray had vacated the chair Watson assumed and Murray went to McGill, where he gave Sir William Dawson endless trouble because Dawson thought he was getting someone who was still Common Sense but had also become an idealist. In Toronto, George Paxton Young had converted to the philosophical idealism of T. H. Green. In 1877, G. M. Grant, who had studied under Edward Caird in Glasgow and as early as 1867 had lectured at the Halifax YMCA on "Reformers of the Nineteenth Century" (Carlyle, Wordsworth, and Coleridge), became principal of Queen's. In 1899, another student of Edward Caird, T. B. Kilpatrick, went to Manitoba College as Professor of Philosophy and Apologetics and later to Knox College. The sweep was almost complete. It was now time for what Brian Fraser has called the "Presbyterian Progressives."

The unknown author of the *Letter to the Hebrews* ends his long list of the heroes of the faith with the question, "And what more shall I say? For time would fail me to tell of Gideon, Barak, Samson, Jephthah, of David and Samuel and the prophets" (11:32). Similarly, there is simply not time to speak of other Presbyterian theologians or to tell the next part of the story. This essay began with the question, Can we speak of a distinctively Canadian Presbyterian theology? It is evident that the writers noted here did not seek the deliberate cultivation of a Canadian theology, yet they produced a theology "with a local habitation and a name" which is indeed worthy of our respect and careful attention. Their work is a distinctive and significant contribution to Canadian life and culture.

NOTES

1. If John Watson, professor of philosophy at Queen's University, Kingston, from 1872-1922 and the author of several studies of Kant's philosophy, had been asked this question, he would have replied, "Definitely not."

2. S. F. Wise, "Sermon Literature," in J. M. Bumsted, ed., *Canadian History Before Confederation. Essays and Interpretation.* (Georgetown: Irwin-Dorsey, 1979), 248ff.

3. Wise, "Sermon Literature," 249.

4. Gerald R. Cragg, "The Present Position and the Future Prospects of Canadian Theology," *Canadian Journal of Theology* 1 (1955): 5.

5. Leslie Armour and Elizabeth Trott, *The Faces of Reason* (Waterloo: Waterloo Lutheran University Press, 1981).

6. Ramsay Cook, *The Regenerators: Social Criticism in Late Victorian English Canada* (Toronto: University of Toronto Press, 1985).

7. A. Brian McKillop, *A Disciplined Intelligence* (Montreal: McGill-Queen's University Press, 1979), and *Contours of Canadian Thought* (Toronto: University of Toronto Press, 1987).

8. Ramsay Cook, *The Regenerators*, 6.

9. Sydney E. Ahlstrom, "The Romantic Religious Revolution and the Dillemas of Religious History," *Church History* 46 (1977): 149-70.

10. Sydney E. Ahlstrom, "The Scottish Philosophy and American Theology," *Church History* 24 (1955): 257-72.

11. Ahlstrom, "Romantic Religious Revolution," 149-70.

12. Ahlstrom, "The Scottish Philosophy and American Theology," 268.

13. Armour and Trott, *Faces of Reason*, 4. See also McKillop, *A Disciplined Intelligence*, 24-32, on "The Scottish Legacy."

14. Cf. George Rawlyk, *Ravished by the Spirit* (Kingston and Montreal: McGill-Queen's University Press, 1984), 8. There is an extensive literature on Alline. See J. M. Bumsted, *Henry Alline 1748-1784*, Canadian Biographical Studies (Toronto: University of Toronto Press, 1971); James Beverley, "Introduction"

to *The Life and Journal of The Rev. Mr. Henry Alline* (Hantsport, NS: Lancelot Press, 1982), 9-25; Maurice W. Armstrong, *The Great Awakening in Nova Scotia 1776- 1809* (Hartford: The American Society of Church History, 1948); Gordon Stewart and George Rawlyk, *A People Highly Favoured of God: The Nova Scotia Yankees and the American Revolution* (Toronto: Macmillan, 1972), 79-97; H. H. Walsh, *The Christian Church in Canada* (Toronto: Ryerson, 1968), 19-21; Fred Cogswell, "Henry Alline (1748-1784)," in *Literary History of Canada*, ed. Carl F. Klinck (Toronto: University of Toronto Press, 1965), 74-77; and James S. Thomson, "Religious and Theological Writings," in Klinck, *Literary History of Canada*, 551-52.

15. Halifax, 1902, 23, quoted by H. H. Walsh in *The Christian Church in Canada*, 6.

16. Rawlyk, *Ravished by the Spirit*, 13.

17. Alline, *Life and Journal*, 30.

18. William James, *Varieties of Religious Experience* (London: Longmans, Green, 1920), 173-75, 217-20.

19. Alline, *Life and Journal*, 88.

20. Armstrong, *Great Awakening*, 86.

21. Quoted in George Patterson, *Memoir of the Rev. James Mcgregor, etc.* (Philadelphia: Joseph M. Wilson, 1859), 351.

22. Rawlyk, *Ravished by the Spirit*, 15.

23. See J. L. Blau, "Cabala," *The Encyclopedia of Philosophy*, vol. 2, ed. Paul Edwards (New York: Macmillan & The Free Press, 1967), 1-3.

24. Henry Alline, *The Anti-Traditionalist* (Halifax, 1783), 24 quoted by Armstrong, *The Great Awakening*, 96.

25. Alline, *Two Mites*, 45.

26. Alline, *Two Mites*, 15, quoted in Maurice W. Armstrong, *The Great Awakening*, 103.

27. John Wesley, Letters, VIII, p. 182 quoted in Maurice W. Armstrong, *The Great Awakening*, 104.

28 H. H. Walsh, *Christian Church in Canada*, 121. See also S. D. Clark, *Church and Sect in Canada* (Toronto: University of Toronto Press, 1948), xi.

29. H. Northrop Frye, "An Introduction" to Thomas McCulloch, *The Stepsure Letters*, New Canadian Library No. 16 (Toronto: McClelland & Stewart, 1960), ix.

30. "Archibald Bruce," *Dictionary of National Biography* (DNB), vol. 7, 89. The collected edition of Archibald Bruce's works is to be found in the Library of New College, Edinburgh. Among these is *The Catechism Modernized*, 1791. To give the reader a taste of Bruce's satire, the first two questions and answers are reproduced. Since it can no longer be assumed that the corresponding questions of the *Shorter Catechism* are known, these are given first in italics: ("Quest. What is man's chief end? Answ. "Man's chief end is to glorify God and enjoy Him forever.") "Quest. What is the chief end of a modern clergyman? Answ. To obtain a presentation, and enjoy the benefice and favour of the patron all the days of his life. (Q.2. What rule hath God given to direct us how we may glorify and enjoy him? A. The word of God, which is contained in the scriptures of the Old and New Testaments, is the only rule to direct us how we may glorify and enjoy him") Q. What rule is given to direct him in attaining this desirable end? A. The established

maxims of church polity contained in the scriptures of the old canon law and the new acts of parliament and assembly, illustrated by the speeches, writings and practices of the true sons of the church" (9).

31. Thomas McCulloch, *Calvinism, The Doctrine of the Scriptures* (Glasgow: William Collins, n.d.) The copy in the National Library, Ottawa, has a handwritten subscription dated 1848.

32. "John Taylor," *Schaff-Herzog Religious Encyclopedia*, vol. 11, 284-85, *DNB*, vol. 55, 439-40.

33. *DNB*, vol. 61, 28-30.

34. McCulloch, *Calvinism*, xiv.

35. McCulloch, *Calvinism*, 24.

36. McCulloch, *Calvinism*, 149.

37. McCulloch, *Calvinism*, 151.

38. Armour and Trott, *The Faces of Reason*, 65.

39. McCulloch, *Calvinism*, 255.

40. McCulloch, *Calvinism*, 257.

41. McCulloch, *Calvinism*, 257.

42. McCulloch, *Calvinism*, 269-70.

43. Alasdair MacIntyre, *Whose Justice? Which Rationality?* (Notre Dame, IN: University of Notre Dame Press, 1988), 324.

44. MacIntyre, *Whose Justice?*, 248.

45. Daniel F. Rice, "Natural Theology and the Scottish Philosophy in the Thought of Thomas Chalmers" in *Scottish Journal of Theology* 24 (1971): 24.

46. J. H. S. Burleigh, *A Church History of Scotland* (London: Oxford University Press, 1960), 293.

47. Ahlstrom, "The Scottish Philosophy," 269.

48. Hugh Watt, *Thomas Chalmers and the Disruption* (Edinburgh, 1943), 6, quoted by Sydney Ahlstrom, "Scottish Philosophy," 259.

49. Quebec: J. Neilson, 1799, 8.

50. Ahlstrom, "Romantic Religious Revolution," 150.

51. Michael Willis, *Pulpit Discourses* (London: James Nisbet & Co.), 382.

52. William Caven, "The Rev. Michael Willis, D.D., LL.D.," *Knox College Monthly* 4 (January 1886): 99.

53. Michael Willis, *Collectanea graeca et latine* (Toronto: Henry Rowsell, 1865), iii.

54. Caven, "Willis," 98.

55. Willis, *Pulpit Discourses*, 366.

56. *Presbyterian Record*, November 1849, quoted by Richard Vaudry, "Theology and Education in Early Victorian Canada, Knox College, Toronto, 1844-1861," *Studies in Religion / Sciences Religieuses* 17 (June 1988): 445.

57. Willis, *Pulpit Discourses*, 28.

58. This sermon was preached on the occasion of the death of Henry Esson in April, 1853. Willis, *Pulpit Discourses*, 242.

59. Willis, *Pulpit Discourses*, 245.

60. Willis, *Pulpit Discourses*, 246.

61. Willis, *Pulpit Discourses*, 212, 79.

62. Willis, *Pulpit Discourses*, 333.

63. Willis, *Pulpit Discourses*, 116.

64. Willis, *Pulpit Discourses*, 117.

65. Willis, *Pulpit Discourses*, 122-23. The position which Willis adopts is the softer "infralapsarian" one compared with "supralapsarianism" which ascribed both election *and* reprobation to God's sovereignty.

66. I am indebted for this material to David R. Nicholson, *Michael Willis: Missionary Statesman, Social Activist, Christian Educator, and Reformed Theologian* (M.A. thesis, Toronto School of Theology, n.d.), 58-85.

67. Perry Miller, ed. *American Thought, Civil War to World War I* (New York, 1954), ix quoted by Sydney Ahlstrom, "The Romantic Religious Revolution and the Dilemmas of Religious History," *Church History* 46 (1977): 150, n. 4.

68. F. Tracy, "The Scottish Philosophy," *University of Toronto Quarterly* 2 (Nov. 1895): 1-15 quoted by A. B. McKillop, *A Disciplined Intelligence*, 57.

69. Ahlstrom, "The Scottish Philosophy," 269.

Canadian Presbyterians and Princeton Seminary, 1850-1900

Richard W. Vaudry

Writing in August 1878 on the occasion of the death of Charles Hodge, the editor of the *Presbyterian Record* commented that "to say that he was the greatest theologian America has produced, is not to say enough. No theologian of the age was better known or more universally respected. His great work on *Systematic Theology* is a text book in many lands."[1] While not all would agree with the editor's judgment, his comments certainly indicate the high regard in which Hodge was held by his Canadian contemporaries; perhaps no other American theologian had as much influence among nineteenth-century Canadian Presbyterians. His only serious challenger to that claim would be his eventual successor in the chair of theology at Princeton, Benjamin Breckenridge Warfield. Together with the other members of the faculty of Princeton Theological Seminary, they constituted the single most important American theological influence on Canadian Presbyterianism. Still, the dominant external influences—both ecclesiastical and theological—were undoubtedly Scottish. Scotland's traditions, people, and ideas had dictated the church's controversies, filled its pulpits, and guided its thinking. Its disruptions and reunions of the nineteenth century mirrored such Scottish events as the Disruption of 1843 and not such American ones as the New School/Old School schism of 1837, the reunion in 1868, or the excision of the Southern Presbyterians on the eve of the Civil War. Nonetheless, while American influences, though not dominant, were persistent, exhibiting increasing strength as the century wore on, the relationship was not entirely one directional. Canadians were joint participants in ventures with Princeton theologians, and Canadian scholarship, particularly that of John William Dawson of McGill was noted (and quoted) by American theologians at Princeton and elsewhere.

Before considering in some detail the relationship between Canadian Presbyterians and Princeton Seminary, it is necessary to pause and briefly examine the place of Princeton in American Presbyterianism and the general contours of its theology. In so doing, it is worth noting that in theological and philosophical terms, Scotland, Canada, and Princeton constituted a North Atlantic intellectual triangle.[2] Princeton College and Seminary were built on some of the same Scottish foundations as was Canadian Presbyterianism. From John Witherspoon to James McCosh Scottish influences at Princeton College were readily apparent. While none of the Princeton theologians under consideration were born in Scotland they did draw on certain Scottish traditions in their work, and many had warm personal relationships with their counterparts in Scotland.[3]

Princeton Seminary and the Princeton Theology

Princeton was the largest and arguably the most influential Presbyterian seminary in nineteenth-century America. By 1912 it had enrolled 1,000 more students than any other American seminary and by the 1930s had graduated nearly 6,500 students.[4] Its influence was confined neither to the Presbyterian Church nor to the national boundaries of the United States. Five bishops of the Protestant Episcopal Church were Princeton Seminary graduates, and the writings of the various Princeton theologians in book form and in the pages of the variously titled *Princeton Review* spread the seminary's influence beyond its graduates.[5] Indeed, the bulk of Hodge, Warfield, and Machen's writings are still in print.

From its founding in 1812 until its reorganization in 1929 (when Machen et al. left to found Westminster Seminary, Philadelphia), Princeton Seminary was dominated by four men: Archibald Alexander (1772-1851), Charles Hodge (1797-1878), Benjamin Breckinridge Warfield (1851-1921) and J. Gresham Machen (1881-1937). Thus John Gerstner has commented that "in a sense Hodge laid the foundation, Warfield perfected the building, and Machen spent most of his time moving it from one location to another."[6] Other men, to be sure, were important to the seminary's development—perhaps most notably Archibald Alexander Hodge (1823-1886), son of Charles Hodge and his immediate successor in the chair of theology, and Francis Landey Patton (1843-1932), Professor of the Relations of Philosophy and Science to the Christian Religion, Woodrow Wilson's predecessor as President of Princeton University and later President of Princeton Seminary.[7] Yet Alexander, Hodge, Warfield, and Machen were the most influential.

Of course, these men lived in distinct eras, faced separate challenges and fought different battles. They had different interests and possessed distinct personalities. Warfield, for example, unlike either Hodge or Machen was not much involved in controversy in the courts of the Presbyterian Church. Moreover, he was a postmillennialist and accepted theistic evolution, which Hodge would not.[8] He never wrote a systematic theology, relying instead on Hodge's *magnum opus*, and spent a considerable amount of his time fighting the theology of Albrecht Ritschl, on the one hand, and such things as subjectivism, perfectionism, and what he called counterfeit miracles, on the other. Perhaps more than the others he was the consummate polemicist—most of his work appeared originally in the form of articles and reviews. Hodge, as David Wells has shown, was concerned primarily with such doctrines as original sin, the imputation of Adam's sin, and regeneration, and in so doing did battle with various contemporaries such as the New School theologian Nathaniel Taylor of Yale, Horace Bushnell, Charles Finney, and the Unitarians.[9]

Despite their different foes, Alexander, Hodge, Warfield, and Machen all regarded themselves as heralds and apologists for Protestant orthodoxy. Andrew Hoffecker's comment concerning Warfield is appropriate: "His task at Princeton, like his predecessors', was to produce ministers who were so thoroughly trained in Reformed theology that they could effectively proclaim the gospel and refute any teaching that did not conform to the high standard of Calvinistic orthodoxy."[10] Each regarded himself as building on and continuing the theological tradition of his predecessors. The senior theologian often saw himself passing the torch to his successors. Thus Archibald Alexander called Charles Hodge to his death bed and presented his walking stick to him with the words, "You must hand this to your successor in office, that it may be handed down as a kind of symbol of orthodoxy."[11]

Whatever differences may appear among the four (owing chiefly to the distinctions noted earlier), they shared a number of basic theological affirmations. Mark Noll, in the introduction to his anthology of Princeton writings, has identified four pillars of the Princeton position: their attitude to Scripture, their Reformed confessionalism, their commitment to the Scottish Common Sense philosophy, and their emphasis on religious experience. It is perhaps best to alter Noll's order somewhat and first consider Princeton's commitment to Scottish realism, because this constituted their epistemological foundation. The Scottish philosophy of Common Sense was developed in the eighteenth century by Thomas Reid and James Beattie as an antidote to the idealism of Bishop Berkeley and the skepticism of David Hume. John Witherspoon took it to Princeton in the 1760s and it continued as the dominant philosophical perspective at Princeton College and Seminary throughout the nineteenth century and was infused with renewed vigour by its last great American proponent, James McCosh, who became President of Princeton College in 1868. It is worth noting that use of Scottish Common Sense did not imply a commitment to any particular theological system. It was a common weapon in the apologetic arsenal of English evangelicals of the Clapham Sect variety, Scottish ones like Thomas Chalmers, and was common stock of Canadian Free Church Presbyterians (among others).[12] It had been developed, however, by theological moderates in the Church of Scotland and was regularly employed by those at more liberal schools than Princeton, like Harvard, Yale, and Oberlin. And it was by no means the preserve of the Presbyterians.[13]

The major contribution of Common Sense was in the area of memory and perception. It asserted that the observer, in the act of observing or remembering, perceived what was actually there without ideas or points of view interposing themselves between subject and object. This Common Sense perception was usually linked to a

Baconian inductive scientific method in which the correct method of procedure was the gathering and ordering of objectively perceived facts. "Speculative hypotheses" were to be avoided. Thus the mind could arrive at objective and universal truth. Accordingly, the Princeton apologists constructed an argument from design, asserted the harmony of science and Scripture, and used what today might be called an evidentialist approach. Yet lest we portray them in sharp, angular relief, it is worth noting that Warfield, for example, was very astute in uncovering the philosophical presuppositions of those who "denied the supernatural and wanted to reinterpret Christianity on naturalistic terms."[14] And, as John Gerstner has pointed out, Hodge was fully aware of the noetic effects of sin.[15] Moreover, "Hodge was not a rationalist but an advocate of Christian rationality," and "what is crystal clear is that Hodge recognized the absolute necessity of supernatural, divine illumination for anyone who was ever 'persuaded' savingly that the Bible is the Word of God."[16]

The Princeton commitment to this Common Sense/Baconian synthesis, as George Marsden has suggested, may well have contributed to their idea of the inerrancy of Scripture. Marsden notes that Hodge saw the theologian's task as one of systematically arranging the "hard facts" of Scripture and that "such a scientific model, combined with a high view of God's role in inspiring the Biblical writers, fit extremely well with the conclusion that God would do nothing less than reveal the facts of Scripture with an accuracy that would satisfy the most scrupulous modern scientific standards."[17] At the same time, the Princeton theologians took seriously the humanity of Scripture and rejected any theories of mechanical dictation.[18]

Princeton was also noted for its Reformed confessionalism. Its theologians regarded themselves as standing in the tradition of sixteenth- and seventeenth-century Calvinism, affirming its major doctrines and drawing on its English, Dutch, and Swiss theologies and confessional statements. The seminary used the theological institutes of the seventeenth century scholastic Calvinist Francis Turretin as its principal theology text until Hodge's own *Systematic*

Theology appeared in 1873.[19] Yet Turretin was by no means the only reformed theologian consulted, and while he was a major, he was not the dominant theological influence that some have suggested.[20]

Though they sometimes appear to be arid rationalists, these Princeton theologians always sought to combine high academic standards and precise theological thinking with a warm-hearted evangelical piety. They balanced these concerns in their own lives, emphasized them in their writings, and sought to foster them in their students.[21]

The four pillars which thus constituted the Princeton theology were, as Noll has pointed out, "simply the common intellectual affirmations of the day."[22] What seems distinctive about Princeton, however, was its particular blend of these traditions and the fact that it continued to affirm and defend these affirmations after they had ceased to be fashionable in many other quarters.

Princeton and Canada

The earliest substantial contact between Canada and Princeton Seminary arose because of the Free Church controversies of the 1840s. In late 1843 and early 1844 the newly formed Free Church of Scotland, in an effort to procure funds and the support of public opinion, sent deputies to tour North America. These delegates included William Cunningham, later Principal of New College, Edinburgh, and Robert Burns of Paisley, guiding force behind the Glasgow Colonial Society and later pastor of Knox Church, Toronto, and Professor of Church History and Christian Evidences at Knox College. Cunningham arrived at Princeton for the first of his visits in late December, 1843. By February of the following year, Burns and Henry Ferguson, an elder from Dundee, had been there, George Lewis of Ormiston was expected, and a rumour was circulating that Chalmers himself might visit the following summer. All of this prompted James Waddell Alexander to comment that "the Scotch delegates thicken upon us."[23] Chalmers never did make the trip across the Atlantic, but Burns, Cunningham, and the others were warmly received. Money was raised for the Free Church, and Charles Hodge subsequently wrote an article in the *Biblical*

Repertory and Princeton Review on the "Claims of the Free Church of Scotland."[24] Cunningham returned to Princeton in March of 1844, "chiefly," so J. W. Alexander tells us, "to gather some hints about theological instruction."[25]

James Waddell Alexander, eldest son of Archibald Alexander and himself a professor at Princeton College and later at the Seminary, has given us a valuable glimpse into their visit. Writing to Reverend John Hall, he offered the following description of Burns's first visit to Princeton in February, 1844:

> Burns, you know, is in Witherspoon's pulpit at Paisley; he has been settled there thirty-three years. He is one of the most learned men in Scotland—had edited Haleyburton's works, Woodrow's history, and is author of Memoirs of Prof. McGill. Burns's manner in the pulpit is more outré than Cunningham's. But his sermon was noble, rich, original, scriptural, and evangelical, and in diction elegant: and his closing prayer was seraphic.[26]

Burns returned to Princeton in March and again preached, prompting Alexander to comment that [in] "spite of my prejudices, I must say he preached ... one of the very noblest discourses I ever heard ... It was teeming with Scripture, but even the most familiar texts were brilliant by their setting and connexion."[27] Burns kept up some connections with Alexander, for three years later, by which time Burns was settled in Toronto, Alexander noted a visit by Burns to New York City, where Alexander was now pastor of Duane Street Presbyterian Church,[28] and remarking, "I think he has more exactness and extent of knowledge, and a greater outpouring of it in vehement and often affectionate discourse, than any man I ever met: unless I except Chancellor Kent, whom he resembles in his contempt of all conventionalities."[29] Alexander subsequently left his New York pastorate to become Professor of Ecclesiastical History at Princeton Seminary.

It is also known that Burns was an avid reader of the *Biblical Repertory and Princeton Review*, referring to it in a letter to Charles Hodge as "your quarterly visit" and adding that "I almost wish you were '*a monthly.*'"[30] George Paxton Young was also a reader of the *Princeton Review*. In 1855 Young wrote to its editor (Charles Hodge) offering for publication an article on Sir William Hamilton's "doctrine of Sensitive Perceptions *in particular*" adding that "I disagree with him [Hamilton] in almost every thing except the grand point of the immediacy of our sense perceptions."[31] It has also been established that Hodge's works—particularly his commentaries on Ephesians and Romans—were used as texts at Knox College.[32]

Thus there were a number of personal and literary connections between the Canadian Free Church and Princeton. Yet it appears that no Canadians went south to study at Princeton before the 1860s. The reasons for this are not entirely clear, but it may be surmised that the obstacles of distance and money were too great, the inducements too few. The men who were presenting themselves as ministerial candidates would find that Knox College under Willis, Burns, and Young provided a more than adequate theological education. Indeed the trend toward studying abroad seems to belong primarily to a later period. While there were few inducements for Canadians to attend Princeton in this early period, there were significant obstacles in the way of Americans entering the Canadian Free Church. New School ministers were not considered fully orthodox in their theology (interestingly enough, on the very points that Hodge and Cunningham had "collaborated," i.e., the imputation of Adam's sin and Christ's righteousness). On the other hand, Old School ministers, while their theology was considered acceptable, had to be sound on the slavery issue, which the Canadian Free Church firmly opposed.[33]

However, in the period following the union of the Free and United Presbyterian synods in 1861 and the end of the U.S. Civil War in 1865, increasing numbers of Canadian students attended Princeton. Charles William Gordon, in his biography of James Robertson, ascribed this migration to deficiencies at Knox:

> The work being done in Knox College at this period was not up to that high standard demanded by the ministry of the Presbyterian Church, and there was, consequently, considerable dissatisfaction among the students. Hence, when the College opened in the autumn of 1866, a large number of Canadian students found their way to Princeton, which, under the Hodges, was then attracting men from both continents.[34]

Robertson himself felt that if Knox College was "to serve the purposes of the Canadian Presbyterian Church, it must be overturned and laid on better principles," adding that "I hope they may start a college at Montreal and get some men from Britain."[35] He was also concerned that many Canadians who attended Princeton would be induced to remain in the United States by the greater opportunities it presented—which in fact happened in many cases.

Whether the deficiencies at Knox were the reasons for so many Canadians attending Princeton is an open question. Certainly changes had occurred at the Toronto college since the 1850s. After the union of the Free and United Presbyterian Synods in 1861, Knox absorbed the United Presbyterian seminary which had been established at London in the 1840s under William Proudfoot. Certainly, the 1860s and the early 1870s were a transitional period for Knox, between the settled times of the 1850s and those of the post-1875 period. Accordingly, Burns resigned as Professor of Church History and Christian Evidences in 1864; George Paxton Young resigned the same year and Willis stepped down as principal in 1870. William Caven was appointed Professor of Exegetical Theology (which included evidences, Biblical criticism, and the interpretation of Scripture) in 1866, becoming principal in 1873. William Gregg took up the chair of apologetics in 1872 and William McLaren was appointed Professor of Systematic Theology the following year.[36] The appointments of Caven and McLaren in particular served as stabilizing forces at Knox until beyond the turn of the century. Moreover, while the Knox-Princeton connection had been established during the Free Church era, it was maintained and indeed deepened during the tenure of Caven and McLaren.

While it is clear that increasing numbers of Canadians attended Princeton Seminary in the last third of the nineteenth century, establishing precise figures and drawing a composite profile are problematical. However, it is possible to draw at least an impressionistic educational profile of the ministers in the Presbyterian Church in Canada. By far the most popular location for theological study was Knox, Toronto, followed at some distance by the second and third most popular places—Presbyterian College, Halifax, and

Presbyterian College, Montreal. Tied for fourth place were New College, Edinburgh, and Princeton Seminary.[37]

It is also difficult to generalize about the careers of these Canadians who attended Princeton. Several patterns emerge: some went to Princeton after graduating in arts in Canada; after study at Princeton, some returned directly to Canada to occupy pulpits; some served charges in the United States and then returned to Canada; some never returned to Canada; and some returned to Canada but then ended up in the United States.

Among the more prominent Canadian graduates of Princeton Seminary were George Leslie Mackay, missionary in Formosa, James Robertson, superintendent of missions in western Canada; William Cochrane of Zion Church, Brantford, moderator of the 1882 General Assembly and one of the guiding forces behind Home Missions; Louis Henry Jordan, author of a number of books on comparative religion;[38] and James Frederick McCurdy of University College, Toronto.[39]

Canadian students were also exposed to Princeton influences both inside and outside the classroom. The writings of Charles Hodge were in evidence in at least two of the Canadian seminaries. His *Systematic Theology* was used at Presbyterian College, Halifax, as were parts of Turretin's *Institutio theologiae elenticae*. At Presbyterian College, Montreal, the third-year systematics course included the American theologians Hodge and James Henley Thornwell, and the honours course used Hodge on the Atonement.[40] Donald Harvey MacVicar, Professor of Systematic Theology and Principal of the Presbyterian College, Montreal, was known as an admirer of Charles Hodge and as a defender of the inerrancy of Scripture.[41]

Princeton influences were, of course, far from absent at Knox College, Toronto. Two of its professors had completed part of their theological training at Princeton. James Ballantyne, after graduating from Princeton Seminary in 1883, studied in Edinburgh and Leipzig and was appointed to the chair of apologetics and church history at Knox College in 1896, succeeding William Gregg.[42] As well, George Livingstone Robinson, a native of New York State and a graduate of Princeton Seminary and the University of Leipzig, was appointed Professor of Old Testament Literature at Knox in 1896.[43] Robinson left Knox for McCormick Seminary in 1898 and was a contributor to *The Fundamentals*[44] on the subject of the unity of the Book of Isaiah.

The Knox-Princeton connection was anchored in the person of William Caven (1830-1904). Born in Wigtownshire, Scotland, he emigrated to southwestern Ontario in 1847, where he received his theological education at the United Presbyterian Theological Hall. He was ordained in the United Presbyterian Synod in 1852 and became Professor of Exegetics at Knox College in 1866. He was appointed principal in 1873, combining with that position the chair of New Testament Literature and Exegesis. He never produced a theological tome, but he did contribute articles to *The Presbyterian and Reformed Review* and served on its editorial board under the direction of B. B. Warfield.[45] He also contributed an article, "The Testimony of Christ to the Old Testament," to *The Fundamentals*, which appears to have been originally published in *The Presbyterian and Reformed Review*.[46] Caven's colleague and eventual successor as principal, William MacLaren, also had Princeton connections. He sat on the board of directors of the American Bible League along with Francis Landey Patton of Princeton and C. I. Scofield, and was vice-president of the Toronto branch of the Bible League along with many of the most important Canadian evangelical leaders.[47]

Moreover, two Princeton professors are known to have made the trek north to give special lectures at Knox. On at least two occasions, Francis Landey Patton, a native of Bermuda and a former student at the University of Toronto, Knox College, and Princeton Seminary, lectured at Knox. In 1885, at the close of the college session, he lectured on the "History of Theistic Discussion" and "the proper equipment of a Theological College."[48] At the Knox College Jubilee in October 1894 he spoke on "Supernatural Religion."[49] B. B. Warfield also ventured north in October 1895. He preached at St. James' Square Presbyterian Church in Toronto before beginning a week-long series of lectures at Knox College. He lectured twice a day—in the mornings on systematic theology and in the evenings on the inspiration of Scripture.[50]

The wider public at large also had access to Princeton via the writings of its professors. Notwithstanding the American editions which would have been accessible to those living in Canada, a number of Princeton publications were issued by Canadian publishers. In 1881 James Bain of Toronto published as a twenty-four-page pamphlet an article by Charles Hodge on "Arminianism and Grace," which had been originally published in the *Princeton Review*, with the comment:

> The Rev. Dr. Hodge, presumed to be the author, was distin-guished for the clearness of his views of Scripture truth, and acknowledged to have been the ablest writer on Systematic Theology in the present day—it is therefore with confidence we re-issue this tractate as a help to the promotion of scriptural views on the subject of which it treats.[51]

In 1887, Toronto publisher S. R. Briggs published an edition of B. B. Warfield's *An Introduction to the Textual Criticism of the New Testament*. At that time Warfield was teaching at Western Theologi-cal Seminary in Allegheny, Pennsylvania, but the following year he left for Princeton.[52]

Although there was a well-established connection between Princeton Seminary and Knox College, one of the more interesting ties to Princeton was through John William Dawson of McGill. His connection suggests that the lines of influence not only ran from Princeton to Canada but in the opposite direction as well. By the time of his main connection with Princeton in the 1870s, Dawson had been Principal of McGill for some fifteen years, had written extensively on geology, and had established a reputation as Cana-da's foremost natural scientist and as one of the leading anti-Darwinian critics in the English-speaking world. He was an active Presbyterian layperson who helped lay the foundations for the Dominion Evangelical Alliance.[53] It was not entirely surprising, then, that in 1878 Princeton tried to recruit Dawson as Professor of Geology, thus relieving Arnold Guyot of half of his teaching responsibilities.[54] This was not Dawson's first contact with

Princeton—either the College or the Seminary. Dawson and James McCosh of Princeton College corresponded concerning various subjects in the early 1870s. McCosh looked to Dawson for suggestions concerning his proposed school of science at Princeton. He also wanted Dawson to give a series of lectures on paleontology in the fall term, 1872. Dawson for his part tried to get Princeton to award his son an honorary degree—which it finally did in 1877, though only that of Bachelor of Science.[55]

Then in 1878 Professor Guyot expressed a desire to abandon the teaching of geology. The Princeton trustees were prepared to agree to this if "we can secure a man of eminence to take Paleontology with perhaps certain branches of biology."[56] The trustees wanted Dawson. The offer contained in a letter (March 23) was an attractive one: a reduced teaching load, thereby providing more time for research and travel; travel expenses to the fossil beds of Wyoming and Colorado; a salary of $3,000 from Princeton College; a house; and an offer from Princeton Theological Seminary for an annual series of lectures on the relationship of science and religion for which the Seminary would pay $1,000. The material inducements were thus very attractive. McCosh then brought to bear on the situation a series of other considerations (which are also interesting for their view of Providence). He thus wrote:

> We give you this call. It looks to me as if it were a call from God. It is unsought on your part. There is a concurrence of all parties in this place. The College and the Seminary unite in you not only cordially but with intense eagerness and earnestness. The friends of religion, anxious about the cause of Christ in these critical times will rejoice to hear of your acceptance. Your influence will reach over an immense body of young men in the College, in the School of Science, and in the Church. Your sphere of influence will have no bounds except those imposed by your strength.[57]

On April 4 McCosh again wrote to Dawson, imploring him to accept:

> The fact is that if you decline, which I hope you may not, we do not know where to look for a geologist of repute who is not a Darwinian. We feel it to be of vast moment not only for ourselves but for the country to have you in the United States to guide

opinion at this critical time. It is surely a providence that both the College and the Seminary have been able unanimously to unite on you. Vast consequences depend on your decision. I may be wrong but I believe you might with the Blessing have more weight over public opinion here than you have in Montreal. The United States are not after all so wild as England is. You might help to keep us stable on this continent.[58]

Two days later, Charles Hodge, then Chair of Princeton College's Board of Trustees, added his own arguments and weight to the persuasive process. He stressed the Presbyterian character of Princeton College, the warmer climate, and the great need for men like Dawson. "We are sadly in want in this country," he wrote, "of scientific men who are firm believers in the Bible. You cannot be more needed in Montreal than you are here."[59] Dawson declined the offer on April 15, 1878, writing to Hodge that the threat from Ultramontanism would keep him in Montreal, "for unless the gospel and the light of Modern Civilization can overcome popery in French Canada our whole system will break up."[60] McCosh continued to woo Dawson for the next few months, but by the fall of 1878 he had apparently given up trying to change Dawson's mind.[61]

Dawson's connections with Princeton did not end here. Between 1878 and 1881 he contributed eight articles to the *Princeton Review* on various aspects of the relationship of Christianity to science. At this point, however, the *Princeton Review* had nothing officially to do with the Seminary, though a few of its professors along with a number from Princeton College contributed articles.[62] Because of his stature as a Christian and scientist, Dawson was occasionally quoted as an authority by Princeton theologians. Perhaps the most interesting of these occurs in the controversial 1881 essay by A. A. Hodge and Warfield, "Inspiration," with its defence of verbal inspiration and its insistence on the inerrancy of the Bible's original autographs. In the section titled "Proof of the Doctrine," which Warfield wrote, Dawson (among others) is cited:

> The fact that at this date scientists of the rank of Faraday and Henry, of Dana, of Guyot and Dawson, maintain that there is no real conflict between the really ascertained facts of science and the first two chapters of Genesis, rightly interpreted, of itself

demonstrates that a supernatural intelligence must have directed the writing of those chapters.63

Dawson's experience was undoubtedly unique. Perhaps no other Canadian of his era was as highly regarded by the Princeton theologians as was the Principal of McGill. Certainly no other Canadian was quoted as often, nor were any others offered positions at the seminary.

The deaths of Dawson, MacVicar, Caven, and MacLaren, all occurring within a decade of each other, mark the close of the first phase in the relationship between Canadian Presbyterians and Princeton Seminary. Rooted in the Free Church era of the 1840s, nurtured and sustained in the second half of the nineteenth century, the Princeton influence in Canada, while not pervasive, was nonetheless continuous and strong. Its reformed confessionalism and evangelical piety meshed well with the Free Church tradition as it developed in the nineteenth and continued in the twentieth century.64 Though it is beyond the scope of this paper, it is worth noting with Keith Clifford that Princeton made a contribution to the dissidents' position during the debate over church union.65 Finally, it is clear that a number of Canadians with strong Princeton connections also contributed to *The Fundamentals*. While this is an interesting connection, more must be known about the nature of Canadian fundamentalism before any firm conclusions can be drawn from it. However, as one would expect, it is clear that the Princeton influence was generally on the side of conservatism within the Presbyterian Church in Canada—both theologically and ecclesiastically. In short, in an age of theological change and uncertainty, many Canadian Presbyterians looked south to Princeton for clear directions on Scripture, the Westminster Confession, and the defence of the faith.

NOTES

1. *Presbyterian Record*, August 1878, 205.

2. Cf. Marsden's comment that "from the time of the Puritans down through the awakening to the end of the nineteenth century British and American evangelicalism had been in many respects part of a single transatlantic movement." George Marsden, "Fundamentalism as an American Phenomenon, A Comparison with English Evangelicalism," *Church History* 46 (1977): 216.

3. See for example the relationship between Charles Hodge and William Cunningham of New College, Edinburgh. Robert Rainy and James Mackenzie, *Life of William Cunningham* (London, 1871), 205, and Charles Hodge, *The Orthodox doctrine regarding the extent of the atonement vindicated by C. Hodge. With a recommendary preface by Rev. Dr. Cunningham* (Edinburgh: John Johnston, 1846). *National Union Catalog, Pre-1956 Imprints*, vol. 249, 107.

4. Mark A. Noll, *The Princeton Theology 1812-1921* (Grand Rapids, MI: Baker, 1983), 19-20. The exact total was 6,386.

5. Noll, *Princeton Theology*, 20. See the table in Noll, 24 re: Princeton periodicals.

6. John H. Gerstner, "The Contributions of Charles Hodge, B. B. Warfield, and J. Gresham Machen to the Doctrine of Inspiration," in *Challenges to Inerrancy*, ed. Gordon Lewis and Bruce Demarest (Chicago, 1984), 372.

7. Francis Landey Patton, *Dictionary of American Biography*, vol. 14, 315-16.

8. W. Andrew Hoffecker, *Piety and the Princeton Theologians* (Grand Rapids, MI: Baker, 1981). Hoffecker on Warfield in David Wells, ed., *Reformed Theology in America: A History of its Modern Development* (Grand Rapids, MI: Eerdmans, 1985), and David N. Livingstone, "B. B. Warfield, the Theory of Evolution and Early Fundamentalism," *The Evangelical Quarterly* 58 (1986): 69-83.

9. David Wells, "Charles Hodge," in Wells, ed., *Reformed Theology in America*, 37.

10. W. Andrew Hoffecker, "B. B. Warfield," in Wells, *Reformed Theology in America*, 60.

11. Quoted in Hoffecker, *Piety and the Princeton Theologians*, 48, n. 14.

12. Cf. Roger Anstey, *The Atlantic Slave Trade and British Abolition* (Atlantic Highlands, NJ: Humanities Press, 1975); Daniel F. Rice, "Natural Theology and the Scottish Philosophy in the Thought of Thomas Chalmers," *Scottish Journal of Theology* 24 (1971): 23-46; Richard W. Vaudry, "Theology and Education in Early Victorian Canada: Knox College, Toronto, 1844-1861," *Studies in Religion/Sciences Religieuses* 17 (June 1988).

13. Cf. George M. Marsden, "Everyone One's Own Interpreter? The Bible, Science, and Authority in Mid-nineteenth-Century America," in *The Bible in America: Essays in Cultural History*, ed. Nathan O. Hatch and Mark A. Noll (New York and Oxford: Oxford University Press, 1982), 82-85.

14. Hoffecker in Wells, *Reformed Theology in America*, 69-71.

15. George M. Marsden, *Fundamentalism and American Culture* (New York: Oxford University Press, 1980), 114-15.

16. Gerstner in Lewis and Demarest, *Challenges to Inerrancy*, 356-58.

17. Marsden, "Bible, Science and Authority," 90; *Fundamentalism and American Culture*, 110-15.

18. Marsden, "Bible, Science and Authority," 91-92; Noll, *Princeton Theology*, 25-26.

19. Wells, *Reformed Theology in America*, 36.

20. Noll, *Princeton Theology*, 28-29.

21. Hoffecker, *Piety and the Princeton Theologians*.

22. Noll, *Princeton Theology*, 28-29.

23. James Waddell Alexander, *Forty Years' Familiar Letters of James W. Alexander, D.D. constituting, with the notes, a memoir of his life, edited by the surviving correspondent John Hall, D.D.*, 2 vols. (New York and London, 1860), vol. 1, 388.

24. *National Union Catalogue, Pre-1956 Imprints*, vol. 249, 104.

25. Alexander, *Letters*, vol. 1, 390.

26. Alexander, *Letters*, vol. 1, 388.

27. Alexander, *Letters*, vol. 1, 391.

28. *New Schaff-Herzog Encyclopedia of Religious Knowledge*, vol. 1, 122.

29. Alexander, *Letters*, vol. 2, 68.

30. Princeton University Library, *Charles Hodge Papers*, Burns to Charles Hodge, November 5, 1859, Box 14, Folder 42.

31. Princeton University Library, *Charles Hodge Papers*, George Paxton Young to [Charles Hodge], November 5, 1855, Box 19, Folder 60.

32. Cf. Vaudry, "Knox College, Toronto, 1844-1861."

33. Cf. Richard W. Vaudry, "The Free Church in Canada, 1844-1861" (Ph.D. diss., McGill University, 1984), 259-60.

34. Charles W. Gordon, *The Life of James Robertson: Missionary Superintendent in Western Canada* (Toronto: Westminster, 1908), 44.

35. Gordon, *Life of Robertson*, 45.

36. A. F. Kemp, F. W. Farries, and J. B. Halkett, *Handbook of the Presbyterian Church in Canada*, 1883, 90. Cf. D. C. Masters, *Protestant Church Colleges in Canada* (Toronto: University of Toronto Press, 1966), 45-47.

37. *Handbook of the PCC., 1883*, 169-250. Queen's taught arts and theology and thus it is difficult to distinguish arts from theology graduates in the P.C.C. Handbook. Queen's may well be slightly ahead of New College, Edinburgh or Princeton Seminary in my list.

38. "Louis Jordan," *Who Was Who, 1916-1928*, 567.

39. On McCurdy see John S. Moir, *A History of Biblical Studies in Canada: A Sense of Proportion* (Chico, CA: Scholars Press, 1982).

40. *Handbook of the PCC., 1883*, 108-111, 133.

41. John H. MacVicar, *Life and Work of Donald Harvey MacVicar* (Toronto, 1904), 113, 201. H. Keith Markell, *History of the Presbyterian College, Montreal 1865-1986* (Montreal, 1987), 19-20.

42. *Handbook of the PCC., 1883*, 90; H. J. Morgan, ed., *The Canadian Men and Women of the Time* (1898), 46; N. Keith Clifford, *The Resistance to Church Union in Canada, 1904-1939* (Vancouver: University of British Columbia Press, 1985), 54.

43. Morgan, *Canadian Men and Women*, 874.

44. Mark A. Noll, *Between Faith and Criticism: Evangelical Scholarship and the Bible in America* (San Francisco: Harper & Row, 1986), 40, 42; *Schaff-Herzog Encyclopedia*, vol. 10, 60.

45. "William Caven," *Who Was Who*, 1897-1916, 126; Noll, *Princeton Theology*, 24 n. 35.

46. Noll, *Between Faith and Criticism*, 42, 221 n. 14, 20. Warfield cited this paper by Caven in "The Real Problem of Inspiration," *The Presbyterian and Reformed Review* (1893), reprinted in Warfield, *The Inspiration and Authority of the Bible*.

47. Ernest Sandeen, *The Roots of Fundamentalism: British and American Millenarianism 1800-1930* (Chicago and London: University of Chicago Press, 1970), 202; Clifford, *Resistance to Church Union*, 39.

48. *Presbyterian Record*, May 1885, 122.

49. *Presbyterian Record*, November 1894, 285.

50. Toronto *Daily Mail and Empire*, October 3, 1895, 12, 15-18.

51. Charles Hodge, *Arminianism and Grace* (Toronto: James Bain, 1881).

52. Benjamin B. Warfield, *An Introduction to the Textual Criticism of the New Testament* (Toronto: S. R. Briggs, 1887).

53. On Dawson see Charles F. O'Brien, *Sir William Dawson: A Life in Science and Religion* (Philadelphia: American Philosophical Society, 1971); H. Keith Markell, *History of the Presbyterian College, Montreal 1865-1986* (Montreal, 1987), 8-9.

54. The best account of this can be found in the Dawson Papers in the McGill University Archives. A good account is in O'Brien, *Sir William Dawson*; a less satisfactory account which never mentions Princeton Seminary is in S. B. Frost, *McGill University* (Montreal: McGill-Queen's University Press, 1980), vol. 1, 225ff.

55. McGill University Archives [MUA] *William Dawson Papers*, McCosh to Dawson, December 21, 1871; September 4, 1872; October 30, 1876; June 25, 1877.

56. MUA *Dawson Papers*, McCosh to Dawson, March 23, 1878.

57. MUA *Dawson Papers*, McCosh to Dawson, March 23, 1878.

58. MUA *Dawson Papers*, McCosh to Dawson, April 4, 1878.

59. MUA *Dawson Papers*, Charles Hodge to Dawson, April 6, 1878.

60. Dawson to Charles Hodge, April 15, 1878. Quoted in Frost, *McGill University*, vol. 1, 225.

61. MUA *Dawson Papers*, McCosh to Dawson, April 18, April 25, June 3, 1878.

62. *The Princeton Review*, 1878-1883. Copy in Seattle Public Library. Dawson also had some contact with Warfield in the 1890s. On March 5, 1890, Warfield wrote to Dawson asking for a paper for a symposium on "What is Animal Life?" MUA *Dawson Papers*, Warfield to Dawson, March 5, 1890. Also, Warfield in his article "On the Antiquity and the Unity of the Human Race," *The Princeton Theological Review* (1911) quotes from Dawson's *Relics of Primeval Life* (1897) reprinted in Warfield, *Biblical and Theological Studies* (Philadelphia: Presbyterian and Reformed Publishing House, 1952), 235-58.

63. Quoted in Noll, *Princeton Theology*, 230. It is not possible in a paper of this length to consider the historiographical debates concerning the Princeton theology and theologians. Simply put, they seem to revolve around two distinct questions: (1) what was the impact of the Princeton Theology on American fundamentalism? (2) In what sense was Princeton and its doctrine of Scripture an innovation and thus out of step with the Reformed tradition of the Westminster Confession of Faith, etc.? On question one Sandeen ought to be balanced by Marsden. On question two, one should consult Sandeen and Rogers and McKim on the one side and John Woodbridge, Randal Balmer and John Gerstner on the other.

64. Cf. Ian S. Rennie, "Conservatism in the Presbyterian Church in Canada in 1925 and Beyond: An Introductory Exploration," *Canadian Society of Presbyterian History* (1982): 29-59.

65. N. K. Clifford, "The Interpreters of the United Church of Canada," *Church History* 46 (June 1977): 212-14.

Recovering the Reformation Conception of Revelation: Walter Williamson Bryden and Post-Union Canadian Presbyterianism

John A. Vissers

A future historian who attempts to understand and evaluate the development of the Presbyterian Church in Canada in the half century following 1925 will find himself [sic] very clearly confronted with the fact of Walter W. Bryden. He will not find the name appearing often in the minutes of the General Assembly nor among those serving on important committees which are supposed to wield great power in the shaping of the Church's life. But as he examines the convictions which have moved men to action and asks why the ministry of this Church has moved in certain directions and not in others, he will come upon innumerable trails all leading back to the classroom of this one man. It can be said that he moved the Church at the level of its faith and its deepest thinking as has no other man in its history.[1]

These words were written by the late James D. Smart in 1956, some four years after the death of Walter Williamson Bryden. In Smart's estimation it is not possible to understand the development of the Presbyterian Church in Canada following 1925, including its contribution to Canadian culture, apart from understanding the significance of Bryden's life, ministry, and theology. As Professor of Church History and the History and Philosophy of Religion at Knox College in Toronto, Bryden shaped an entire generation of theological students in preparation for the pastoral ministry of the then Continuing Presbyterian Church. In this context Bryden's influence was considerable. Joseph C. McLelland assesses that influence in these words:

The quarter-century and more during which Bryden taught the theologues of Knox was the most critical in the history of the Presbyterian Church in Canada. Behind lay mixed motives and

traditions, ahead an uncertain future, no clear theological position emerging, but rather a struggle over the Church's relationship to its subordinate standard, the Westminster Confession of
Faith. This was Bryden's hour. Occupying one of the highest and
most influential educational positions in the Church, he brought
his considerable intellectual gifts to bear on the practical issue of
theological education—the teaching of those "teaching elders"
who must minister to a Church undergoing a crisis of identity.2

For many students Bryden's influence was a personal one—the
influence of a revered professor on the lives of those theologues
who sat in his classroom week by week. But Bryden's leadership
extended beyond his personal relationships with students to the
substance of his theological thought. He taught a generation
of ministers to think theologically and thereby contributed to a
theological awakening in the church.

The substance of that theological thought, however, has never
been thoroughly and carefully examined. Bryden's theology is usually described as "Barthian" or "neo-orthodox" without any real
comprehensive assessment of his theological program. For example, in speaking of Bryden's significance for the Presbyterian Church
in Canada in *Enduring Witness,* John Moir says:

> Within Knox College and Presbyterian College the majority of
> faculty members were older men who showed little interest in
> theological trends and seemed content to repeat well-worn
> lectures despite student dissatisfaction with such uninspiring
> material. The notable exception was W. W. Bryden of Knox, whose
> own theology had been much influenced by Barth's conservative
> "neo-orthodoxy," which Bryden said, had driven him back to the
> Bible. Through his classes and writing Bryden did much to shape
> and challenge a generation of younger ministers.3

A similar description of Bryden's theology may be found in
N. Keith Clifford's book *The Resistance to Church Union in Canada
1904-1939*:

> Thus they [i.e. those who opposed church union and constituted
> the Continuing Presbyterian Church] did not bind their church
> to any theory of biblical inerrancy, premillennialism, or
> dispensationalism, and they did not insist that their church adopt

an anti-ecumenical stance. Consequently, after 1925 the Presbyterian Church in Canada was completely free to follow Walter Bryden, their new young theologian at Knox College, beyond modernism and fundamentalism to neo-orthodoxy.[4]

Moir's description of Bryden's theology as having been influenced by Barth's conservative neo-orthodoxy, and Clifford's description of Bryden's theology as a neo-orthodoxy which moved beyond fundamentalism and modernism are not inaccurate, but they certainly do not tell the whole story. What is missing in the study of the significance of Walter Bryden for the Presbyterian Church in Canada after 1925 is a careful assessment of the substance of that so-called Barthianism and neo-orthodoxy. Such a study will demonstrate that Bryden's theology, while certainly influenced by Barth and the emerging neo-orthodox theological consensus of that period, was primarily the result of Bryden's own conscious theological program, that program being the recovery of the Reformation conception of revelation, particularly Calvin's doctrine of the knowledge of God, for the Presbyterian Church in Canada after 1925. It is the purpose of this paper to give a preliminary theological analysis of Bryden's theology from this perspective in order to redress this lacuna in the study of Walter Bryden and his significance for the Presbyterian Church in Canada.

This study of Bryden's theology will take the following form. First, a sketch of Bryden's theological development, setting forth his life and ministry, will be given. It will be argued that Bryden's theology was shaped in the Canadian context by Scottish liberal evangelical Calvinism of the late nineteenth and the early twentieth centuries as well as by Barth's theology. Second, a survey of the key themes of Bryden's doctrine of revelation will be set forth, demonstrating the extent to which he sought to recover the Reformation conception of revelation. Third, the implications of Bryden's conception of revelation for his ecclesiology will be examined. It will be argued that this conception of revelation and the church emerged as the theological rationale for the post-union Presbyterian Church in Canada, providing the church a theological basis for its continuing existence in the context of Canadian society.

The Life and Ministry of Walter W. Bryden

Walter Williamson Bryden was born on a farm near Galt, Ontario, on September 18, 1883.[5] As a young boy he injured his right arm in a shooting accident near his home. The resulting disfigurement was to be a distinctive feature of his appearance throughout life and the cause of much personal suffering.

The Bryden family attended Knox's Presbyterian Church in Galt. Presbyterianism had been part of the fabric of the culture in Galt since at least the early part of the nineteenth century when the area had been settled by Scottish immigrants. The years during which Walter Bryden was associated with this congregation (1883-1902) were periods of growth and activity in the life of the congregation. In 1889 the Sabbath school enrolled a record number of 679 students, with fifty-two teachers and officers. The Reverend Alexander Jackson of Pittsburgh, whose ministry was conducted in the congregation during Bryden's childhood and teenage years, was strongly Calvinistic in his theology and evangelistic in his preaching. In 1894, a record 159 new members were added to the rolls of the church, and in 1895 five men from the congregation were studying at Knox College for the Presbyterian ministry. In sum, at Knox's Church Bryden was raised in a vibrant congregation of the Scottish Reformed tradition, with its strong Calvinism, its presbyterian form of church government, and its dissenting Free Church heritage.[6]

In 1901 Bryden graduated from the Galt Grammar School where he had received a classical education in preparation for university studies upon which he embarked in 1902. At the University of Toronto he studied moderns in his first year, and philosophy and psychology in his second, third, and fourth years, graduating in 1906 in honours philosophy and psychology. In 1907 he presented a thesis for the Master of Arts degree in psychology called "A Verification of the Law of Weber, By the Method of Mean Gradations, With Reference to Great Differences of Light Intensities," and was granted the degree with honours standing.[7] During Bryden's study at the University of Toronto he was exposed to the school of philosophical idealism which had been espoused by

George Paxton Young, although Young himself had died in 1889, long before Bryden's arrival on the campus. Nevertheless, Young's emphases on metaphysical idealism, the doctrine of free will, the ideal of self-realization through the use of reason which was understood as the inner structure of all reality, were still very much at the centre of philosophical thinking during Bryden's years of study at the University of Toronto. It was against this exalted view of human reason as the arbiter of all reality which had shaped his early philosophical and theological convictions, that Bryden later set forth his program to recover the Reformation conception of revelation.[8]

In 1906 Bryden also began studies in theology at Knox College, Toronto, in preparation for pastoral ministry in the Presbyterian Church in Canada. With the death of Principal Caven in 1904 the college was in a period of theological transition and institutional reorganization. The faculty represented a variety of emphases within the Reformed tradition, reflecting both the decline of post-Reformation orthodox theology in the form of Presbyterian creedalism and the rise of liberal Protestantism which was sweeping in from continental Europe, largely mediated and moderated by British scholars. Bryden studied Old Testament under John McFadyen, who taught his students the newest insights of the developing historical-critical method of biblical interpretation. At the same time he studied Reformed theology under Principal William MacLaren, who represented the more conservative nineteenth-century Princeton approach to theology. Bryden's later theological work was an attempt to recover what he considered to be the best of each tradition, a Reformed theology that reached back beyond the period of post-Reformation scholasticism to the Reformation itself, and an enlightened critical approach to Biblical interpretation adequate to provide the basis of a post-Enlightenment theological epistemology.[9]

Bryden spent his second year of theological study (1907-08) at the United Free Church College in Glasgow, an experience which was to have a decisive impact on his theological development. His studies under James Denney, T. M. Lindsay, James Orr, and George Adam Smith exposed him in varying degrees to the

Scottish liberal evangelical Calvinist theology being set forth in response to both classical Reformed theology and the rising tide of Ritschlian theology. It was James Denney who figured prominently in Bryden's theological development. Bryden later referred to Denney as "the prince of Scottish theologians," whose "terse observations, as the years go by, seem to become ever more pregnant with meaning."[10] Denney pointed Bryden to a theology that could be preached, and helped him understand that the knowledge of God which issues from faith in Christ is a paradox.[11] Bryden became convinced that the relationship between the finite and the infinite could only be addressed in terms of the incarnation and Atonement, even though this paradox could never be rationally or ethically comprehended. Further, he began to see the importance of the testimony of the Holy Spirit as an essential element in a Reformed doctrine of revelation which would be adequate to the contemporary context.[12] T. M. Lindsay also influenced Bryden, who later referred to "the things I learned in Principal Lindsay's classroom while a student in Glasgow."[13] Lindsay persuaded Bryden that the doctrine of revelation and Scripture espoused by post-Reformation scholasticism, especially in its expression of the nineteenth-century Princeton school, was not the doctrine taught by Calvin and the Reformers.[14] Denney and Lindsay, together with James Orr, George Adam Smith, and later the British theologians P. T. Forsyth and John Oman, helped Bryden to see the possibility of developing a Reformed theology which might weave a mediating path between liberal Protestantism and evangelical orthodoxy.

Bryden returned to Canada to complete his final year of theological study (1908-09), and after graduation he was ordained to the ministry of word and sacraments in the Presbyterian Church in Canada, taking up an appointment as the minister of St. Andrew's Church, Lethbridge, Alberta. Bryden referred to this ministry as "spade work in western Canada," as he was involved in the establishment of a new congregation in the northern part of the town.[15] In Lethbridge Bryden came into contact with the miners struggling to organize the labour movement in western Canada. Coming into contact with the Western Miner's Federation and the Industrial

Workers of the World, he recognized the challenge of Marxism to the Christian tradition, and was forced to rethink his understanding of the New Testament. Politically and economically Bryden's sympathies lay with the socialists, although he could not accept what he saw as the reductionist and domesticated message of the Social Gospel. Nevertheless, throughout his life Bryden found himself on the moderate left of the political spectrum, and a faithful supporter of the CCF after its inception in the 1930s.[16]

In September 1910 Bryden married Violet Nasmith Bannatyne, whom he had met in Scotland. Their first son, William Bannatyne Bryden, was born on August 10, 1911 in Lethbridge and died on August 25, 1925 in Woodville, Ontario. Their second son and only surviving child is Walter Kenneth Bryden, Professor Emeritus of Political Economy at the University of Toronto.[17]

In 1912 Bryden was called to be the minister of Knox Presbyterian Church, Woodville, Ontario, a position he held until 1921. He later referred to this experience as ministry in "a quiet little village in the heart of old Ontario."[18] In 1921 the Bryden family moved to Melfort, Saskatchewan, where Bryden succeeded W. A. Cameron as the pastor of St. James Church. Most of his first book, *The Spirit of Jesus in St. Paul* (1925), was written during this pastorate, which ended in 1924 with Bryden's resignation due to the ill health of his wife. From Melfort they moved back to the Bryden family farm in Galt, and Walter Bryden served as supply preacher in Kirkland Lake and other places, spending much of his time with colleagues discussing the issue of church union in preparation for the vote which was to take place at the June 1925 General Assembly. In the aftermath of that assembly Bryden accepted a call from the continuing Presbyterians in Woodville to once again be their minister.[19] Significant for Bryden's theological development during this period was the fact that his struggle to articulate a Reformed doctrine of revelation occurred in the midst of his own pastoral ministries, and more specifically in the context of the church union controversy. Bryden's theology was the theology of a preacher, pastor, and churchman who was much concerned for the life of the church and the furtherance of the Christian gospel in Canada. In 1927 he wrote a pamphlet called *The Christian Ministry* in which he set forth the theological rationale for Reformed ministry in an effort to enlist new pastors for the continuing Presbyterian Church. In an address to the convocation of Presbyterian College, Montreal in 1929 Bryden reflected upon his own theological and pastoral pilgrimage:

> I have to confess that my particular ministry has been a fairly limited and modest one and perhaps a little unusual. I have never for instance had the privilege of being the minister of what is known as an influential city pulpit. For nearly half of the sixteen or seventeen years I spent in active congregational work, I was employed in what they call "spade work" in western Canada. The other portion was spent in a quiet little village in the heart of old Ontario. I am persuaded, however, that this kind of ministerial career has its advantages and compensations. You get to know real life as other men do not know it, and your own life is tested by the inwardness of things rather than by the outwardness of conventions which after all do not matter. Besides, you are not so likely to be encompassed by exacting church duties and if you have the will, you may train your mind and heart on those far greater things. As I see it now, my true student days began after I left the college halls; and had I to do it all over again, I surely would choose the same kind of ministry.[20]

Like his teacher James Denney, and in parallel to the experience of Karl Barth, Bryden worked out his theological program in the context of the church, for the church. What makes Bryden's experience especially unique, however, was that his theology was forged in the context of a church undergoing a national crisis. And as painful as the decision was for Bryden, he was not persuaded to enter the new United Church of Canada on the basis of the arguments advanced in its favour.

In 1925 Bryden was invited to lecture on church history at Knox College on a part-time basis while he continued his ministry in Woodville. This he did for one year, but in 1926 the family moved to Toronto, and in 1927 Bryden was appointed to the two chairs of church history and the history and philosophy of religion by the General Assembly of the Presbyterian Church in Canada. Bryden taught church history, the history of religions, and the philosophy of religion as a church theologian, introducing his students to both the Reformed tradition and the latest theological thinking. During the academic year 1937-38 Bryden also taught systematic theology. On April 12, 1928 the degree of Doctor of Divinity (*honoris causa*) was conferred upon him by Presbyterian College, Montreal. In 1945 Bryden assumed the principalship of Knox College, which he held until his death in March 1952.

During the first twenty years after church union, Knox College was in considerable turmoil as an institution as those associated with it struggled to provide theological education for the continuing Presbyterian Church in Canada. Nevertheless, in addition to his teaching and administrative responsibilities Bryden wrote *Why I Am a Presbyterian* (1934), "The Presbyterian Conception of the Word of God" (1935), *The Christian's Knowledge of God* (1940), and *The Significance of the Westminster Confession of Faith* (1943), as well as a variety of articles and book reviews for both academic journals and more popular Christian papers. It was also during the period from the late 1920s through to the 1940s that his engagement with the theology of Karl Barth began, whom he referred to as "the stern, new prophet of Europe" and "the modern scion of the Reformation spirit," and whose theology he described as "real Calvinism in a modern dress."[21] The theology of Karl Barth pointed Bryden back to the Bible and his old teacher James Denney, and it provided Bryden with the categories to explicate more fully the recovery of the Reformation conception of revelation which he had been struggling to articulate in the Canadian Presbyterian context. The mediating path of liberal evangelical Calvinism developed into a Reformed neo-orthodoxy for Bryden. In sum, on the basis of this survey of Bryden's life, ministry, and intellectual development, it may be concluded that Bryden's "conservative Barthianism" or "neo-orthodoxy" must be understood in terms of his own theological development along the lines of Scottish liberal evangelical Calvinism, parallel to but apart from the theology of Karl Barth and the unique Canadian Presbyterian context in which he worked out this theological program. Moreover, the material aspect of that theological program was the recovery of the Reformation conception of revelation in the theology of John Calvin for the new

Enlightenment and post-union context of the Presbyterian Church in Canada.

The Conception of Revelation in the Theology of Bryden

Bryden addressed the question of the conception of revelation and the knowledge of God throughout his theological writings. Already in his first book, *The Spirit of Jesus in St. Paul*, Bryden had noted that what one means by the knowledge of God is the most difficult and yet important question that may be asked of a religious person.[22] In *The Christian's Knowledge of God* he argued that a genuine knowledge of God in the modern church has been lost because of the loss of a Reformation understanding of revelation.[23] Revelation, Bryden contends, is neither to be identified merely with a general human religious experience, human reasoning about that religious experience, human ethical ideals, culture or history, nor is it to be identified as a series of propositional eternal truths set forth in the Bible. According to Bryden, revelation is the gracious act of God in which a genuine knowledge of God by faith breaks upon the individual soul of the Christian. God is both the object of such knowledge for the human soul and the means whereby such knowledge is apprehended. God is mediated only by God.

The locus of this revelation and the knowledge of God for Bryden is the Word of God, and this recovery of a Reformation theology of the Word forms the centre of his theological program. Bryden explicitly affirms that it is to be a sixteenth-century conception of the Word of God which has to be recovered by the Presbyterian Church in Canada after 1925. "It is not too much to hold," Bryden argues, that it was a "completely fresh and living apprehension of the Word of God which constituted the primal inspiration of the Reformation movement as a whole," and especially for Calvin.[24] Bryden recognized that while it is impossible, in any literal way, to go back to Calvin, it was imperative that if Presbyterianism was to remain true to its distinctive features, it had to get back to something of the understanding of the Word of God which had created Calvin and the Reformed faith.[25]

Bryden's recovery of Calvin's Reformation conception of revelation is characterized by a dialectical christocentric reconstruction of the doctrine of the Word of God. For Bryden, the Word of God is the Judging-Saving Word of God in Jesus Christ. The Word of God "is Jesus Christ, and Him crucified, with nothing to be added or subtracted from simply that."[26] Jesus Christ is the mediator of both revelation and reconciliation, and these two aspects of the Christian faith cannot be separated in Calvin's conception of the Word of God, Bryden argues. This Word of God in Jesus Christ encounters human beings in utter negation and completely disillusions them by calling into question their independent human existence and their attempts to domesticate the divine reality. This is the judgment of the Word of God.[27] But the Word of God is also a Word which encounters us in grace and therefore affirms human existence in Jesus Christ. This is the salvation of the Word of God.[28] This Judging-Saving Word is an exclusive, unique, and absolute revelation of God without which genuine knowledge of God is not possible.[29]

In setting forth this interpretation of the Reformation conception of the Word of God, Bryden rejected what he considered to be the inadequate interpretation of a rational orthodoxy or fundamentalism which identifies the Word of God simply with written Holy Scripture, in its wholeness, to be interpreted literally because it is verbally inerrant and plenarily inspired.[30] It is Bryden's contention that such a view does not find its source in Calvin and the Reformation, but that its origin is in the Protestant scholasticism of the post-Reformation orthodox period. Moreover, this interpretation fails to account adequately for Calvin's doctrine of the *testimonium Spiritus sancti internum*, in which the authority of Holy Scripture is self-authenticating and grounded not in human reason but in the work of the Holy Spirit testifying to the Word. This interpretation also makes faith an assent to certain propositional truths rather than an experience of trust in the grace of God.

In setting forth his recovery of Calvin's Reformation conception of the Word of God, Bryden also rejected the interpretation of nineteenth-century liberal Protestantism (i.e., Schleiermacher and Ritschl).

This position Bryden described as a theology of revelation in which the Word of God has been reduced to a religious-ethical ideal, a rational philosophical ideal, and a cultural-historical ideal.[31] Liberalism means primarily by the Word of God:

> those supreme moral and religious values which find unique expression in the Old Testament and especially in the New Testament—but which exist preeminently in the teachings of Jesus especially as these are embraced and find vital expression in the unique perfection of Jesus' life and personality.[32]

This position, Bryden argues, owes its insights not to Calvin and the Reformation but to the Enlightenment philosophy to which it accommodated. Bryden's extensive polemic against the high view of reason emanating from the Enlightenment made him vulnerable to the accusation of being a fideist, or as F. H. Anderson suggested in a critical review of *The Christian's Knowledge of God* in a 1941 edition of *The University of Toronto Quarterly*, an "irrational enthusiast." It may be argued that the negative pole of the dialectic, Bryden's strong judgment of "No!" to rational orthodoxy and liberal Protestantism, operates magisterially and prevents the full reconstruction of a Reformed theology of revelation adequate to the need of his context.

In sum, Bryden's recovery of Calvin's Reformation conception of revelation is characterized by a dialectical christocentric reconstruction of the Judging-Saving Word of God in Jesus Christ; a recovery of the Reformed doctrine of Word and Spirit in revelation; a union of revelation and reconciliation in the Word of God in Jesus Christ; and a conception of faith as personal encounter and trust rather than assent to propositional truths. His rejection of rational orthodoxy and liberal Protestantism is shaped by a desire to recover genuine Reformation theology after the Enlightenment, and in this sense Bryden's theology is influenced by both Scottish liberal evangelical Calvinism and the emerging neo-orthodoxy, but may perhaps be characterized as a "neo-Reformation" theology. While the adequacy of Bryden's interpretation of Calvin and the Enlightenment may be questioned, there can be no question that such a recovery and restatement for the Presbyterian Church in Canada after 1925 was the explicit aim of Bryden's theology. But what were the implications of this theological recovery for Bryden's ecclesiology?

Revelation and the Church in the Theology of Walter Bryden

Bryden's attempted recovery of Calvin's Reformation conception of revelation after the Enlightenment had direct implications for his ecclesiology and his position in the church union controversy. Throughout his writings the relationship between this understanding of revelation and the church is developed. In *The Spirit of Jesus in St. Paul*, a psychological study of Paul's religious experience based upon the Corinthian correspondence, Bryden attempts:

> to study the "soul of Paul" as his inner thoughts and feelings, his ethical appreciations and spiritual aspirations reveal themselves in these two letters. There is also the hope on the part of the writer that such a portrayal of the life of the great apostle may have some practical significance in the understanding of the perplexities of our own modern Church life, and in lending guidance in the discharge of our important and difficult work.[33]

In his book *Why I Am a Presbyterian*, a series of lectures given at Knox College and the University of Toronto, Bryden attempts to explain his personal decision to remain with the Presbyterian Church in 1925, arguing that genuine unity must be grounded in the Gospel of grace given in the revelation of the Word of God.[34] In his essay, "The Presbyterian Conception of the Word of God," Bryden argues that essential Presbyterianism has to do with the conception of revelation and the Word of God rather than a form of order and ministry which emerged in Scotland.[35] In *The Christian's Knowledge of God*, Bryden discusses the nature of the church and its relationship to culture at great length because it is so closely related to his exposition of the doctrine of revelation.[36] *The Significance of the Westminster Confession of Faith* addresses the nature of the confessional and confessing church in the Reformed tradition.[37] While Bryden does not develop a full dogmatic ecclesiology in any one of his writings, it is not too much to suggest that the church is integral to his recovery of a Reformation conception of revelation.

First, Bryden argues that the church is a creature of the Word of God. The church, he says, must "strive to rediscover the Word of God—that Word, I mean, which in the beginning gave rise to Holy Scripture, and which alone gave existence to the Church of God, and apart from which that Church cannot stand."[38] According to Bryden, "there is a very definite and necessary relation between the New Testament conception of revelation and the New Testament conception of the Church."[39] For Bryden "the Word of God is prior to and transcends both the Scripture and the Church and we may add it is prior to and transcends creation as well. Briefly, the Word of God is the raison d'être of all three."[40] The Word of God gives faith to men and women, a faith which has given existence to the Church of God itself.[41] "Revelation, therefore, and the Church are interdependent existences, so to speak. The latter, at least, possesses no significant meaning except for the former."[42] In sum, the church is constituted by the Word of God. It is a creature of the Word and a fellowship of the Holy Spirit. This is the very nature of its existence.

Second, the church is called to confess the Word of God. Such confession, Bryden argues, emanates from a church living under the constraint of God's Word. In a 1941 article in *The United Church Observer* titled "Continental Movements and the Theological Thought of Tomorrow," Bryden distinguishes between a statement of faith and a confession of faith:

> It is easy to make statements of our faith, but confessions are wrung from men who have been on their knees. A theology which may be acquired objectively is not Christian theology; the latter appears when men are under the power and constraint of God's Word.[43]

A church which has been created by the revelation of the Word of God, and which is continually encountered by that Word in its life, is a church which must confess its faith. In his book *The Significance of the Westminster Confession of Faith*, a revised and expanded version of an address delivered to the sixty-ninth General Assembly of the Presbyterian Church in Canada in 1943 on the occasion of the tercentenary of the Westminster Confession of Faith, Bryden argues that the church must take the subordinate standard seriously as an essential part of its Reformed witness. The Westminster Confession of Faith is not an outmoded expression of Christian thought no longer having any but an historic interest, but it is also not an absolute norm for Christian doctrine. Bryden rejected both historical relativization and a literalistic interpretation of the Westminster Confession of Faith. James D. Smart summarizes Bryden's contribution to the Presbyterian Church in Canada on this point:

> He did two things that are not likely to have to be done again; he commanded an interest and a respect for the faith which speaks in the Westminster Confession of Faith and he destroyed every pretext in our tradition for a literalistic confessionalism that would make the Westminster Confession not a guide to faith but an iron-bound shackle upon the faith of the church.[44]

In sum, the church's confession emanates from its encounter with God's revelation in the Judging-Saving Word of God.

Third, the pastoral ministry and leadership of the church consists of those who have been called to proclaim God's Judging-Saving Word in Jesus Christ because they themselves have been encountered by this Word at the very heart of their existence. In his 1927 tract, *The Christian Ministry*, Bryden sets forth his understanding of the Reformed doctrine of ministry in the context of making an appeal to the youth of the church to consider ministry within the Presbyterian Church in Canada after 1925.[45] The church needs those, he says, who in their encounter with God's Word know the inner reality of Christian experience and the sense of a divine call. His convocation address to Presbyterian College speaks about the nature of Reformed preaching. True preaching, he says, "may be described as the unveiling of one's soul as that soul in the course of life is being touched by God."[46] Preaching, Bryden argues, is a kind of incarnation which is particularly auspicious for this age.[47] In sum, the revelation of God's Judging-Saving Word creates and sustains the preaching ministry of the church.

Fourth, the church's creation by and encounter with God's Judging-Saving Word has important implications for the church's relations with the social, economic, and political powers. As the church stands under the judgment of the Word of God, so that Word judges the self-righteousness and injustices of the world. Only through such judgment can the world know the salvation which God's Word brings:

> Only the judging-saving Word which judges man as such, rich and poor, civilized and uncivilized alike, ever succeeds in truly mellowing the hearts of men in such wise that they will be truly concerned about one another. The Church, it is true, cannot busy herself in creating programs, political or social, which must pass with the passage of time. But in her transcendent Word she must be the judge of everything which adversely affects the lives of men. And only with a profound consciousness of this kind in regard to the world's various needs can the Christian maintain with sincerity that it is the Church's responsibility to "preach the Gospel only."[48]

The Presbyterian Church in Canada existed, Bryden argued, according to God's Word and Spirit and not according to the laws of any particular nation. Therefore, as the church stood under the judgment of God, the church would bear witness to God's Judging-Saving Word which calls into question, indeed even into a crisis, the self-righteousness and injustices in the political, social, and economic realm.

This understanding of the church in relation to the Word of God in Jesus Christ emerged as the post-union theological rationale for the Presbyterian Church in Canada. It was this understanding of revelation and its implications for the constitution of the church, its confession, its ministry, and its relation to society and culture that Bryden saw being threatened by the formation of the United Church of Canada. That this was a post-union rationale is admitted by Bryden in his book *Why I Am a Presbyterian*:

> Such thoughts as I have just given expression to were very much in my mind in 1925 and in the years preceding. But, I confess, they have come to real vitality only in more recent years.[49]

Bryden contends that the impetus for church union came primarily from the desire to establish a larger, more efficient, and better organized national church in Canada, rather than from a desire for the unity of the church which came from its creation as a fellowship of the Spirit by the Judging-Saving Word of God. This concern for external organization, he argues, was not a sufficient basis for church union since its considerations were "primarily sentimental, expedient, utilitarian, and humanitarian, rather than ecclesiastical and theological."[50] However, the maintenance of a Scottish Presbyterian ecclesiastical system or a rational orthodox theology, the rationale used by some of those who opposed church union, was not sufficient reason to oppose church union.[51] According to Bryden, the only reason sufficient to oppose church union was the Gospel itself. For him, the knowledge of God revealed in the Judging-Saving Word of God in Jesus Christ, witnessed to in the Scriptures, giving life to the church and its confession in the world, was the only genuine basis for church union. Such a church, he concludes, being conscious of the Gospel and the missionary mandate, is truly catholic.[52] In providing this rationale for the Presbyterian Church in Canada Bryden helped prevent a retreat of the Presbyterian Church into sectarianism and voluntarism, thus enabling a continuing Presbyterian contribution to Canadian culture.

Conclusion

Why has the Presbyterian Church in Canada moved in certain directions and not in others since 1925? It may be concluded that much of this has to do with the influence of Walter Williamson Bryden. Bryden's influence must be understood theologically as well as personally. His theology is to be interpreted formally as a neo-Reformation theology seeking to weave a path between liberal Protestantism and what Bryden saw as a rational fundamentalist orthodoxy. Bryden's development owes as much to Scottish liberal evangelical Calvinism as to the later influence of Karl Barth and neo-orthodoxy. Bryden worked out his theology within the context of the Canadian church. The theology of Walter Bryden is to be understood materially as an attempt to recover Calvin's Reformation conception of revelation and the knowledge of God in the Word of God after the Enlightenment. This doctrine is characterized by a dialectical christocentric reconstruction of the Word of God; a recovery of the Reformed doctrine of Word and Spirit; a union of revelation and reconciliation in the Word of God in Jesus Christ; a conception of faith as personal encounter rather than as assent to propositional truths; and an understanding of the church as a creature of the Word of God and a fellowship of the Holy Spirit whose confession and ministry took a certain shape in the world. It was this conception of revelation and its implications for ecclesiology which formed the heart of Bryden's theological contribution to the Presbyterian Church in Canada in 1925. It is to be hoped that this approach to the study of the neo-Reformed theology of Walter Williamson Bryden will provide the historical and theological framework within which further study and critical reflection may proceed. That this approach represents his self-understanding may be seen in a letter Bryden wrote to Allan L. Farris in 1945:

> I stand firmly by the Reformed faith, subject to Scripture which I believe cradles God's living Word for those who have ears to hear it. That about sums me up—whatever lies before.[53]

NOTES

1. James D. Smart, "The Evangelist as Theologian," in W. W. Bryden, *Separated Unto the Gospel*, ed. D. V. Wade (Toronto: Burns and MacEachern, 1956), vii.

2. Joseph C. McLelland, "Walter Bryden 'By Circumstance and God,'" in *Called to Witness*, vol. 2, ed. W. Stanford Reid (Don Mills, ON: Presbyterian Church in Canada, 1980), 120.

3. John Moir, *Enduring Witness* (Don Mills, ON: Presbyterian Church in Canada, 1975), 235.

4. N. Keith Clifford, *The Resistance to Church Union in Canada* (Vancouver: University of British Columbia Press, 1985), 4.

5. "Death of Principal of Knox College," *Presbyterian Record*, May 1952, 9.

6. Interview, W. Kenneth Bryden, May 27, 1986. See also W. J. McKeown, "Memoirs of Dr. Bryden," *Presbyterian Record*, October 1975, 8; "History of Knox's Church, Galt," Presbyterian Church Archives, AR4; John S. Moir, *Enduring Witness*, 137-42; W. S. Reid, "The Scottish Protestant Tradition in Canada," in *The Scottish Tradition in Canada*, ed. W. S. Reid (Toronto: McLelland & Stewart, 1976), 118-19.

7. Walter Williamson Bryden, "A Verification of the Law of Weber, By the Method of Mean Gradations, With Reference to Great Differences of Light Intensities," M.A. thesis, 1907, University of Toronto, University of Toronto Archives, T79-0076-(.93).

8. Leslie Armour and Elizabeth Trott, *The Faces of Reason: An Essay on Philosophy and Culture in Canada 1850-1950* (Waterloo: Wilfrid Laurier University Press, 1981), 87. See also W. W. Bryden, *The Christian's Knowledge of God* (Toronto: Thorn Press, 1940), 221.

9. Moir, *Enduring Witness*, 189ff. See also "Death of Principal of Knox College," *Presbyterian Record*, May 1952, 9; J. E. McFadyen, "Foreword," in W. W. Bryden, *The Spirit of Jesus in St. Paul* (London: James Clarke and Company, 1925), 7-8; "Our Colleges," *Presbyterian Record*, October 1927, 291-94.

10. W. W. Bryden, *The Significance of the Westminster Confession of Faith* (Toronto: University of Toronto Press, 1943), 27; W. W. Bryden, "The Presbyterian Conception of the Word of God, unpublished manuscript, Knox College Archives, 206/0019.

11. Bryden, *Significance of Westminster Conf.*, 27.

12. Bryden, *Significance of the Westminster Conf.*, 27ff.

13. Bryden, *Separated Unto the Gospel*, 66.

14. J. D. Douglas, "T. M. Lindsay," *The New International Dictionary of the Christian Church*, ed. J. D. Douglas (Grand Rapids, MI: Zondervan, 1978), 597. See also J. B. Rogers and Donald McKim, *The Authority and Interpretation of the Bible* (San Francisco: Harper and Row, 1979), 380-85.

15. Bryden, *Separated Unto the Gospel*, 131. See also William Hay, *History of the Presbyterian Church in Lethbridge*, Presbyterian Church Archives, AR4.

16. W. K. Bryden, "Interview." See also Donald V. Wade, "The Theological Achievement of Walter Bryden," a paper presented to the Karl Barth Society of North America, Barth Colloquium, March 22, 1974, Toronto, Ontario, 3.

17. W. K. Bryden, "Interviews." See also Walter Williamson Bryden, University of Toronto Archives, A73-0026/043.

18. Bryden, *Separated Unto the Gospel*, 131.

19. Wade, "Theological Achievement of Walter Bryden," 3. See also R. A. Mackay, "Founding of Woodville Congregation," *Presbyterian Witness*, October 30, 1924; "History of Woodville Reveals How Village Character Was Shaped," *The Lindsay Post*, April 17, 1957, 6, Presbyterian Church Archives, AR4. Mrs. B. Whittome and Mrs. C. Rush, "St. James Presbyterian Church History," Presbyterian Church Archives, AR4 S3M45S3.

20. Bryden, *Separated Unto the Gospel*, 131.

21. Bryden, *Separated Unto the Gospel*, 135. See also Bryden, "The Presbyterian Conception of the Word of God," unpublished manuscript, 49.

22. Bryden, *The Spirit of Jesus in St. Paul*, 152.

23. Bryden, *The Christian's Knowledge of God*, 1-2.

24. Bryden, *Separated Unto the Gospel*, 179.

25. Bryden, *Separated Unto the Gospel*, 178.

26. Bryden, *The Christian's Knowledge of God*, 173.

27. Bryden, *The Christian's Knowledge of God*, 132-34.

28. Bryden, *The Christian's Knowledge of God*, 135-38.

29. Bryden, *The Christian's Knowledge of God*, 138, 148.
30. Bryden, *Separated Unto the Gospel*, 181.
31. Bryden, *The Christian's Knowledge of God*, ix-x.
32. Bryden, *Separated Unto the Gospel*, 188.
33. Bryden, *The Spirit of Jesus in St. Paul*, 36.
34. Bryden, *Why I Am a Presbyterian*, 9-20.
35. Bryden, *Separated Unto the Gospel*, 175-80.
36. Bryden, *The Christian's Knowledge of God*, 220ff.
37. Bryden, *The Significance of the Westminster Confession of Faith*, 7-12.
38. Bryden, *The Christian's Knowledge of God*, x.
39. Bryden, *The Christian's Knowledge of God*, 4.
40. Bryden, *The Christian's Knowledge of God*, 14.
41. Bryden, *The Christian's Knowledge of God*, 132.
42. Bryden, *The Christian's Knowledge of God*, 180.
43. W. W. Bryden, "Continental Movements and the Theological Thought of Tomorrow," *United Church Observer*, June 15, 1941, 11, 28.
44. Smart, "The Evangelist as Theologian," xi.
45. W. W. Bryden, *The Christian Ministry* (Toronto: Upper Canada Tract Society, 1927).
46. Bryden, "The Triumph of Reality," *Separated Unto the Gospel*, 133.
47. Bryden, "The Triumph of Reality," 140-42.
48. Bryden, *The Christian's Knowledge of God*, 259.
49. Bryden, *Why I Am a Presbyterian*, 104-5.
50. Bryden, *Why I Am a Presbyterian*, 111.
51. Bryden, *Why I Am a Presbyterian*, 21-52, 170.
52. Bryden, *Why I Am a Presbyterian*, 169.
53. Letter W. W. Bryden to Allan L. Farris, August 6, 1945. Used by permission.

The Role of Women in the Preservation of the Presbyterian Church in Canada: 1921-28

Roberta Clare

It is interesting that historical writing on women in the Presbyterian Church in Canada focuses on famous women who happen to be Presbyterian, rather than on Presbyterians who happen to be women. This is to say that like much scholarly work on Canadian Presbyterianism, it emphasizes biography. While well-written essays of this *genre* recreate the fascinating characters of Presbyterian history, important historical events sometimes become consumed by the character sketch.

The biographical approach is particularly evident in materials touching on the role of women in the years 1921 to 1928. For example, in an essay in *Enkindled By the Word*, Priscilla Lee Reid outlines the contribution of Mrs. D.T.L. McKerroll as follows:

> Another was Mrs. D.T.L. McKerroll, wife of the minister of Victoria Church, Toronto. Although always known as a strong leader and forthright person, it was in 1925, following the disruption that she earned the title "woman of the hour." Elected the first president of the W.M.S. (W.D.), reorganized in June of that year, she, by word and example, rallied the Presbyterian women and gave them the spirit to go forward with confidence.[1]

Dramatic though this portrait is, it neglects Mrs. McKerroll's activity before 1925 on the executive of the Toronto branch of the Women's League of the Presbyterian Church Association. Her contribution as one of the major decision makers of the League is arguably as important as her role as "the woman of the hour."

Although Professor Keith Clifford devotes two pages to the Women's League in his volume, *The Resistance to Church Union in Canada: 1904-1939*, only one working paper has been prepared on the role of women in the Presbyterian Church.[2] Using mostly primary source material, this essay will argue that during the crisis years 1921 to 1925, Presbyterian women acquired unprecedented influence over church affairs. In the aftermath of 1925, women made a major contribution to rebuilding the church, even though their activity was restricted to the Women's Associations (W.A.) of local congregations and the Women's Missionary Society.

The General Assembly of 1916 stepped up the campaign for church union despite—or perhaps because of—a significant increase in the opposition. Calling the Assembly a "Western Stampede," which threw the church into disruption, the opponents to union decided to organize to fight the unionist tide.[3] Specifically, they launched the Presbyterian Church Association with a mandate to "preserve the Presbyterian Church in Canada." The Association was immediately successful. Within the year, the radical dissidents, with the help of the moderates, forced the unionists to retreat from their position that union was "an accomplished fact."[4] However, in the long run the moderates may have hindered the dissident cause more than they helped it. The momentum of the Association was lost at the General Assembly of 1917 in Montreal, when a truce was declared between the two parties. Without a cause to champion, the Presbyterian Church Association lost steam and one year later became dormant.

The church union issue was shelved for four years until 1921 when the Union Committee was reappointed to deal with a number of overtures that asked the church to clarify its official position on union. The West had honoured the truce, but the issue would not go away. A large number of union congregations had come into existence during the truce. By 1921 the number of united congregations in the synods of Manitoba, Saskatchewan, and Alberta had risen to four hundred.[5] Tensions were already building again, and it seems that the re-appointment of the Union Committee was all it took to rekindle open animosity between the unionists and the dissidents. As before, the dissident movement was slow to organize, but this time it had difficulty regaining the momentum it had rallied in 1916-17. Meetings did not take place until the summer of 1922, when the lay leaders finally made the financial commitment to reorganize. The revived Association was plagued with problems from the start. Once it got off the ground organizational clashes between the Ontario and Quebec executives of the Association, and chronic financial problems impeded its effectiveness in countering the unionist campaign.[6]

There is no evidence that women had played a significant role in the union question up to this time. But the General Assembly of 1922 that prompted the Presbyterian Church Association to emerge phoenix-like from its ashes also took a stand on the role of women in the church. Two significant historical events prompted the Presbyterian Church at this particular time to open debate over women's ordination.

First, women had recently played a more significant role in the political and economic life of the country. In the Great War (as would also happen in World War II) political leaders had convinced women it was their patriotic duty to leave their homes and join the war effort. With most men overseas, women took over the jobs of men. After the war, of course, these same leaders urged women to return to their homes.[7] Thus the General Assembly was also subject to a general societal pressure for women to return to their subordinate roles in society.

Although most women did leave the work force, the clocks could not entirely be turned back. The role of women in the war effort was a major factor in winning them the right to vote in 1922. The movement toward the emancipation of women also showed its strength in ecclesiastical circles. In 1921 the Methodists agreed to the ordination of women in principle but voted against it because they feared it would impede the negotiations for union.[8] Nevertheless, Congregational women had been granted the right to sit on their church courts.[9] The Methodists, for their part, had allowed women access to the courts by 1918, but did not permit the ordination of women.[10] Therefore, it was time for the Presbyterians to respond to the advances in both society and in other reformed churches, especially those involved in the proposed union.

The Presbyterian Church did not exactly show leadership in this matter. At best, the report of General Assembly of 1922 is a superficial study on the role of women that only partially takes into account the current developments in church and society. Predictably, the report argues that there is no historical precedent for the ordination of women. But it does not address the question theologically. In its second argument, it acknowledges the practices of other churches but dismisses them as insignificant:

> Present day instances of the ordination of women can be quoted; yet they are not so numerous that an argument for the introduction of the practice in our communion should be based upon them, and there is no evidence of a widespread demand for the ordination of women throughout the membership of our church.[11]

The Assembly also argues the point from a more overtly bigoted point of view:

> The question is really two-fold and concerns the nature of the task on the one side, and the possibility of effective service on the other. In view of the variety, the intimacy, the gravity and the burdensome nature of the work of the Ministry on the one side, and in view of limitations, necessarily involved in the fact of sex on the other, the Assembly is not prepared to direct that women be ordained to the office of the Ministry.[12]

Presbyterian women remained ineligible for ordination either as ministers or elders, and therefore continued to have no representation in the church's courts—the Presbytery or the General Assembly.

Although women had no voice in the government of their church, they had discovered much earlier their own kind of ministry. In 1876 women had taken up the example of the Methodists and established the offices of deaconess and home and foreign missionaries. The Women's Missionary Society grew rapidly and Presbyterian women gained a reputation for efficient business management, in particular, in the administration of their property and funds. They had never been in debt. The Societies were independently organized and administered by women and were not controlled by the church's Mission Board.[13] They sought a closer connection with the church. In 1924 it was reported that "some years ago the W.M.S., anxious for closer cooperation and better understanding approached the General Assembly asking for representation on its Home and Foreign Boards—a request that has not yet been granted."[14] Therefore, while officially the W.M.S. operated under the auspices of the church and submitted reports to General Assembly each year for routine approval, in reality it operated more as an independent organization with minimal contact with the church.

And so it is not surprising that in the crisis years the W.M.S. remained silent on the national affairs of the church. The Toronto branch of the Women's League notes in its minutes: "The position of the women in the W.M.S. was discussed and it was felt that they must before long make a declaration as society in regard to the question."[15] There is no evidence a stand by the W.M.S. was ever taken. Moreover, women were instructed not to express opinions on the union question in Women's Associations. The minutes of April 16, 1923 state: "It does not seem possible to reach the membership through the women's organizations as they have had their last meeting for this season. It has been reported that they have been instructed to remain neutral."[16] Women could not express their opinion in the patriarchal structure of the church, even in a crisis.

In light of these factors the only way women could play a part in opposing union was to form another independent body outside the structure of the church. Their initial support came from laymen, not clergymen. Professor Clifford argues that the Women's League was formed when women realized that "without their being consulted, all their funds and property were to pass into the United Church of Canada."[17] However, this alone does not fully explain the fervour of the Women's League. The predicament of women was compounded by the fact that the funds and property were considered to be the legal possession of a church body that had declined to participate in W.M.S. management.

Just as the church had declined to represent the interests of the W.M.S. by participating on its boards, the Presbyterian Church Association regarded the Women's League as an independently run organization despite requests from the League that it be run under the auspices of the Association.

According to Professor Clifford, the idea that the women of the Presbyterian Church in Canada should be separately organized in defence of the church originated with John Penman, the great organizer of the dissident movement. He realized that the women of the church could prove helpful in getting the momentum of the Presbyterian Church Association going again. But Penman underestimated the extent of the role they would play.

The first meeting of the Women's League was held in Montreal in January 1923. Mrs. J. J. McCaskill was elected recording secretary of the Presbyterian Women's League, and two months later she became organizer for the Presbyterian Women's Leagues throughout Quebec and Ontario.[18]

The Women's League never really became a Montreal-based national organization. In spite of efforts by the Presbyterian Church Association to convince Mrs. McCaskill to form a national organization,[19] the branches seem to have been organized regionally, generally according to synod. In both the minutes of the Toronto branch of the Women's League and the correspondence between Mrs. McCaskill and the secretary of the Association, Reverend John MacNamara, there is no reference to Mrs. McCaskill acting as national League president, although she did travel a great deal on speaking tours. Nor is there any reference to either an administrative or organizational connection with the Montreal group. (The Toronto Branch handed over the money directly to Mr. MacNamara.) Moreover, while Montreal boasted the honour of being the pioneer organization,[20] it was by no means the most successful. The Women's League of Toronto may well claim this honour. It operated out of the same premises as the Presbyterian Church Association—St. Andrew's Institute (once part of St. Andrew's Presbyterian Church at King and Simcoe Streets).

The relationship between the Women's Association of St. Andrew's Church and the Toronto Branch of the Women's League is significant. The W.A. dutifully observed the request to "remain neutral": there is no record of any discussion regarding union in the minutes of the W.A. in the 1921 to 1925 period. The first meeting of the Toronto Branch of the Women's League took place March 1, 1923 in St. Andrew's Institute, the same building where the St. Andrew's W.A. met regularly. In fact, more than half the meetings of the League were held in the same building as the W.A., yet there is no reference to any of these meetings in the W.A. minutes. The puzzle is solved when the names on the list of the executive of the Women's League are noted. Many of the leaders of the W.A.—Mrs. Stuart C. Parker, wife of the minister, Mrs. Arthur McMurrick, Mrs. George Cook, Mrs. C. S. McDonald, Miss M. Buchanan, Mrs. J. W. MacNamara (wife of J. MacNamara, secretary of the Presbyterian Church Association), Mrs. George Dickson— were all elected to the executive of the Women's League in its first month of existence.[21]

The first task the executive committee of the Toronto branch of the Women's League undertook was to outline its mandate and submit it for approval to the executive committee of the Presbyterian Church Association. In its minutes, the recording secretary presents a seven-point mandate that outlines "the manner in which women members can serve in the crisis with which the Presbyterian Church in Canada is confronted."[22] The minutes make clear that the women were trying to avoid the unsatisfactory relationship that existed between the W.M.S. and the church. The women wanted direct representation on their executive from the Men's Association (as they called the Presbyterian Church Association). The issue is complicated by the fact that, at the same time, the committee was responding to a request from the executive to appoint a woman organizer.

The proposal to appoint a woman organizer was a heated issue within the ranks of the Men's Association. T. B. McQuesten of Hamilton declared that such an appointment would be "a major mistake because to have a woman organizing women would lead to all sort of petty jealousies."[23] As all political organizers knew, McQuesten argued, the best results in organizing women are to be obtained by a male organizer.

The request for the appointment of a woman representative was turned down—not by the men but by the Women's League.

The League wanted to be part of the Association, not an auxiliary of it, and the appointment of a woman representative would distance women from the main organization. In outlining its position on the matter, the committee at first argues against the appointment of a woman representative quoting traditional arguments concerning the role of women:

> The Committee do not consider the appointment of a woman organizer advisable. In order to work effectively and success-fully, such an officer would need to be in close personal communication with the men's committee under which direction she would be working and would be bearing the responsibility to the Church and to the general public ... This would involve full membership on the Executive Committee which would be undesirable for many reasons. Furthermore, the experience of the Committee in other religious and altruistic work leads them to the belief that a woman who is a paid official is handicapped in making an appeal, which demands in others disinterestedness and sacrifice.[24]

However, it becomes clear that the committee is not arguing that women have no role to play because they are the inferior sex, as McQuesten claimed. Rather, the committee argues at great length that any effectiveness women might have would be hampered because of their sex:

> The Committee do not recognize any difference whatever in the position of men and of women in regard to the preservation of a Church in which their obligations of membership are identical, and believe that any method of rousing the Church members to a sense of the present danger, which divides the sexes, merely causes delay and adds to the overhead expense.
>
> The members of the Committee approve of the place by which the Church is governed by men officials, and believe, therefore, that the work of educating and rousing the members can be done much more effectively by men who appeal to the large body of the people, irrespective of sex ... This system of government enables a man, through his position in or influence on the Session and Board of Managers, to force the issue and gain an entrance to a Church where the minister is in favour of Union.[25]

Therefore, the Committee recommended that

the women members of the Presbyterian Church in Canada be permitted to serve individually as may be necessary, or required *under the direction* and at the request of the Executive Committee of the Presbyterian Church Association, *but that the official education and organization of the entire membership be undertaken by qualified men exclusively.*[26]

Ironically, this did not happen. The Toronto Branch of the Women's League remained neither an integrated part of the Men's Committee nor within the confines of its mandate. Within two months, the League had outgrown and extended its mandate. (In February 1924 it submitted a new mandate to the Men's Committee.[27]) It became so successful that the general rule for organizing opposition to union was to organize a Women's League based on the model of the Toronto Branch. In a July 1923 letter to the Reverend J. A. MacGillivray, the secretary of the Men's Association, wrote:

Now as to organizing in Guelph City and Presbytery, do not you think steps should be taken as soon as possible to get such organization and to get a Women's League started? We must do something at once to counteract the vote of your Commissioners in the Assembly.[28]

The Toronto Branch of the Women's League contributed to three main areas of the anti-union campaign: finances, literature, and membership drives. The League bore the bulk of the financial burden of the Toronto Presbyterian Church Association. The League's minutes report on March 26, 1923 that just three weeks after the League was formed, Mr. C. S. McDonald, treasurer of the Men's Association, had written to the League's treasurer noting that "expenses of this Association had been borne by a few but that help from others would now be welcomed."[29] A budget of $25,000 had been prepared for Ontario, $1,000 of this to be spent in the Toronto district. By December the League's treasurer had reported that "we are the only organization contributing to the enormous expense under which the Association is laboring."[30] In less than two years, the Women's League raised $5,293.25. In addition, they paid for their own expenses such as stationery, postage, etc.

More important, as the March 14, 1924 minutes noted, they paid for the services of Crussel, the Association's lawyer:

> In view of the expenses that will be incumbent in connection with the Conference and the engagement of Crussel to represent us before Parliament, the motion of the last meeting providing payment of $500 to the Men's Committee be rescinded. Carried.[31]

The drive for funds was independent of the Men's Association. Initially, memberships to the League cost ten cents each. Later the fee was increased to a quarter. The League collected $100 at each prayer meeting held at St. Andrew's Church. These seem to have been held at least once a month and were advertised in the local papers. At least three public rallies were organized in two years at Cook's Church. The facilities at Knox Church and Cook's Church were used for public meetings. Top name speakers were brought in for these engagements, and the League covered the speaker's fees. The events were big enough to warrant newspaper coverage. Permission from ministers was sought to set up tables in local churches on Sunday to recruit members. Moreover, the League responded to the shortage of anti-union literature by producing its own pamphlets, such as "Our Church Crisis: A Challenge to Presbyterian Women."

The Women's League was generally better organized and less cautious than the Men's Association. In fact, two major campaign drives were vetoed by the Men's Committee. The Toronto Branch adopted the practice of the Montreal group and issued membership cards to paying members. This was part of a major campaign strategy to rally support in preparation for the debate on the Union Bill in the House of Commons. Because the unionists had tried wherever possible to vote in clerks of sessions and moderators of presbyteries who were unionists,[32] the cards of the Women's League were a safe way to prove the strength of the dissident movement. The cards issued by the Toronto Branch read simply, "I am a petitioner for the continuance of the Presbyterian Church in Canada."[33] However, three days after the women launched their campaign MacNamara advised them that "the issue of a Petition had been the subject of discussion between the Men's Committee and Crussel and Messrs. Lafleur, K. C. and Campbell, K. C. of Montreal and 'the time is not yet ripe for such a petition to be released.'"[34] The men instructed the women to continue "preparatory work of an educational character."[35] Similar instructions were issued in a stronger tone to the Women's League in Montreal:

> Our Committee feel that this is a matter where very great caution should be exercised. They are not sure that it would be advisable as yet to publish any information as to the strength of the League beyond general information that is growing rapidly. You see the different Branches have been organized only recently and are not in a position yet to reveal their full possibilities.[36]

It is not clear exactly what MacNamara meant when he referred to the "possibilities" of the Women's League. Perhaps he still hoped that a national organization for the women could be formed. In any case, by September 1923 the League recorded in its minutes that "sufficient organizational work had been done."[37] And in its meeting of March 11, 1924, the women decided that it was "time to go public" and they made plans to organize a large conference modelled after the conference in Montreal the year before.[38] There is no indication that they sought the approval of the Men's Committee to launch their public campaign.

The second campaign which the Men's Committee failed to endorse concerned the W.M.S. In a letter addressed to MacNamara marked "personal," Mrs. McCaskill in Montreal requested MacNamara to outline the policy the Women's League in Toronto had adopted concerning any approach to the W.M.S. Mrs. McCaskill was upset because the president of the local W.M.S. Auxiliary had received literature from the unionists addressed to her officially as well as personally. She explained: "Our League has decided not to touch that department of the Presbyterian Church until some move might come from the W.M.S. The League feels that it does not wish to disturb the smoothly running machinery of that organization."[39] However, noting that MacNamara had indicated that he had "had splendid response from ladies who are prominent in the different departments of the church," she made the following suggestion:

> If any of these ladies you mention, as being prominent in Church work, are workers in the W.M.S. would they wish us to make any move as a League toward sending in a resolution against union? If the unionists are beginning to work in the W.M.S., should we not do so?[40]

Once again, MacNamara, on behalf of the Presbyterian Church Association, advocated a conservative line echoing his earlier statement to the Women's League of Toronto:

> We have been careful not to interfere with the W.M.S. in any way. Whatever literature has been sent out has been sent either in packages to congregations or to individuals as such. We do not intend to depart from that until justification arises. I feel that inevitably the conflict will affect the women's organizations and that the members will find it necessary to declare themselves on one side or the other, but that had better be left to the women themselves.[41]

Whether MacNamara was politically naive or simply let his sense of fair play determine the Association's campaign strategy, he played into the hands of the unionists who had a reputation for playing dirty.

Therefore, it is not surprising that by 1924, the Toronto branch of the Women's League had become less involved with the Men's Association. One of the major projects of the Toronto Branch in 1924 was to send a letter to the members of Parliament in anticipation of the union debate. The letter reveals the extent to which the Women's League had outgrown its original mandate and become the driving force of the dissident movement. In its first meeting held March 1, 1923 the Women's League had insisted that it operate as part of the Presbyterian Church Association. One year later, its mandate had changed drastically. It had assumed the responsibility of an advocacy organization representing and defending the concerns of its constituency—women in the church—in the union debate. In addressing the members of Parliament, the letter was hard hitting in arguing that the present predicament of women was to be blamed on the unionists as well as the church itself. In effect the Women's League was arguing for the right of women to have a say in the administration of the church in matters that affected their concerns. Ironically, one may speculate that had the men responded to the original request that representatives of the Men's Association sit on the executive of the League, the League's position may never had become so advocacy oriented:

> It is estimated that the membership of the Presbyterian Church is more than sixty percent women. As our Church is constituted, none of the courts have women as members. It is a well-known fact, however, that in all branches of church activity and support, the women bear no small part, the W.M.S. alone in 1922, did [sic] work that called for expenditures of over $450,000. The work done by Ladies' Aid Societies in congregations, while not tabulated apart from local reports, is well known to all church Boards of Management, when questions of building furnishings or repairs are under consideration ...

> If the question of Church Union, involving, as it does, property rights which the sixty percent membership of women have had no small share in securing, can be settled in the church courts, where there are no women representing women, [this means] 60 percent of the Presbyterian Church has had no voice or part in the disposal of the church property [which] they have, through the years, helped to secure and maintain ...

> As women of the Presbyterian Church, unrepresented in our Church courts, we have had no opportunities, apart from the cards referred to above, to express our opinion on this legislation now before the Federal House, and we appeal to your sense of justice and fair play, to your British abhorrence of coercion in every forum, to your belief that trusts should be administered as directed and cannot in honour and justice be diverted to another purpose, to see that this Bill, which disregards and coerces the individual in matters of conscience and religion, is so amended as to permit freedom of conscience to all concerned, with a just and fair division of property, which belong to all alike, together with adequate protection to all trusts according to the terms of their bequest.

Once the Union Bill became law, the Women's League believed its job was over, and on May 10, 1926 the Toronto Branch officially disbanded.[42] However, the work of the Women's League was far from over. Women continued to work for the "preservation of the

Presbyterian Church in Canada," even though they were restricted now to working within the structures of the church. Their contribution is evident in two areas: the work of the local Women Associations in rebuilding the Presbyterian Church, and the new role of lay leaders under the direction of the W.M.S.

It is no coincidence that the driving forces behind the W.M.S. and the W.A. were the women who had held important positions on the Executive of the Women's League. For example, as noted above, Mrs. J.T.L. McKerroll turned her attention from the Women's League to the W.M.S. She was joined by two other women who travelled the country reorganizing the W.M.S. (W.D.): Helen Mackenzie Thompson, daughter of a Presbyterian minister and granddaughter of Prime Minister Alexander Mackenzie, was president of the W.M.S. from 1928 to 1932,[43] while Laura Pelton was sponsored by her lay father to travel to reorganize the Women's Missionary Society (W.D.). She later helped to organize the Canadian Council of Churches.[44]

At the local level, Mrs. Stuart Parker, Mrs. George Cook, Mrs. A. McMurrick, and Miss Mitchie, who had served on the executive of the Toronto branch of the Women's League, were all elected to the executive of the W.M.S. at St. Andrew's Church in January 1926.[45]

Once the union question was settled, the W.M.S. picked up its campaign to have the relationship between the W.M.S. and the General Assembly's Mission Board redefined. In his book, *The History of the Presbyterian Church: 1875-1925*, Thomas MacNeill quotes Mrs. John MacGillivray, president of the W.M.S.:

> Does it not seem a paradox that it should be the Church (we speak of our own) into which she (woman) has put her best work and thought, where the seeds of training for service were first sown, which should be the last to let down the bars? ... We do not refer to the missionary as such, but to the woman in the pew. We are not pleading for women to enter the pulpit (though the public press headlines would understand it so). Our women are conservative on that point, but where the need arises and she is academically prepared, and is actually doing the Church's work under the appointment of the Assembly's boards, why should

recognition be withheld in the courts of the Church? Has the day not come also when the relationship of the Women's Board of the W.M.S. to the Assembly's Mission boards should be co-operative rather than auxiliary?[46]

With the shortage of ministers after union, laypersons, women and men, took over pulpits under the direction of the W.M.S., especially in the West. This became an accepted practice until the first post-union theology students graduated, and ministers could be lured to Canada from the United States and Scotland. At the request of the W.M.S., General Assembly's Committee on Public Worship issued *Service Helps* in 1927, and *Aids for Worship in Church, Camp and Sunday School* in 1930, which limited the role of the layperson and discouraged preaching.[47] If behind the W.M.S. request for literature was a scheme to prompt the church to establish the lay preacher (male and female) as a permanent fixture, the strategy backfired. A backlash to women leaders was evident in the Committee that was publishing the books. In 1936, the Committee on Church Worship reported:

> One of the Committee is quite concerned—and with reason— over services that are wholly placed, at times, in the hands of young people. He writes: "Should we encourage young people (other than young men who are candidates for the ministry) to conduct a service of Public Worship? ... I must admit that when I read 'The Young People Took the Service' I do not like it ... I feel that the pulpit should be left to the minister." The following advertisement appeared in a city newspaper: "GIRLS! GIRLS! GIRLS! Girls in middies will usher! Girls will take the service. Girls will preside at the organ. A choir of girls!" The matter, then, suggested by our correspondent should be seriously considered by our Sessions.[48]

The second contribution women made to the church in the aftermath of union concerned the financial appeals of congregations that were trying either to rebuild or to buy back property that had been turned over to the newly formed United Church. In 1927, the W.A. and W.M.S. at St. Andrew's Church took on two joint projects. On January 19, 1927, their executives dealt with the first appeal:

> Many town churches are taking booths for the Fairbanks Church
> Bazaar in Cook's Church in aid of their property fund. Executive
> would prefer to give lump sum of money instead of having
> booth—suggested $1,200. The object is to buy land for a new
> church as they lost theirs in the division of property after the
> Union just after the burning of the mortgage. Property since
> assessed at $6,500.[49]

The women at St. Andrew's contributed more than money.
On October 31 the W.A. responded to a second appeal, this time
from St. James Church, Winnipeg. The W.A. put on a musical and
sold 200 tickets at $1.00 each to raise money. They donated $300 to
St. James Church, a library of fifty books, and 100 hymnals.[50]

These special projects were taken on in addition to the regular
altruistic work of the W.A., which amounted to approximately
$2,000 annually, including the funding of "Holiday House" (which
cost about $500 to run per year). In 1927 the W.A. spent about
$4,000, half of which was designated for rebuilding or buying back
churches. It was difficult for the W.A. to carry the increased expen-
ditures. In 1928 it considered abandoning its efforts to fund and
furnish Holiday House as an ongoing project. But it never considered cutting back its donations to struggling churches.

The work of the W.A. across the country to rebuild and refur-
nish Presbyterian churches went unnoticed, whereas the Women's
League had been a visible and celebrated lobby group. At the Presbyterian Congress which preceded the General Assembly of 1925,
Mrs. Bumstead was honoured for the work that the League had
carried out in preserving the Presbyterian Church.[51] The W.A. enjoyed no such recognition, even though this paper has established
that it too made a significant contribution. The W.A. was a different
kind of organization. It was not an outside group and did not
exercise the brashness of an advocacy group. In responding to the
appeals of struggling churches, the W.A. perceived its work as a
matter of duty and part of the rubric under which it had always
operated. It did not run to the streets with a cause that involved
protecting its own interests. Douglas Campbell argues that by succeeding in their task women "devalued their position to the status
quo ante."[52]

However, I think Dr. Campbell goes too far in stating that women "preferred their inferior position in the Presbyterian Church to the promise of equality in the other one."[53] Before union, women had a strong voice through the Women's League and had gained credibility in both public and ecclesiastical circles. Both the Congregational and Methodist churches had seriously considered the ordination of women. Moreover, respected Presbyterians had supported the ordination of women in 1922. Principal MacVicar of St. Andrew's College had advocated it, and Knox College had already graduated women students with distinction from its theology program.[54] Thus Presbyterian women in the post-union years were not unrealistic in thinking it was only a matter of time before ordination would be available to them.

Then why did the Presbyterian Church in Canada take so long to ordain women to the Ministry of Word and Sacrament? First, as in the case of Principal MacVicar, most theologians were unionists and joined the United Church. Second, the Presbyterian Church and the United Church were very different institutions in the aftermath of 1925. Winners can afford to be cocky and introduce reform and change in more drastic measures than the losers would ever consider. It is clear that the Presbyterian Church was the loser in the union issue. For ten years it scrambled to pick up the pieces—to reorganize and regain some of its former strength. The Presbyterian Church could not afford to revive a potentially volatile issue when its main objective was survival.

NOTES

1. W.M.S. is the Women's Missionary Society. W.D. is Western Division. Neil G. Smith, ed., *Enkindled by the Word: Essays in Presbyterianism in Canada* (Toronto: Presbyterian Publications, 1966), 117.

2. Douglas Campbell, "Putting Women in their Place: Women and Church Union," Working Paper No. 19, PCA.

3. N. Keith Clifford, *The Resistance to Church Union in Canada: 1904-1939* (Vancouver: University of British Columbia Press, 1985), 99.

4. Clifford, *Resistance to Church Union*, 100.

5. Clifford, *Resistance to Church Union*, 117.

6. Clifford, *Resistance to Church Union*, 130.

7. Campbell, "Putting Women in their Place," 2.
8. Campbell, "Putting Women in their Place," 3.
9. Campbell, "Putting Women in their Place," 3.
10. Campbell, "Putting Women in their Place," 3.
11. *Acts and Proceedings of the General Assembly of the Presbyterian Church in Canada*, 1922, 279.
12. *Acts and Proceedings*, 1922, 279.
13. Clifford, *Resistance to Church Union*, 133.
14. The Women's Missionary Society, *Call and Response* (Toronto: Presbyterian Publications, n.d.), 116.
15. *Minutes of the Women's League, Toronto Branch*, November 11, 1923, Presbyterian Church Association Papers, PCA.
16. *Minutes of the Women's League, Toronto Branch*, November 11, 1923.
17. Clifford, *Resistance to Church Union*, 133.
18. Clifford, *Resistance to Church Union*, 133.
19. Mrs. Francis McCaskill to Rev. J. A. MacNamara, May 12, 1923, Presbyterian Church Association Papers, Case 5, File 10, PCA.
20. Rev. J. MacNamara to Miss Kate Campbell, Vice-President, Montreal Branch of the Women's League, September 27, 1923, Presbyterian Church Association Papers, File 4, Box 2-1, PCA.
21. *Minutes of the Women's League, Toronto Branch and Minutes of the St. Andrew's Church Women's Association: 1918-1926*, King Street, Toronto.
22. *Minutes of the Women's League, Toronto Branch*, March 14, 1923.
23. Clifford, *Resistance to Church Union*, 133.
24. *Minutes of the Women's League, Toronto Branch*, March 26, 1923.
25. *Minutes of the Women's League, Toronto Branch*, March 26, 1923.
26. *Minutes of the Women's League, Toronto Branch* (emphasis added), March 26, 1923.
27. *Minutes of the Women's League, Toronto Branch*, March 26, 1923.
28. The Rev. J. A. MacNamara to Rev. J. A. MacGillivray, July 9, 1923, File 34, Box 3-IV, Presbyterian Church Association Papers, PCA.
29. *Minutes of the Women's League, Toronto Branch*, March 26, 1923.
30. *Minutes of the Women's League, Toronto Branch*, November 20, 1923.
31. *Minutes of the Women's League, Toronto Branch*, March 14, 1923.
32. Clifford, *Resistance to Church Union*, 176.
33. *Minutes of the Women's League, Toronto Branch*, March 23, 1923.
34. *Minutes of the Women's League, Toronto Branch*, March 23, 1923.
35. *Minutes of the Women's League, Toronto Branch*, March 23, 1923.
36. McCaskill to MacNamara, May 30, 1923, Case 5, File 10, Presbyterian Church Association Papers, PCA.
37. *Minutes of the Women's League, Toronto Branch*, September 14, 1923.
38. *Minutes of the Women's League, Toronto Branch*, March 11, 1924.
39. McCaskill to MacNamara, March 16, 1923, Case 5, File 10, Presbyterian Church Association Papers, PCA.

40. McCaskill to MacNamara, March 16, 1923, Case 5, File 10, Presbyterian Church Association Papers.

41. McCaskill to MacNamara, March 28, 1923, Case 5, File 10, Presbyterian Church Association Papers.

42. *Minutes of the Women's League, Toronto Branch,* May 10, 1926.

43. *Minutes of the Women's League, Toronto Branch,* May 10, 1926.

44. Brian Fraser and Mary Whale, *Conversations With Our Past* (Toronto: Board of Congregational Life; Presbyterian Church in Canada, 1983), 14.

45. Fraser and Whale, *Conversations,* 19.

46. *Minutes of the Women's Association, St. Andrew's Church: 1918 to January 1926.*

47. John T. McNeill, *The Presbyterian Church in Canada: 1875-1925* (Toronto: Presbyterian Church in Canada, 1925), 154.

48. "Aids for Worship," *The Presbyterian Record,* 51 (1931), 8.

49. *Acts and Proceedings ,* 1936, 108.

50. *Minutes of the Joint W.M.S. and W.A.: January 1927 to October 1929,* St. Andrew's Church, King Street, Toronto.

51. *Minutes of the Joint W.M.S. and W.A., January 1927 to October 1929,* October 31, 1927.

52. Campbell, "Putting Women in their Place," 6.

53. Campbell, "Putting Women in their Place," 6.

54. Campbell, "Putting Women in their Place," 6.

55. McNeill, *Presbyterian Church in Canada,* 152.

Contributors

ROBERTA CLARE, a graduate of Knox College and Union Theological Seminary, New York, has been the Presbyterian-United Chaplain at McGill University, Montreal, and is presently pursuing doctoral studies at Union and Columbia University.

N. KEITH CLIFFORD, author of *The Resistance to Church Union in Canada, 1904-1939*, was Professor of Religious Studies at the University of British Columbia.

MICHAEL GAUVREAU, author of *The Evangelical Century*, is in the Department of History, McMaster University.

WILLIAM KLEMPA is Principal of Presbyterian College, Montreal and Lecturer in Theology at McGill University, Montreal.

PAUL LAVERDURE, a graduate of McGill and the University of Toronto, has been a researcher for the Redemptorist Order.

D. BARRY MACK is a Ph.D. graduate of Queen's University with a thesis on George M. Grant. He is minister of St. Andrew's Presbyterian Church, St. Lambert, Québec.

JOSEPH C. MCLELLAND is Emeritus Professor of Philosophy of Religion of both McGill University and Presbyterian College and editor of the works of Peter Martyr Vermigli.

JOHN S. MOIR, author of *Enduring Witness*, was Professor of History at the University of Toronto and Adjunct Professor of Church History at Knox College, Toronto. He is retired and living in Simcoe, Ontario.

JACK ROBINSON teaches English at Grant McEwan College in Edmonton, Alberta.

RICHARD W. VAUDRY, author of *The Free Church in Victorian Canada, 1844-1861*, and teaches history at The King's College, Edmonton.

JOHN A. VISSERS is Professor of Systematic Theology, Ontario Theological Seminary, Toronto.

B. ANNE WOOD, author of *God, Science and Schooling: John William Dawson's Pictou Years, 1820-1855*, is Professor of Education, Dalhousie University, Halifax.

Index of Names